13,75

D0085564

After Mao What ?

BY J. P. JAIN

Documentary Study of the Warsaw Pact

China Pakistan and Bangladesh

India and Disarmament : Nehru Era

Nuclear India
(in two volumes)

Soviet Policy Towards Pakistan and Bangladesh

China in World Politics

After Mao What ? Army Party and Group Rivalries in China

After Mao What ?

Army Party and Group Rivalries in China

J. P. Jain

Westview Press
Boulder, Colorado

ISBN: 0-89158-528-1

Copyright 1975 in New Delhi, India
by Radiant Publishers

Published 1975 in New Delhi, India
by Radiant Publishers

Published 1976 in the United States of America
by Westview Press Inc.
  1898 Flatiron Court
  Boulder, Colorado 80301
Frederick A. Praeger, Publisher and Editorial Director

Printed in New Delhi

Library of Congress Cataloging in Publication Data

Jain, Jagdish P   1930-
    After Mao what?

    Bibliography: p.
    Includes index.
    1.   China--Politics and government--1949-
I.   Title.
DS777.55.J255   320.9'51'05   75-31534
ISBN 0-89158-528-1

Contents

List of Appendices

List of Tables and Charts

Abbreviations

AC	Administrative Committee
CC	Central Committee
CCP	Chinese Communist Party
Chm	Chairman
Cdr	Commander
Dept	Department
Dir	Director
Dy	Deputy
GPD	General Political Department of the PLA
HQ	Headquarters
MAC	Military Affairs Committee
MD	Military District
Mem	Members
MR	Military Region
NPC	National People's Congress
PLA	People's Liberation Army
Pol. Csr	Political Commissar
PRC	People's Republic of China
Secy	Secretary
Secy-Gen	Secretary-General
Vc-Chm	Vice-Chairman

Preface

Mao Tse-tung has dominated the Chinese domestic scene for well over four decades now. Ever since the 1935 Tsunyi Conference, he has been successful in asserting his leadership over the Chinese Communist Party and the People's Liberation Army—the two main *loci* of power within China. However, in the process, Mao has had to face many a challenge to his authority. At times, it appeared as if the reins of control over the Party and the PLA were slipping out of his hands and that the country was relapsing into a period of warlordism, or heading towards army dictatorship or rule by a Party hierarchy, not loyal to Mao and his dogma. But Chairman Mao has somehow managed to retain his supremacy over the major components of the Chinese political system by deposing or liquidating all those who dared usurp his throne. Mao's successors are unlikely to have either the charismatic personality or the stature of the great helmsman. Therefore, what follows after Mao is a matter of great significance and acute concern for both the Chinese people and the world at large.

After the session of the Fourth National People's Congress, there may not appear sufficient reason for being unduly worried about the problem : Who after Mao ? The promotion of Teng Hsiao-ping as Vice-Chairman of the Party Central Committee and member of the Standing Committee of the Politburo, and his appointment as the senior-most Vice-Premier and Chief of Staff of the armed forces seems to have enabled the Party to avert the possiiblity of a crisis should Mao Tse-tung and Chou En-lai both become incapacitated or pass away. Teng enjoys the confidence of veteran Party, armed forces and government cadres and, therefore, may succeed in establishing his supremacy in the country. But even if there is no succession struggle immediately after the death of Mao and/or Chou, group rivalries and factional struggles are likely to continue and may possibly become more intense. To prepare for the future, the veteran cadres (the so-called moderates) are busy taking as many key Party and government positions in the country as possible, while the radical Leftists are seen active in launching politico-ideological campaigns to discredit and dislodge them. Besides, the army is a factor to be reckoned with and Lin Piao's followers, who are still firmly entrenched in military units, both at regional and provincial-district levels, may still be a source of some trouble to the Party leadership. The disunity among the Party leadership and the existence of factional differences is reflected, among other things, in the failure to fill the vacancy left by the death of Tung Pi-wu in the Politburo, nine vacancies in the Party Central Committee, and a few vacancies of First Secretaries in the Provincial Party Committees.

The present study discusses in detail the question of political control over the People's Liberation Army, the inter-action between the Party and the PLA, and the present state of group rivalries within the Chinese leadership, which will greatly help in understanding the problems of post-Mao succession. The book examines the role of the army and the political commissar system within the PLA and the impact of the Cultural Revolution on the Party-Army relationship and the domestic politics of China. It also examines in depth and in proper perspective the fall of Lin Piao, the problem of regionalism, the leadership pattern, both at the centre and in the provinces, the role of the army, and the system of checks and balances, that had been evolved among personalities, different sections of society and various groupings.

The large number of appendices, tables and charts, it is hoped, will prove to be of great help in understanding the intricate web of Chinese politics.

The views expressed in this study are entirely the personal views of the author and are not to be attributed to any institution, organization or body. I thank my son Rajendra for his help in editing the manuscript and other members of my family for their assistance of various kinds.

New Delhi   J. P. Jain

Introduction

After the establishment of the People's Republic of China in 1949, Chairman Mao Tse-tung had been successful, to a great extent, in suppressing the so-called *bourgeois* military line of Kao Kang, Peng Teh-huai, Lo Jui-ching and Lin Piao (who, for over 40 years, was credited for faithfully following the Maoist military line. He was even named as Mao's successor at the Ninth Party Congress in 1969). The General Political Department (GPD) and the commissar system operating under its direction were the key instruments for promoting Maoist military thinking within the People's Liberation Army (PLA). However, that system was perceptibly shaken in the internal upheaval called the Cultural Revolution. The power and prestige of the army commanders, on the other hand, was considerably enhanced. Since the Tenth Party Congress in 1973, persistent efforts have been made to restrict the political role of the military and to assert Party leadership and control over the army. Yet the PLA is far from being a spent force or a non-entity in Chinese politics. Moreover, the *bourgeois* rights and socio-economic conditions, that give rise to *bourgeois* military thinking, have not altogether disappeared.

Will Mao, in the short span of life left to him, succeed in establishing an absolute leadership of the Party over the PLA so as to forestall forever the danger of warlordism or military rule reappearing in China ? Will China continue to be ruled by a unified political leadership at the Centre ? These are important questions occupying the serious attention of the

Chinese people and of all those interested in or concerned with China.

The problem of exercising effective political control over the army has not been an easy one, particularly in a country which has a long tradition of warlordism. Ever since the founding of the Chinese Red Army in 1927, there had been a ceaseless struggle between two lines of thinking, *viz.* whether to place the army under the Party's absolute leadership and follow the principle that the Party commands the gun or to oppose the Party's leadership and have the gun command the Party. Lin Piao is denounced for pursuing a *bourgeois* military line by preaching "the fallacy that the gun commands the party," by undermining the Party's absolute leadership over the army and for asserting that the army should decide the character and fate of the Party and the state power. Lin Piao is, thus, accused of following the footsteps of Kao Kang and Peng Teh-huai.

The *Red Flag* article, "Our Principle is that the Party Command the Gun—Critique of Lin Piao's Crime in Opposing Party Leadership Over the Army" by Tien Chun, asserts that Chairman Mao had always fought for the principle that the "Party commands the gun, and the gun must never be allowed to command the Party." It is stated that when Mao proclaimed that "political power grows out of the barrel of a gun," he was not trying to establish the supremacy of the military over the Party. He was actually emphasizing the importance of the armed struggle and the armed forces for the Party. According to Mao, of the seven sectors, *viz.* industry, agriculture, commerce, culture and education, the army, the government and the Party, "it is the Party that exercises overall leadership." The Chinese Red Army (renamed PLA in 1946) is said to be "an armed group carrying out revolutionary political tasks" laid down by the Party. "It is not only a fighting force but also a work force" and should serve as an instrument for the Party. Under no circumstances should the gun be used "as a tool by individual careerists." The *Red Flag* article criticized Lin Piao for seeking to establish his personal leadership over the army, the government and the Party. Lin is denounced for catering to the interests and wishes of imperialism, revisionism and reaction by following a *bourgeois* military line.[1]

In the 1920s both Chinese and Soviet leaders shared a common military theory, style or experience which laid great stress on ideological and revolutionary fervour. Subsequently, however, the USSR, owing to its different set of circumstances —experiences, military capabilities and political considerations —moved away from the doctrines of protracted war, strategic withdrawal and the defensive-offensive concept, and its tremendous faith in the power of ideology and Party control over the military. The Kremlin preferred to adopt more modern concepts of integral strategy and professionalism, massed firepower, the offensive defensive, etc. and a short war, fought with megaton nuclear weapons and intercontinental ballistic missiles. Chairman Mao, on the other hand, could not wholly reconcile himself to the Russian strategy of modern warfare, partly because of his personal predilections and partly because of the conditions prevalent in China. To Mao, the increasing influence of Soviet advisers during 1946-1960 and the upsurge of professionalism and modernization within the PLA under Peng Teh-huai seemed to indicate a gradual erosion of Maoist military theory and a decline in his own personal power status both within the military and the Party. It was, perhaps, not unthinkable that he might have thus felt "an increasing Soviet threat to his own long-term political survival and to his vision of China's future."[2]

Confucius, one of the most influential leaders in China's national life during the last 2500 years, was neither a military hero nor a messiah, but a school master. Under his spell, the warrior temperament of ancient China remained submerged for a long time and the army career came to be despised by the literati. Soldiers came to be regarded as "something more than parasites on society and agents of destruction."[3] The prevailing attitude toward the soldiers was best summed up in the proverb : "Good iron is not beaten into nails; a good man does not become a soldier."[4] Thus, there was little or practically no glorification of military genius so characteristic of the West.

However, with Mao's stress on war as "the highest form of struggle between nations, states, classes or political groups"[5] and the advocacy of the Marxist-Leninist principle of "seizing political power with arms and solving problems with war,"[6] the concept of the soldier could no longer possibly remain the same. Nevertheless, one finds many similarities between the traditional aspects of Chinese military institutions and the Maoist military ethic and style. In his paper "Military Continuities : The PLA and Imperial China," Edward L. Dreyer comes to the conclusion that the principal legacy of the imperial past to contemporary Chinese military practice is an institutional syndrome characterized by failure to separate political ends and military means, dominance of a generalist ideology and consequent failure to develop military professionalism, and the assignment of soldiers to farming and other non-military duties in peace-time. This legacy, Dreyer adds, "is, of course, not the only doctrinal force operating within the Chinese military establishment, but it has been most compatibly wedded to the doctrine of People's War and both have grown in influence during the decade of the 1960s."[7]

Of all the social strata and political groupings, Mao held the proletariat and the Communist Party to be "politically the most far sighted" and as such entitled to lead the masses of China's peasantry and urban petty *bourgeoisie* which had a limited political outlook.[8] The army, which was recruited largely out of the peasant masses, was also subjected to Party leadership for that matter. At the same time, Mao instructed the entire Party "to pay great attention to war, study military matters and prepare to fight," to give "preferential treatment to soldiers' families" and help the troops in meeting their material needs. He advanced the slogan : "Let all the people be soldiers." He even went to the extent of asserting that without an army of the people there would be nothing for the people.[9] Despite this emphasis on the role of armed struggle and the mobilization of masses to that end, the army has all along been regarded a tool in the hands of the Party. The Party cadre was required to exercise a strict control over the soldier and assign him his tasks both in the field of production and of fighting. If the soldier was provided with somewhat better food than the ordinary masses it was to keep him contented and satisfied and make a better use of him for achieving Party ends.

PART ONE

The Past

1 Maoist Military Thinking

Chairman Mao's military thinking has been greatly influenced both by the traditional Chinese military theories as well as by Marxism-Leninism. Mao seems to have been particularly impressed by the ideas expounded in Sun Tzu's unique classic, *The Art of War*, written around 400-320 B.C., if not earlier. The translator of this military classic, Samuel B. Griffith, considers it to be "the source of Mao Tse-tung's strategic theories and of the tactical doctrine of the Chinese armies." On examination, one finds a close similarity between Mao and Sun Tzu on many points. For instance in their stress on deception and mobility in war, in considering war as a conscious act and defence and offence as complementary to each other, in keeping the enemy under strain and then wearing him down, in believing that, externally, one should make alliances with powerful leaders and states and, internally, one should pursue an agro-military policy, the two seem to hold similar views. Likewise, both Mao and Sun Tzu laid considerable emphasis on the human factor in war and on unity and fellow feeling between officers and men. Of all the factors making for success in war, Sun Tzu observed, the foremost was moral influence, *i.e.* that which causes the people to be in harmony with their leaders, so that they would accompany them in life and unto death without fear of mortal peril.[10]

The strategy and tactics of Mao Tse-tung were, at the same time, the result of the integration of Marxism-Leninism with the special circumstances obtaining in a vast semi-colonial, peasant-based country that China was. His military thinking is a curious mixture of armed struggle and politics. The hard core of Mao's thinking consists of armed struggle, reliance on the support of the countryside, and continuous fighting from secure bases. The armed struggle was linked with the peasants' struggle in agrarian revolution. Relying on the support of the broad masses of peasantry, the Chinese Red Army launched widespread guerilla warfare, which helped it to conserve its strength. The adoption of the strategy and tactics of mobile war also enabled the PLA to deal crucial blows to the enemy and to gradually expand its bases. The so-called "People's Army," consisting of peasant masses mobilised for fighting, spread out like a multitudinous sea to drown the enemy.

The peasant-oriented Maoist military philosophy had its origin in the special circumstances obtaining in China during the civil war : lack of sufficient weapons and training facilities, and very few opportunities to have access to major industrial and administrative centres. The Maoist philosophy laid stress on the priority of men over weapons, politics in command, guerilla tactics and a highly decentralized command and control system. It emphasized the concept of "people's war" and the organization of para-military forces, such as the militia and the people's armed police. Although the nature of modern warfare has relegated the militia and guerilla aspects of "people's war" to a minor role, it, nevertheless, continues to occupy an important place in Mao's military ethic and style.

Militia

In his political report to the Seventh National Congress of the Communist Party of China in April 1945, Chairman Mao Tse-tung put the strength of the army at 910,000 men and that of the rural militia "who are not withdrawn from normal productive work" at "more than 2,200,000." He described the militia as "the vast armed organizations of the masses" fighting in coordination with the army.[11] At the time of the founding of the People's Republic, the strength of the people's militia was estimated at about 6 million. Purges and dismissals, that were carried out at the end of the civil war, reduced its strength to less than 4½ million. It rose again to 12 million by 1953 and 15 million just before the establishment of the communes in 1958.

With the establishment of communes, the militia movement was revived with intense vigour and its strength grew to the gigantic size of 250 million because, under the slogan "Everyone A Soldier", all able-bodied men and woman of military age were automatically absorbed into it. However, it was believed that only about 30 million were in any reasonable state of training and military preparedness and this included the 20-odd million ex-regular army reservists.[12]

The milita is said to be endowed with the following characteristics :

1. It is an armed force of the masses of the people under the firm and strong leadership of the Party and not divorced from production. It is an organization which combines labour with military force and which is at once civilian and military in character.
2. It is organized under voluntary and democratic principles, and adopts a system of democratic centralism in its everyday life.
3. It is an armed organization of the whole people. It is a huge organization with enormous membership widely distributed in the cities and the countryside and in all professions and trades.[13]

Chieh-fang-Chun Hua-pao of 16 March 1962 defined the militia as "an armed organization of the masses which is under the leadership of the party and does not detach itself from production."[14] It is a military organization, an educational organization as well as an organization for physical culture. It is "a useful assistant to and a powerful reserve" of the Chinese People's Liberation Army. As a useful assistant, it relieves the regular armed forces of any worry about the rear, thereby enabling it to concentrate its full attention to combat tasks. As a great reserve, the militia makes possible the expansion of the regular army "on a grand scale and at high speed" at any time so desired. The existence of militia ensured "the continuous supply to the regular army of large number of reinforcements" and this was considered "an important guarantee of victory in the war."[15]

While the militia combines in itself the two tasks of fighting and production, (the militiaman is described as one who takes "a gun in one hand and a hoe in the other") the one or the other task may, at any given moment, be emphasized depending on the exigencies of state policy. Thus, during the economic crisis of 1959-61, militiamen were instructed to subordinate "all their other activities to their participation in production and construction."[16] Han Tung-shan, Commander of Hupeh Military District, in a broadcast, emphatically stated that military training "must not take precedence over production tasks."

The basic duties of militiamen, as described in *Chieh-fang-chun Hua-pao*, were as follows :

1. To take an active part in socialist construction and to play a leading role in production;
2. To assist the army in consolidating coastal, frontier and air defenses, in guarding against the enemy's secret agents, and in maintaining peace and order;
3. To get ready to join the army and go to war at any time for the purpose of striking against aggressors and defending the motherland.[17]

To carry out these "glorious duties" assigned by the Party and the State, militiamen were directed to listen to "what the Party and Chairman Mao say" and to try "seriously" to comply with certain requirements, which included, among others, obeying the leadership of the Party; abiding by the laws and decrees of the government; obeying the orders of superiors; exposition of "evil persons and evil deeds" (though not defined, but the obvious reference seemed to be to enemies, *viz.* the reactionaries or revisionists and their activities); and the study of politics and the military art.

Party Commands the Gun

When Mao speaks of the Party ruling the gun, he expresses something more than merely his notion of civil-military relations. His objective is to use the PLA as a militant arm of the Party. According to Maoist precepts, the PLA, as a political instrument, must not be too preoccupied with "purely military" duties but must, instead, become consciously a political institution engaged in the education and mobilization of its own members and the larger civilian community. Those holding the alternative view have argued that, although the military certainly has an obligation to the people, its principal function must remain professional—the "management of violence" for national defence.[18]

As early as 1931, the Party apparently sought to circumscribe the role of military professionals, restrict them to a relatively narrow sphere of activity and limit command authority to professional military matters. By placing the military under the overall supervision of a Party organ—the Revolutionary Military Council (later renamed the Military Affairs Committee) —and by having military activities monitored by "Party-soldiers" (General Political Department military commissars), the Party hoped to keep the military responsive to the Party's authority at the national and local levels.[19]

The establishment of a GPD within the PLA in 1931 was an important step taken by the Chinese Communist Party in its attempt to play a dominant role in all political as well as military affairs. A major reason for its creation was the Party's desire to inspire and measure "redness."[20] But while the Party was instrumental in establishing an institutional framework of the commissars, the latter, in comparison to the former, had a separate identity of its own. Thus, there were, in fact, two hierarchies of political control over the Chinese armed forces. The first consisted of the Party committee—a strictly Party body which was parallel to, but indipendent of, the military structure at every level down to the regiment. The second was a system of the General Political Department (with its commissars), which was established as an integral part of the army's structure and existed at all levels in the PLA.

At the lower military organizational levels, the two hierarchies tended to merge with one another. At company level, for instance, the Political Department was represented by a political officer, while the Party structure was continued through the Party group or cell. The company political officer, who was appointed by his regimental Political Department, was also in charge of the company cell, and thus combined both the control and educational functions of the political system, providing the essential link between the decision-making process and chain of command and the rank and file which carried out such decisions and commands.[21]

Although it is easy to argue that the commissars and the Party form one body, Whitson points out, it is more accurate to distinguish the one from the other, especially after 1950.[22] A. Doak Barnett explains this distinction in the following words :

> The commissar system operating under the GPD has been a unique institution in many respects, tied to but different from both the regular professional military command and the civilian Party bureaucracy. The commissars have been a part of the army, operating within its structure, yet they have been distinct from the principal military command hierarchy. And although, when the GPD's influence has been at its peak, its political officers have constituted the core of the "Party within the army," their outlooks have differed in many ways from those of the men staffing the civilian hierarchy of the Party. While subject to both army and Party direction, they have not really been fully integrated into either, and the GPD has functioned in some respects as a separate institution, often competitive with both the regular Party apparatus and the regular military command structure.[23]

After 1950, the GPD's revolutionary (non-military) functions of mobilizing the masses were taken over by the Party, which asserted its primacy in civil administration. However, the GPD and its cadres (commissars) were left free to perform their principal functions of education, indoctrination, and counter-intelligence *within* the Red Army. Thus, a separate system of "military party" developed within the PLA. This institutionalized framework consisted of an elite military "priesthood" that was better educated, more thoroughly indoctrinated, and ostensibly more conscious of the political implications of military action than either the Party or professional commanders.[24] However, commanders tended to prefer a military organization that minimized intermediate *political* authorities between themselves and available military power. They often disliked, resented and even opposed the commissars' interference in their affairs. Likewise, in the enhancement of the status and functions of military commissars, Party officials often suspected the diminution, if not complete erosion, of their power and influence.

Despite the vigorous attempts made by the Party and the institution of military commissars to establish their effective leadership over the PLA, it was not always found easy to keep the gun under the control of the Party. During many long periods (*e.g.* prior to 1950 and after the spring of 1967), the military dominated the Party rather than the reverse.[25] The current emphasis on "Party controls the gun and the gun should never be allowed to control the Party" is probably the last attempt to resurrect the Maoist principle during Chairman Mao's life-time.

2 The Chinese Army : Early Phase

The success of the Chinese Red Army would have been impossible had it not identified itself with agrarian revolution and if the agrarian revolution had not been made the content of the armed struggle. Thus Mao enunciated the idea of "mutually integrating military with political struggles." He also asserted that the decisive factor in determining the outcome of a war was the human factor, *i.e.* the political factor, and not the weapons. In the absence of superior equipment, Mao naturally laid stress on exploiting the subjective factor, *i.e.* the infusing among the soldiers of "highest revolutionary heroism" through inculcation of ardent love of the motherland, deep hatred of the enemy,[26] and "a spirit of resolute militancy which recognizes no insurmountable difficulties and is determined to overcome all difficulties" (Chu Teh).[27]

In addition to engaging in combat, Mao's fighting hordes had to work for land reform, for the "people's power" and act as the propagandists and organizers for the Party. The ability to "administer a state and ensure its domestic security," to use an old Chinese saying, was also required of them.[28] Thus, the roles of fighter, politician and administrator were all combined in one. All this was made a rule at the Kutien Congress of the Fourth Red Army of the CCP when a resolution, drawn up by Mao Tse-tung, was passed. The resolution defined the tasks of the PLA as "by no means confined to fighting." Besides fighting, the Red Army also had the great responsibility of educating, organizing and arming the masses, helping them to establish revolutionary political power and to set up Party Organizations.[29] In these circumstances, a purely military viewpoint—that the army should not engage in mass work—was not feasible at all.

During the Civil War, the PLA lived on the country as it passed through or grew its own food. Since the Red Army could exist and expand its influence or area of control only with the cooperation and support of the peasants, it could hardly afford to detach itself from the mass of the people. The PLA could not be allowed more comforts or a higher standard of living than that obtaining among the masses. Nor could officers in the army be given a privileged position, as compared to the rank and file, and permitted to assume an air of superiority. Both officers and men ate the same kind of food and their uniforms too were of the same type and quality. Thus, there was not much scope for contradictions emerging either between the army and the people or between the officers and rank and file of the army.

Kutien Conference and the Commissar System

The principles of political work in the Red Army, enshrined in the "Resolutions of the Ninth Congress of the Fourth Red Army of the Communist Party of China," were drafted personally by Mao Tse-tung at the Kutien Conference in 1929. These principles, later called "basic" and of "historic significance" by the devotees of Mao,[30] were : to educate the troops in the programme and policy of the Party; to educate the troops in the revolutionary spirit so as to achieve unity in the ranks of the people's army; to achieve unity between the people's army and the people as well as the people's government; to bring the army entirely under the leadership of the Party; to raise the fighting capacity of the army; to carry out the work of demoralising the enemy troops and attain the goal of unity within its "own ranks"; defeating the enemy and securing the freedom and emancipation of the people.

The political control structure over the PLA dates back to April 1928, when Chu Teh joined Mao Tse-tung on Chingkangshan and the Fourth Field Army came into existence, with Chu as commander-in-chief and Mao as its political commissar. After Kutien, Mao endeavoured to assert control over the expanding army through his own commissar appointees and his increasing use of both commissars and commanders to mobilize and govern the civilian populace. In this connection, W. W. Whitson states :

> From the origins of the Red Army at Nanchang on August 1, 1927, and as a result of his experience at Chingkangshan and in Kiangsi, Mao Tse-tung conceived of the military as an instrument to achieve domestic political mobilization and goals. The 1964 "Learn from the PLA" and the 1966 "Make the PLA a great school of revolution" movements were recent expressions of that ideal which was perhaps best articulated by Mao at the Kut' ien Conference. The commissar system, especially after Kut' ien, became the institutional expression of the Maoist concept that the joint exercise of authority by commissars and commanders would insure that military operations were directed toward appropriate political objectives.

The concept of the commissar's role came to be evolved in 1924 when an immediate need was felt for political control over and direction of "the gun," *i.e.* the commander. These commissars focused their energies on controlling the gun by emphasizing indoctrination and mobilization of friendly military forces. This was essentially a *defensive* effort designed to guard against disaffection, sustain morale, provide a rationale for warfare, encourage unity, and counter enemy subversion and intelligence operations. Fundamentally, W. W. Whitson states, the commissars had utilized every means of creating and preserving a loyal, politically reliable central army, and especially an officer corps so imbued with a sense of mission and an *esprit de corps* as to be capable of inspiring acts of personal and unit heroism. Under the Party representative system, a commissar was given the power to veto the directives of a selfish or politically unreliable commander, even if those orders were ostensibly operational.

A resolution, passed by the Communist Senior Cadres Conference on 1 September 1942, prescribed that Party Committee Chairmen at sub-bureau and provincial levels concurrently serve as political commissars of the military regions and military districts respectively. A similar phenomenon, Whitson points out, occurred during the 1965-68 period of the Cultural Revolution, when many commissars had an opportunity to expand their influence beyond the purely military arena, to create and manage Revolutionary Committees, and to challenge, if only briefly and unsuccessfully, their rivals—the civil Party cadres. Before 1946, the success of a commissar in turning an apolitical peasant into a motivated fighting man, who might very well have to enter battle without a weapon, could provide an increment to firepower that would help a Communist force prevail over a better-armed enemy.[31]

In the conditions in which the Communists were struggling to seize political power in China, it was not possible for the leadership to assume full responsibility for provisioning the army. The officers and rank and file in the Red Army not only worked together to carry out the political tasks assigned to them by the Party but they also engaged themselves in production work in order to support themselves. Although Mao was convinced that "even under socialism" there could not be absolute equality as regards distribution of material things, yet he considered it necessary to decree that the distribution of material things in the Red Army "must be more or less equal, as in the case of equal pay for officers and men."

3 Modernization and Professionalism in the Army

The establishment of peace-time conditions after the victory of the Communists in the civil war and the arrival of over 3,000 Russian officers, advisers and technicians after the signing of the treaty of alliance with the Soviet Union brought about a significant change in the character of the Chinese army. Greater attention came to be paid to raising the technical level of the army by studying the developed military science of the USSR. Formalism set in and the officers' status and prestige were openly upheld under Russian guidance and influence and made much more apparent. The Korean War accelerated this trend.

The military theory, evolved in the course of the long years of the civil war, had so far proved workable. It had enabled Mao to be victorious against Chiang Kai-shek. But when the PLA confronted the superior, modernized army of the United States during the Korean War, the tactics and techniques employed in the civil war did not prove to be very effective. "Now to defeat these new aggressors who differ from all our past enemies," to use the words of Peng Teh-huai, was, indeed, a very grave problem which could only be tackled by mastering modern weapons and learning to use them. Peking sought to exploit the subjective factor to the utmost by infusing among the so-called "People's Volunteers" ardent love of the motherland and deep hatred for the "aggressors" but the "highest revolutionary heroism," thus aroused, was found to be only of limited value.

The experience of the Korean War made Communist China openly admit the "many shortcomings," in the army, in comparison to that of the USA, "in the matter of modern weapons."[32] Thereafter, Peking set in earnest to transform the Red Army by "absorbing the highly advanced military science of the Soviet Union." Speaking on "The Tasks of the PLA," on the occasion of the 24th anniversry of the founding of the PLA, Commander-in-Chief Chu Teh observed : "Our troops *must* actively study technique and raise their technical level." He added :

> The Chinese PLA must build up its various arms, strengthen itself in modern technical equipment and strengthen its combat training and its fighting power, so as to undertake the historic tasks of defending the Motherland and opposing imperialist aggression.[33]

Even Hsiao Hua, the Deputy Director of the Political Department of the People's Revolutionary Military Council, had to admit the necessity of studying "modestly the highly developed military science of the Soviet Union." He affirmed the "Party's leadership in the army" and the application of Mao's principles of army building. At the same time, he recognized the need of making the PLA "a powerful modernised and regular national defence army."[34] Speaking on the occasion of the 25th anniversary of the founding of the PLA, Chu Teh observed :

> The Chinese People's Liberation Army is marching towards the goal of modernised powerful army of national defence. This is a great historic change in the history of the Chinese People's Liberation Army.[35]

It was, thus, clear that after the Korean War, the stress in army building was decidedly on modernization. Many distinctive features of the egalitarian model were discarded or modified and the PLA began to resemble the Soviet Army. Occasionally, however, it was asserted that "a basic factor in defeating any enemy" always remained the high morale and excellent political quality of the PLA.[36]

Before the Korean War, the PLA was an incongruous mass

of peasant-soldiers, and, therefore, it was not very difficult to divert it to production work. The Common Programme, the basic law of the land before the adoption of the Constitution in 1954, enjoined that, in addition to its duty of defending the "independence, integrity of territory and sovereignty of China," the PLA "shall, during peace time, systematically take part in agricultural and industrial production, assist in national construction work, on the condition of not hindering military tasks."[37] The necessity of setting up a political work system in the army and of educating the commanders and soldiers "in the revolutionary and patriotic spirit" was also mentioned in the Common Programme. The PLA's energies came to be directed to construction work when Mao Tse-tung, in his capacity as Chairman of the People's Revolutionary Military Council, issued a directive to that effect on 5 December 1949. In the directive, he stressed that the PLA was "not only an army of national defence, but an army of production to help the people throughout the country conquer the difficulties left behind by a long war and to speed up the construction of a New Democratic economy."[38] The officers and men in the PLA set to implement, in right earnest, the directive without any complaint.

The next time when the PLA was called upon to devote its energies on a large-scale to production work was in 1958, when the programme of the "Great Leap Forward" was launched. However, by 1958, the PLA had been transformed into a compact, highly-trained, modernized force with a status-conscious routinised and formalised officer corps. This was in marked contrast to the state of affairs existing before 1949 or even several years thereafter when the PLA was a huge, sprawling, semi-guerilla force, its soldiers were irregulars, its command structure rudimentary and equipment hetrogenous and, for the most part, obsolete. In 1957, it was stated that the size of the Chinese army, including recruits was 2.7 million less than in 1949.[39] (In 1949, the PLA was $4\frac{1}{2}$ million strong.) This sizable reduction in the numerical strength of the Chinese army signified that the primary stress was being laid not on the role of the human factor, but, on the material building of the army, *i.e.* on arms and equipment, technical facilities, industries that directly served army-building, communications and transport, etc. A network of military schools was set up. Professional and technical competence of the PLA made much headway under the guidance of Soviet officers and advisers. A military Academy of Science was opened in 1958 to train senior commanders.

The 1954 Constitution, adopted during this period of transformation of the PLA, made no mention either of diverting the armed forces to production work or of any political work in the army. Article 20 of the Constitution, the only article concerning the armed forces of Communist China (as compared with seven Articles in the Common Programme), stated that the duty of the armed forces, which belonged to the people, was "to safeguard the gains of the people's revolution and the achievements of national construction, and to defend the sovereignty, territorial integrity and security of the country."[40]

The Conscription Law, that came into effect in July 1955, sought to do away with the necessity of relying on "volunteers" for military personnel. It brought into sharp focus the distinction between the amateur citizen-soldier and the professional officer and thus helped regularisation. Far more conducive to the growth of professionalism in the Army was the adoption in February 1955 of the "Regulations on the Service of Officers." These regulations fundamentally altered the egalitarian and informal nature of the Chinese officer corps. They classified officers into categories based on their respective fields of specialisation and established a regular channel for entry into the officer corps and for advancement on the basis of professional competence.[41] These regulations defined ranks. Smart uniforms were also designed, distinguishing badges of rank came to be worn, saluting was made compulsory and good conditions of service were prescribed. Officers no longer took off their coats and set the example in working parties. Instead, they became aloof and detached.[42]

Shortly after the promulgation of the Regulations, the old system of providing both the officers and men with food and a small allowance in lieu of salaries was abolished in favour of cash payments. The scale of pay ranged from US $2.50 per month for a private to US $192-$236 for a full general. This was indicative of new differentiations. With the conferment of military titles and honours on Army leaders in the autumn of 1955, Chinese officers acquired all the trappings typical of a regular army.[43] In this context, Edgar O. Ballance observes :

> During the next three years these privileges, under the encouragement of the Russian Military Mission, increased and the Red Army officers' corps swelled, preened and glittered under the horrified gaze of the political officers and the older veterans, who, even if they did not exactly want all men to be equal, certainly did not desire such ostentatious differentiation.[44]

With the emergence of a professional officer corps—a step encouraged by the institution of ranks in 1955 and the introduction of strict disciplinary codes in 1953—the links between higher and lower levels in the PLA were considerably weakened. It was, therefore, not surprising that Tan Cheng, a former Deputy Minister of National Defence and Director of the GPD from late 1956 to 1964, complained in September 1956 of the Army's failure to maintain the traditions of democracy and of unity between the officers and the men. Relations between the two came under close examination in the rectification campaign that followed the "Hundred Flowers" movement of early 1957 and which was concerned with the military as much as with the rest of the population.

Prior to 1950, during periods of civil war and defence of the homeland, the commissars had greater opportunities for an active role than they subsequently had during the Korean War or thereafter. The creation of an increasingly modernized army seriously restricted their role within the armed forces. Besides, the introduction of conscription, ranks and a host of technical schools, plus the arrival of many Russian advisers, were causing concern to Mao personally and commissars generally, for these events spelled the increasing isolation of commanders (and their commissars) from the masses. After 1950, the Party was able to divest commanders of civil administrative functions, but it permitted them maximum authority within their professional sphere. As a result, the role of the GPD in collective decision-making was apparently reduced to an all-time low by the time Peng Teh-huai was dismissed in 1959. W.W. Whitson points out :

During the Korean War, the advent of ultra-professionalism in the PLA seriously undermined the credibility of the commissars, especially at the unit level. By 1954, with the formal reorganization of the PLA along Russian lines, the institution of ranks, conscription (in 1955), pay scales, and so forth, the commissar found his role seriously confined. During the war, his traditional right to countersign all orders was frequently ignored, especially at the company level where battle pressures are most acute....After the Korean War, during which the Party had expanded all over China in its efforts to mobilize national resources, commissars found their role within the PLA hampered by "purely military attitudes"—a reaction to United Nations firepower—which seemed to have infected both young commanders and political instructors at the company level. By 1960, the lack of enthusiasm among both groups for company-level political functions was reflected in the total absence of any party branch committees in more than 6,000 companies of the PLA. This undoubtedly was also a manifestation of the general skepticism among commanders regarding the utility of commissars in modern army....In spite of the post-1959 attempt to revive commissar authority at the unit level, the testimony of refugees and the general evidence of the Cultural Revolution suggest that this effort did not fundamentally alter the situation, either before or after the Cultural Revolution.[45]

4 Great Leap Forward and its Aftermath

The CCP launched the "Great Leap Forward" movement at a time when the PLA was fast becoming an increasingly complex, specialized and bureaucratic type of defence establishment and the authority and influence of commissars was on the decline. The Party expected that the army would not lag behind in making a success of the ambitious venture in the economic field. However, the professionals in the army resented any proposal requiring them to go to farms and engage in production work along with the rank and file. They considered it derogatory to their prestige and self-respect and thought that it would adversely affect their task of maintaining discipline. They disliked their energy and time being diverted to non-military purposes. It is pertinent to recall that within a fortnight of his becoming Minister of Defence, Lin Piao (who replaced Peng Teh-huai on 17 September 1959) criticized those "comrades" who, proceeded from the basis of a division of labour between economic construction and the building up of national defence. These "comrades," he observed, held that there was no need for the army to take part in "civilian" business, like the revolutionary struggles of the masses and national economic construction. They regarded such work as "an extra burden for the army" and "an obstruction to training."[46]

The professional officer corps' lack of interest in engaging themselves in the task of national reconstruction threatened to severe the close links between the PLA and the civilian population. Such an attitude also had the effect of undermining the traditional comraderie between the officers and rank and file, that is to say, the links between higher and lower levels. In these circumstances, there was a general feeling of disillusionment with Russian and foreign innovations. The increased professionalism within the PLA, which thrived under Peng Teh-huai, posed a serious threat to the Maoist concepts of a highly politicized, revolutionary, Party army. Consequently, the trend towards professionalism came to be regarded as retrogressive and dangerous.

The *Chieh-fang Chun-pao* (Peking) editorial of 1 July 1958, therefore, deemed it necessary to firmly affirm the need for realizing the "absolute leadership of the Party over the army." It recalled the abolition of the system of Party leadership over the army during the later stage of the "Second Revolutionary Civil War" (1927-36) and of the political commissar system "for a time" during the early period of the Anti-Japanese War (1937-45). In recollecting them, the editorial obviously had in mind the prevailing situation in the army in which military officers threatened the eclipse of the prestige and influence of the political officer within the PLA. Furthermore, in recalling that "only a timely action of the Party centre and Chairman Mao" had rectified the errors of the 1930's and "prevented greater losses," the editorial, it appeared, was seeking to emphasize the necessity of taking similar action in 1958. The paper observed :

> Purely military views, warlordism, and doctrinairism have revived among a part of the personnel. They assert that collective leadership of Party Committee is not adapted to the requirements of modernization and regularization. One-sidedly stressing the suddenness and complexity of modern warfare, they assert that the system of Party Committees will impede the better judgement and concentration of command. They even openly advocate liquidation of the system of Party Committee leadership. Further, in issuing certain orders and conducting military training, they liquidated and restricted the activities of Party Committee in leadership and political work.

A month later, another editorial in *Chieh-fang Chun-pao* (Peking) quoted Mao to the effect that "our army is not and cannot be [any] other type of army than one that must be a tool,

subordinate to the ideological leadership of the proletariat."
The paper pointed out that the army should not only be a
combat group but, at the same time, it must also be a mass
work team and a production team. The principles of army
building, which the editorial emphasized, were : "absolute
leadership of the Party over the army," adherence to the political commissar system and continued strengthening of political
work in the army. It pleaded for "a deeper insight into
Comrade Mao Tse-tung's military thinking and a clearer
understanding of the Marxist military line." The paper
observed :

> In the course of modernized building of our army, a very
> few comrades, because of the influence of bourgeois military
> thinking and doctrinairism, have showed some erroneous
> tendencies. One-sidedly stressing modernization and regu-
> larization they neglected the revolutionary nature of the
> people's army and neglected Party leadership and political
> work. They neglected the principle that the army and the
> people are one and neglected the three major tasks of the
> army. Neglecting the principle that officers and men are
> one, they one-sidedly stressed unification and centralization,
> over-stressed the individual authority of officers and neg-
> lected the promotion of democratic practices and the mass
> line. Based on the principle of military operations, they
> one-sidedly stressed the part of atomic weapons and modern
> military techniques and neglected the role of the people.[47]

On 13 October 1958, the *People's Daily* published Chang
Chun-chiao's article entitled, "Destroy Bourgeois Idea of
Right." Chang was all praise for the "free supply system,"
that was practised in the PLA before 1949, and denounced the
"wage system," which replaced the former in the mid-1950s.
The "free supply system," Chang observed, was a "revolutionary
tradition" and a "communist principle." Any attack on that
system by way of criticizing it as a "rural style" and "guerilla
habit," he stated, was "an attack launched by the bourgeoisie
in order to protect the unequal bourgeois rights." The free
supply system, Chang argued, promoted "proletarian equality"
whereas the "wage system" divided wages into many grades
and thus promoted a "bourgeois system of grades." He praised
the Paris Commune and advocated that all should "live

together, labour together, work together, struggle for communism."

The Party Central Committee and the State Council decided that government functionaries take part in manual work. The GPD of the PLA instructed officers "of all grades" to go to the companies to serve as ordinary soldiers for a month in a year.[48] The official *Hsinhua* news agency reported on 20 October 1958 that, according to incomplete statistics, over 70 generals and 10,000 cadres of the PLA had recently gone to the companies to serve as ordinary soldiers, dressing ordinary soldiers' uniforms, and eating, living, drilling, labouring and playing together with the other fellow soldiers in the companies.[49] By February 1959, James D. Jordan observes, over 150,000 officers, including 160 generals, had "returned to the ranks" and had performed such menial tasks as mess duty, cleaning spittoons, and sweeping out barracks. Even when the extreme measures of the movement were eventually abandoned, "the practice and encouragement of officers to return to the ranks continued at least until 1966."[50]

The Party hierarchy, simultaneously launched a "citizen-soldiers movement," which resulted in the considerable expansion of the people's militia. The militia was said to possess several advantages : making the entire nation militarily alert, inculcating into the people a greater sense of organization and a higher spirit of collectivism, giving members an all-round training in productive jobs and in defence training for the country.[51]

Maoist perspective and military policies, James D. Jordan points out, were reflected in at least six visible spheres :

1. the "men versus weapons theme" ;
2. the rejection of the Soviet military model ;
3. the democratization of the army with the officers to the ranks movement ;
4. the massive "Everyone a Soldier" militia campaign ;
5. the struggle for ideological control within the army ; and
6. the diversion of military resources of men and material into the Great Leap Forward programmes.[52]

Dismissal of Peng Teh-huai

The professionals in the army, as stated earlier, disliked the idea of officers serving as rank-and-file armymen or engaging themselves as auxiliary agricultural workers. They were also averse to the concept of nation-in-arms and its expression in the creation of an enormous untrained militia. These professional elements, in holding such views, evidently had the backing of such high personages as Marshal Peng Teh-huai, Minister of Defence and No. 3 Vice-Premier in the State Council, and General Huang K'o-ch'eng, Peng's senior Vice-Minister who replaced General Su Yu as Chief of General Staff of the Army in October 1958. Peng Teh-huai, was very critical of the Great Leap Forward movement and of people's communes and considered any weakening of war preparations and training tasks "impermissible." At the Lushan meeting of the CC of the CCP in August 1959, Peng found himself in a minority. He was, therefore, denounced for his erroneous thinking and purged, alongwith his associates and supporters.

Thus, Huang K'o-ch'eng and two other Vice-Ministers of National Defence—General Li Ta, Peng's Chief of Staff in Korea, and General Hsiao K'e, Chief of General Training Department—were dismissed in September 1959. General Hung Hsueh-chih (who was Head of the Rear Services of the Chinese People's Volunteers in Korea under Peng, later served as Deputy Head of Rear Services under Huang K'o-ch'eng, and became Head of Rear Services once again when Huang became Chief of Staff) lost his job a month later. At about the same time, the Commander of the Peking Garrison, General Yang Ch'eng-wu, was transferred to the Ministry of Defence, where he did not have command of the troops.[53] General Teng Hua, the Commander of the Shenyang Military Region, who defected to the Communist side with Peng-Teh-huai in the 1920s, was dismissed as Commander of that region. General Su Yu, who had been forced to vacate the post of Chief of General Staff on 12 October 1958 in order to make room for Huang K'o-ch'eng, was rehabilitated and became Vice-Minister of National Defence in September 1959.

The dismissal of Peng Teh-huai and the appointment of Lin Piao as Defence Minister in September 1959 did not immediately lead to any drastic changes in the existing system as such. The new team under Lin Piao proceeded cautiously and gradually. Lin tried to reach a series of compromises acceptable to all contending functional groups—the Party, Maoists, commissars and commanders. Thus neither the argument over the acquisition of nuclear weapons was dismissed nor the question of the modernization of the PLA or the role of the military disappeared. Nevertheless, a vigorous drive to promote political consciousness among the soldiers and the army was launched and greater emphasis was laid on exercising more effective Party control over the Army.

On 1 October 1959, Lin Piao, the new Defence Minister, asserted that the "Party's absolute leadership in the army has been consolidated." He stated that "we criticized... and firmly corrected in time" the wrong view held by "some comrades" about the army being called upon to take part in the "struggles of the masses" and the production work. Replying to the critics of the policy of employing the army in economic construction, he observed: "Only with our national economy developing at a rapid tempo can the modernization of our national defence be attained." Participation by the army in "mass movements," he said, "is a most vivid, fruitful and profound political schooling." He reaffirmed Mao's dictum: "Party commands the gun." Lin declared: "Our army is an army in the service of politics.... If political and ideological work is not done well, everything else is out of the question." Therefore, Lin averred, the strengthening of "theoretical education in Marxism-Leninism" and "in socialism and the general line of the Party" with a view to continuously eliminate from "people's minds the vestiges of bourgeois and petty-bourgeois ideology and enhance their socialist consciousness" would henceforth be regarded "a fundamental task in the building of our army." He criticized those "comrades" who believed that "modern warfare differs from warfare in the past" and attached "importance only to machinery," the mastery of technique and the raising of the technical level of "our army," and, thereby relegated "man's role" in warfare to a secondary place. Lin Piao observed: "We believe that although equipment and technique are important, the human factor is even more important."[54]

Political Work in the PLA under Lin Piao

With Lin Piao's appointment as Minister of National Defence in September 1959, a vigorous drive to promote political consciousness was launched and the army emerged as a kind of testing ground and model for political work methods. Lin Piao had been very closely associated with the PLA's political work programme, the most important plank of which was the study of Mao Tse-tung Thought. Therefore, ever since 1960, when he assumed charge of the day-to-day work of the Military Affairs Committee (MAC) of Party Central Committee, he issued a number of important instructions on strengthening political work within the PLA, based on Mao's Thought.

The meeting of the MAC, held from 14 September to 20 October 1960, adopted an important resolution on "Strengthening Political and Ideological Work in the Army." The resolution regarded Mao's Kutien speech of December 1929 as the basis for political work and laid considerable stress on Mao Tse-tung Thought and the mass line in the building of the PLA. The uninterrupted revolution of society, the resolution of the Military Affairs Committee stated, required an uninterrupted revolution in people's thoughts. History, it asserted, had shown that mighty enemies and powerful weapons "are not always to be dreaded; what is really to be dreaded is political corruption, departure from the masses of the people, ideological disarmament and laxity and even loss of the will to fight". The MAC resolution, therefore, criticized purely military and purely professional viewpoints, the idea of privilege and the absence of democratic spirit in dealing with people. It also deplored the attitude of suspicion and opposition towards the Party's General Line, the Great Leap Forward, and the People's Commune.

The Military Affairs Committee of the Party expressed concern about the fact that a few cadres placed themselves above the collective leadership of their Party branches and often made important decisions by themselves. It noted that, as of October 1960, about one third of the companies (primary units) had no Party branch committees; many platoons had no Party cells; and quite a few small technical units had no Party members at all. It, therefore, laid much emphasis on building Party organizations within the army. The MAC resolution stated: "We must achieve the goal of having Party members in squads, Party cells in platoons and Party branch committees in companies." The Company, it added, was a primary unit for the execution of combat, training and all other duties, including political work. The political officer of a company was "the agent of the political organ assigned to the company to conduct Party and mass work." The MAC criticized the tendency among the political officers to make use of administrative means more often than education and guidance. They were too much concerned with general administrative affairs and too little with political and ideological matters. They were also not very skillful in using the Party organization to bring the masses into action. Some individual political officers or commissars were found "politically impure and inadequately equipped for their duties."

The October 1960 resolution of the Party Military Affairs Committee laid equal emphasis on both modernization and revolutionization of the Army. The PLA, it stated, had always been a combat force as well as a working force—the defender of socialism and a builder of socialism. Accordingly, what was required was the building of a cadre force which was not only red but also expert. The MAC voiced its concern about the fact that a large number of new cadres were growing up under peaceful circumstances; that they lacked training and experience in both combat and practical work. Their original petty *bourgeois* ideology had also remained unchanged. The MAC resolution observed: "While strengthening the revolution of the army, we should also actively improve the quality of our military technique, operations and scientific research in order to speed up its modernization." This, it added, was "an extremely important task in the course of building our Army." Likewise, while carrying on the courses of study on military technique, operations and scientific research, "we must energetically strengthen our political work," successfully carry out "our work in dealing with men, reveal their subjective activity in the control of the technique, and make sure of the greatest possible technical use of equipment in the event of modern warfare."

The Military Affairs Committee was of the opinion that Party Committees at all levels in the PLA should become "the centre of uniform leadership and solidarity in the Army units" and assure to the Party "its absolute leadership over the Army units and the implementation and accomplishment of Party lines, policies, and all other tasks in the Army." Besides, the Party Committees must resolutely struggle with all those thoughts and kinds of behaviour which were in violation of the Party line and policies. The principle of collective leadership of Party Committees, the MAC resolution asserted, must be strengthened. Except in the case of an emergency, where the leader might take immediate action, "all major problems must be deliberated and decided by the Party Committee. No individual should be allowed to monopolize the power of decision or to make arbitrary decisions." Collective leadership, the MAC resolution of 20 October 1960 added, must be integrated with individual responsibility, and neither should be neglected. The Party Committee should place military chiefs and various departments under its unified leadership in order to prevent independent governance. The various leaders and departments should not only make timely reports to and seek instruction from the Party Committee about the scope of their work and its main condition and submit their problems to the Party Committee for deliberation and decision, but should also have the courage to take up responsibilities and accomplish their work in accordance with the decision of the Party Committee. Once a decision was taken by the Party Committee, the political organ must, from the viewpoints of political ideology and policy, supervise and urge various departments and units to execute and implement that decision seriously and thoroughly. The MAC resolution declared:

> We must carry through thoroughly the system of dual leadership of the military system and the local Party Committee over the Army units under the unified leadership of the Central Authorities of the Party, in order to enable the local Party Committee to acquire the leadership and [the power of] supervision over the Army units, to cement the ties of the Army with the local Party Committee, to strengthen coordination and mutual support in our work, and to promote national economic construction and defense construction.[55]

Thus, the MAC resolution was a balanced document. It laid stress on political work and Party leadership but, at the same time, it recognized the importance of military training, scientific research and modernization.

Addressing a conference of high-ranking cadres of the PLA in October 1960, Marshal Lin Piao stated that the principal shortcoming in the Army's political work in the past few years had been "insufficient attention to ideological questions." Therefore, since May 1960, about 120,000 cadres in the entire army were ordered to go down to the companies and basic levels to promote the movement, the first motto of which was "keep firmly to the correct political direction," and engage in political and ideological work "in a big way." Political work, he said, was "very important." It was, as Mao said, "the life line" of the PLA, "the supreme commander, the soul and the guarantor of all work." The "spiritual atomic bomb," *i. e.* man's ideological consciousness and courage, Lin declared, "is much more powerful and useful than the material atomic bomb."[56]

Thereafter, Marshal Lin Piao issued "extremely important directives"—which later came to be known as the "four firsts,"—on the army's political work. These directives pertained to the relationship between weapons and man, that between other work and political work, that between administrative and ideological aspects in the political work, and that between book thought and dynamic thought in ideological work. The principle for the settlement of these four relationships, Lin pointed out, was: "The human factor first, political work first, ideological work first, and dynamic thought first." He added: "What has to be done well is, in the final analysis, the ideological work of man. Such is the direction for our political work in building a modern revolutionary army and for the entire work of Army building."[57]

Accordingly, in the winter of 1960, Lin Piao issued an appeal to the entire Army requiring it to initiate a movement for creating four good companies. He called upon every company to become good politically and ideologically, good in exemplifying the "three-eight" style,[58] good in military training and good in managing daily life. It was believed that the over-all effect of this movement would be to promote political work in the PLA and to consolidate and increase the combat strength of the Army. Li Chih-min's article in *Red Flag*

(1 December 1960), entitled "A Military Expert of the Proletariat Must Also Be A Politician of the Proletariat," asserted that political work was "the prime factor of our army's fighting capacity."[59] On 5 November 1960, the General Political Department of the PLA issued a directive regarding the promotion of the "five good" campaign within the PLA. It required soldiers to be good in political thinking, in military skill, in the "three-eight" working style, in performing assigned tasks, and in physical training.[60]

In subsequent years, Peking authorities at the Centre continued to lay considerable stress on the strengthening of political and ideological work in the army. The declining morale and combat effectiveness of the armed forces, which followed in the wake of the failure of the "Great Leap Forward," the serious agrarian depression and the withdrawal of Soviet aid, was sought to be overcome by Lin Piao's politico-military campaigns, in which great emphasis was laid on "politics in command," *i.e.* on an increasing degree of Party control and indoctrination in the PLA.

Impact of the Economic Crisis, 1959-61

During 1959-1961, China had to face one of the most severe natural calamities "in a century."[61] The aggravation of relations with the Soviet Union, the recall of 1,300 Soviet experts from China in July 1960, the withholding of essential supplies and the continuance of ideological differences—all these further worsened the already bad economic situation. It also tended to create political and ideological confusion amongst the cadres. Peking, thus, came to face a very critical situation which posed a serious threat to Chairman Mao's position.

The documents, consisting of the 29 issues of the secret "Bulletin of Activities" of the GPD of the PLA dated 1 January to 26 August 1961, which were released to scholars by the US State Department on 5 August 1963, revealed that there were recurring civilian and military disorders and, widespread discontent on the mainland in 1960 and 1961. As of July 1960, about 7,000 companies in the Army did not have Party branch Committees while in others the existing Party Committees were stated to have failed to perform their function as a result of the frequent absence of Party branch cadres from the companies. The situation had become so serious that 82% of the total number of Party branches throughout the army had to be "adjusted" during the seven-month period from July 1960 to February 1961. During the same period Party organs at various levels assigned 78,000 cadres "to give concrete assistance to companies." Over 229,000 new Party members were recruited in the PLA in 1960. By March 1961, all the companies that had lacked Party Committees were reported to have established them again. By that time, more than 80% of the platoons were stated to have organized Party cells and over half the squads in the entire army were said to have Party members.[62]

The armed forces suffered from low morale and there were a number of defections from the army, although their extent was not specified in the bulletins. In one army company, 5 per cent of the men were found to be so disaffected that they went to the extent of blaming Mao personally for the country's troubles. In March 1961, 3 out of every 10 soldiers were said to have "wrong" ideas about local Communist Party officials. Serious "disturbances" of peace were reported in 6 of the 7 districts of the Hunan province where civilian militiamen were said to have led the protests, killing Communist Party members, wrecking communication lines and stopping military convoys. The soldiers' thinking was "shaken seriously" during the later half of 1960 and the first three months of 1961. In order to counteract the discontent in the army, the Government gave better rations to troops, accorded preferential treatment to their relatives in the distribution of plots of land, and allowed them to visit military camps to share soldiers' rations. The soldiers were also permitted to take food home.[63]

Against this background, the 9th Plenary Session of the Eighth Central Committee of the CCP (14-18 January 1961) decided that the rectification campaign be carried out throughout the whole country "to help the cadres enhance their ideological and political level, improve their method and style of work and purify the organizations by cleaning out the extremely few bad elements." The Session also took an important step towards strengthening Party control and tightening its grip over the whole country by setting up six Bureaus of the

Central Committee in various regions.[64]

On 2 February 1961, the *People's Daily* reported that the GPD in the PLA had issued a notification on the unfolding of "support the government, love the people" movement during the Spring Festival of 1961.[65] Another movement to "give support to the armed forces and preferential treatment to the dependents of service-men" was also launched simultaneously. The *People's Daily* editorial of 15 February 1961 stated that "concern for their [soldiers] welfare should constantly be shown and assistance should be given in solving their difficulties in production and in their daily life." Such an attitude, the editorial pointed out, was "of great significance in establishing close relations among the Party, the government, the troops and the people, in raising the morale of the troops and in the strengthening of national defence." At the same time, the Party paper reminded the PLA officers and men, that the Chinese army had been built "under the ideological directions of the Party and Comrade Mao Tse-tung" and that the "glorious traditions of the PLA" consisted of "strict observance of the programs, lines, principles, policies and decrees of the Party and the government...protecting the people's interests and unity with the government."[66] There was constant exhortation about the continuing need of preserving harmony between the army and people, loyalty to the Party, its leader Mao and the People's Government.

In July 1961, the Ministry of National Defence promulgated "Regulations Governing PLA Management and Education Work at the Company Level." Drawn on the basis of extensive investigations "throughout the army" of the "conditions in the army units," these regulations emphasized the necessity of "internal unity" among the officers and men. All the cadres and soldiers of the army were declared "class brothers...completely equal politically" with no distinction whatsoever in personal status. The cadres were asked to show love for the rank and file while the latter were required to respect the former.[67] The *Hsinhua* news agency considered the handling of the educational work in the PLA "an administrative and an important political ideological task." Its purpose was: to bolster internal unity; bring into full play the revolutionary enthusiasm of all the troops; tighten organization and discipline;

strengthen and improve the combat strength; and insure "the successful completion of the building of our army and fulfillment of its glorious duties of defending the motherland and peace."[68]

In an article in *People's Daily* on 28 July 1961, Fan Ke stated that professional skill was "subordinate to politics" and that "stress on modernization to the neglect of revolutionization is precisely a reflect of purely military viewpoint" on the questions of army building. He even asserted: "It is precisely because of the assumption of command by politics in the people's army that it is proficient in the military sense." To accord the foremost position to professional skills and technology was an "erroneous tendency" which, he said, must be criticized. The propagation and implementation of Party policies and programmes and the elimination of *bourgeois* ideas, he added, was possible only when the task of army building took place "under the absolute leadership of the Party." The *People's Daily* article stated: "The most fundamental guarantee for strengthening the political work in our army and building our army into a modernized revolutionary army is to arm our army with the Thought of Mao Tse-tung."[69]

In the face of grave internal and external difficulties, the Chinese authorities also laid considerable stress on forging unity inside the army and within the country. *Chieh-fang Chun-pao*, in its editorial of 1 August 1962, observed :

> We must have unity inside and outside the army. Unity must be achieved inside the army between the cadres and soldiers, between the superiors and subordinates, between military work and political work, and between this unit and that unit, and outside between the army and the people, between the army and local authorities. Unity is the most important weapon with which to defeat the enemy. All the people in the army must closely unite together; the soldiers and the people must closely unite together. Thus they will form themselves into a torrent that will drown all enemies.[70]

Writing in *Red Flag* on the occassion of the 35th anniversary of the founding of the PLA, Hsiao Hua described the Chinese army as a new-type army, which must be "completely under Party leadership and carry out both military and political revolutionary tasks." He declared: "There must be strong political work in the army." Military, political and economic democracy, he observed, must be practised within the army "under centralized leadership in order to forge unity in our own ranks and defeat the enemy."[71]

On 28 December 1962, the *People's Daily* reported the GPD's call that urged all armed force units to do their best "to support the production efforts of the masses in the areas where they are stationed, doing so without neglecting military training and the execution of other tasks." However, an exception was made in respect of units stationed in calamity-stricken areas who were asked to "actively cooperate with the local Party and administrative departments in solving the difficulties confronting the masses."[72]

5 All-Army Political Work Conferences

After the Military Affairs Committee of the Chinese Communist Party adopted the "Resolution on Strengthening Political and Ideological Work in the Army" at its meeting on 20 October 1960, a number of PLA Political Work Conferences were convened more or less annually by the General Political Department of the PLA. The first such Conference was held in Peking from 18 October to 11 November 1961. The Conference reviewed and summed up the success and experience acquired by the whole army in strengthening the politico-ideological work over the past year. It also studied the ways and means to extend the campaign to create four-good companies and strengthen the political work in companies.[73] In his report to the PLA Political Work Conference, Hsiao Hua, Deputy Director of the GPD, enunciated ten principles concerning political, educational and ideological work for company units. He emphasized: "We must constantly promote proletarian thought, destroy *bourgeois* thought, remould thought, raise consciousness and increase the fighting will."[74]

All-Army Political Work Conference, 1963

General Hsiao Hua's report to the All-Army Political Work Conference, held from 2 to 27 February 1963, laid stress on continuing "extensively and penetratingly throughout the Army" the movement for creating four-good companies. That movement, it might be recalled, assigned first place to being good politically and ideologically and deemed it to be "the most important of all the factors of our Army's combat strength." Hsiao Hua stated that although the role of weapons and technical equipment had increased in modern war, but the factor which decided the outcome of war remained, as before, "man and not material." Accordingly, what was to be feared was neither the enemy nor the weapons but "political degeneration, separation from the masses of the people, ideological disarmament, and the weakening or the loss of the determination to fight." In fact, the fewer the material things, the greater must be the reliance on the political and ideological work which would turn the spiritual force, (man's courage, consciousness and spirit of sacrifice) into a material force, so that one man can serve as several men and one company as several companies. Therefore, "a high degree of class hatred for the enemy and a positive war-demanding mood" needed to be instilled in soldiers, against US "imperialism", Chiang Kai-shek and all reactionaries. In order to retain the initiative in war, it was considered essential that the soldiers do away with the concept of being "peace-time soldiers." They should always remain in combat readiness, such as in the war of "self-defence" along the Sino-Indian border. "Regular and concrete education in war preparations", Hsiao asserted, must form an important part of their training so that they no longer feared "imperialism, the atom bomb, or any kind of evil thing." On the contrary, they must have confidence in their "certain victory." There must be, he affirmed, "no pacifism or liberalism."

A careful reading of Hsiao Hua's report reveals that while he supported Mao's thesis that the human factor was more important than either equipment or technique and emphasized the need of heightening the "class consciousness and fighting spirit" of soldiers, he did not, at the same time, overlook the necessity of proper military training of the army. "The principal task of the army," he said, was "to fight battles" and the companies' political work must effectively insure the completion of military training tasks. Apparently, political work was a means for achieving this objective. Hsiao Hua also laid stress on the complex nature of modern warfare in the following words :

In the past, training depended mainly on fighting. At present, fighting is learned mainly through training. Besides, the arms and equipment of the Army today are much more complex than those in the past. They cannot be mastered till after proper training....That is why the companies' political work must insure the smooth completion of training tasks and insure mobility, accurate shooting, good communications, good command, and good cooperation. This is an important purpose of political work.

At several places in his report, Hsiao Hua stressed the need for efficiency, physical fitness, technical knowledge and practical experience, although he was careful enough to insert remarks to the effect that political education was necessary for achieving those ends. The emphasis on the leadership of the Party in the army was tempered with by the advice given to the "hard cores of the party branch" to act democratically and "listen humbly to the criticism and opinions of party members, especially those who are warriors" (*i.e.* military experts). Hsiao Hua assigned a place of pride to both political education and military training, *i.e.* both theoretical and practical preparations for combat. He asserted :

If our forces have a high fighting spirit and fine military training and are tough not only politically and ideologically but also tactically and technically, they will be like tigers to which wings have been added and will be always matchless.[75]

It was quite apparent that while the principle of giving supremacy to political work had been established at the meeting of the Military Affairs Committee in October 1960 and Lin Piao's doctrine of the "Four Firsts" had become the official policy of the PLA, divergent opinions advocating the promotion of purely military affairs had not altogether disappeared. Hsiao Hua sought to strike a *via media* between the two viewpoints by pointing out the importance of the study of Mao's Thought and of political work, and, at the same time, laying stress on the complex nature of modern warfare. He asserted that fighting battles was the army's main duty, and called for regular and concrete education in war preparations. In retrospect, it appears that Hsiao Hua's statement that the "principal task of the army is to fight battles" might have contributed to his purge in 1967. It is worth recalling that, during the Cultural Revolution, Ulanfu, former Commander and Political Commissar of the Inner Mongolian Region, was accused of denying the political aspect of the PLA and of claiming that the "purpose of building an army is to fight battles."[76] Lo Jui-ching was criticized, among other things, for having given equal prominence to military affairs and politics and for his argument that politics must find concrete expression in military affairs.

Regulations on Political Work in the PLA, 1963

The All-Army Political Work Conference of 1963 adopted "Regulations on Political Work in the PLA." Absolute Party control over the army was considered essential for enhancing both general morale and military efficiency. Promulgated by the Party Central Committee on 27 March 1963, these regulations, it was stated, gave vivid expression to the Thought of Mao Tse-tung, summed up the rich experiences gained in political work in the army during the past several decades and expounded the major principles of political work in the army and the standards of action for the PLA.[77]

The basic tasks of the Army, as defined in these Regulations, was stated to be not only defence of the "country's sovereignty, territorial integrity and security" and the liberation of Taiwan but also defence of "peace in the East and in the World." Its duty, it was emphasized, was to strive for carrying out the Party's programme and policies and to serve the cause of socialism and communism throughout the world. The Regulations declared : "Our army is the defender and builder of the cause of Socialism." The military line was subordinated to the political line and the PLA was considered a tool for implementing the theories of Mao Tse-tung regarding class struggle, proletarian revolution, the fight against imperialism and modern revisionism. The regulations described Mao as "a great contemporary Marxist-Leninist" of the epoch when imperialism was heading towards collapse and socialism was advancing towards victory. His idea that the decisive factor in a war were human beings, not materials, was affirmed.

Furthermore, the Regulations set out in detail the entire mechanism of relationships between military commanders, political commissars, Party Committees and political departments at all levels from the military region down.

The "positive leadership" of the Party over the army was sought to be ensured by emphasizing the necessity of installing political commissars and political organizations in army units at and above the regimental level, and political instructors at battalion and company levels. The political commissars ordinarily served as the Secretaries—that is the most powerful leaders—of the Party Committees in the PLA. These Party Committees exercised over-all direction and supervision and were stated to serve as "the core for the unified leadership." The army was placed under the "dual leadership" of the military system under the unified leadership of the Party's Central Committee and the local Party Committees. In this system, the political commissar played a crucial role. Therefore, the political commissars, alongwith the military commanders, were described as leading or commanding officers of army units who were "jointly responsible for the work of the army units." In other words, the operational orders, in order to be effective, required the counter-signature of the political commissar.

Some kind of division of labour was sought to be instituted between the military commander and the political commissar whereby questions pertaining to the field of military work were entrusted to the former for the purpose of organizing such work and implementing them. Apparently, the political commissars had to look after the questions pertaining to the so-called political and ideological work. But, the Regulations so defined the main contents of the political work that it was well within the ambit of the Political Commissars' powers to see that the Party's programmes, lines and policies were faithfully carried out and State laws and decrees duly observed. The Regulations also empowered political commissars to assess combat readiness, oversee military research and development, and evaluate the performance of the professional officers. In short, the scope of activity of the military commander was very limited, and that of the political commissar quite extensive. The latter was expected to look after propaganda work, the fighting morale, discipline and the fulfilment of fighting tasks. (See Appendix 6)

Besides, the political commissar was also required to educate

> the entire personnel in developing the internationalist spirit, and seriously carry out well the work of uniting with the allied army and of consolidating the developing militant friendship between our army and allied armies.

Although the exact meaning of "allied army" was not spelled out, any insurgent force that could help in ensuring the "security" of China or in spreading the "cause of socialism," as interpreted by Mao Tse-tung or the CCP could easily be deemed to be an "allied army" with whom it would be necessary for the PLA to collaborate. Although this had dangerous implications for peace in Asia and the world, it nonetheless reflected the "General Line" of the Chinese Communist Party as put forward in its reply letter dated 14 June 1963 to the Communist Party of the Soviet Union.[78]

The revival of "Committee decisions" and commissar counter-signature under Lin Piao's leadership strengthened the hands of the commissars. The new code of Political Work Regulations, drawn up in February 1963 and based on Draft Regulations promulgated in 1954, also gave more authority to the political commissar. By making both the political commissar and the military commander "army unit leaders," the former was, in effect, placed in a position to supervise the activities of the latter. This step was intended to guard against "the tendency of unilaterally pursuing a purely military viewpoint," as *People's Daily* of 10 May 1963 put it. Thus, it was only after 1960 that commissars, whose influence had continued to decline during the era of professionalization and regularization under Peng Teh-huai, were again given a chance to attain parity with the commanders—a process that reached a climax and ultimately provoked commander defiance during the Cultural Revolution. According to W.W. Whitson, the commissars increased their functions and power in a low, erratic manner. He states :

> The 1931 decision to incorporate the commissar system

within the new General Political Department, modeled on its Russian counterpart, led to increasing professionalization and specialization. As the commissar system developed, it gradually eroded the power of other agencies. In order to build and maintain loyalty, commissars sought to establish their control, through the GPD, over *all* military educational curricula ; all morale-building activities, including indoctrination, sports, and organized recreation, "troop-cheering" teams, official military news broadcasts and newspapers, dependent welfare programs (special discounts, housing, rations, and privileges) ; and all discipline-oriented areas, such as the military legal system, the rights and duties of commanders toward their subordinates, and the inspector-general function. At the same time, the need to measure loyalty and *evaluate* political behavior inevitably led commissars to seek centralized control over counter-intelligence and security functions, special investigations, and, ultimately, personnel assignments and promotions.

Although the PLA's earliest commissar system did not clearly place centralized control of these functions among its objectives, the two broad missions of building and measuring loyalty logically led to struggles between the commissars and their competitors. These struggles involved primacy in policy-making, if not command authority. Since they regarded themselves as an "institutional conscience," members of the commissar "priesthood" had a built-in bias against any group that refused to accept their operational ethic, their dictatorial behaviour patterns, and their exclusive right of interpretation.

By late 1966, the post-1960 rise of commissar power relative to commanders and the Party had reached a climax and, in the name of "Maoism" was threatening both military and civil chains of command.[79]

Political Work Conference, 1964

Another All-Army Political Work Conference on questions relating to current political work in the PLA was convened in Peking in the third week of January 1964 by the GPD of the PLA. It called on all members of the army to hold even higher the great red banner of Mao Tse-tung's thinking in the new year, *i.e.* 1964, and urged them to go all out, work vigorously and attain new heights in the work of developing 'four good' companies. The Conference pointed out that the army had stood "the tests of complicated domestic and international class struggles." The PLA, it stated, had proved itself worthy of the name of an army of workers and peasants led by Chairman Mao Tse-tung and the Chinese Communist Party and "worthy to be called a great people's army." By studying the works of Mao Tse-tung and applying them to practice "more often, more effectively and with greater scope," the Conference emphasized, not only would the greatest possible number of cadres and soldiers have "a clear idea of the country" but they would also be immune from the influence of the "spontaneous trend toward capitalism and the bourgeois way of life." The Conference also called upon the whole army to strive to bring about "an all-round rise in its combat capability" and to accomplish with outstanding results the various tasks set for it by the Party and the State.[80] Thus, it was apparent that while the primary stress was laid on raising the political consciousness of the personnel, the aspect of military training was not neglected.

Hsiao Hua's report to the Conference referred to the "complicated international and domestic class struggle," the problem of calamity rescue and relief, the necessity of carrying out "the educational movement in socialist consciousness and in opposing modern revisionism," and the need for further strengthening the role of Party branches over the companies. He also made reference to certain shortcomings in the thinking of the cadres and asked them to "further comprehend the correctness and greatness of Mao Tse-tung's thinking." Outlining the tasks for 1964, Hsiao Hua stated :

> In 1964, it is necessary to strengthen education against modern revisionism and to make the PLA troops perceive clearly, stand firmly, and withstand any test in the complicated class struggle at home and abroad by giving them political and ideological education.

In this connection, Hsiao Hua laid particular stress on the necessity "to manage and utilize newspapers well," in accordance with the "important instructions" of Marshal Lin Piao, issued recently. Under these instructions, newspapers were required to "maintain a firm grip on the living ideology" and "closely observe the spirit of the Party Central Committee, Chairman Mao and the Military Affairs Committee." The

Party Committees, it was stated, should strengthen the leadership over the newspapers.

Although Hsiao Hua's report was mainly devoted to strengthening political education in the army, he pleaded, at one place, for "further understanding" the importance of military training. "Political work," he said, "must guarantee fulfilment of the mission in military training for 1964 and, on the basis of socialist education, motivate the activism of cadres and soldiers in a still satisfactory way in order to bring about a new upsurge in military training." All military cadres should, at the same time, undertake "ideological work during military training." Thus, in accordance with the well-known Chinese practice of "walking on two legs," he emphasized the need of being "both politically red and professionally proficient," though the main thrust of his argument was towards "politics in command."[81]

The campaign "Learn from the Experience of the PLA in Political and Ideological Work" was launched by the *People's Daily* editorial of 1 February 1964. It signified that the army's excellence in political work must be emulated in other sectors, such as industry, commerce and government. In particular, the techniques of political education and control (in force in the army since 1960 when Lin Piao assumed charge of the day-to-day work of the Military Affairs Committee), *viz.* the "four firsts," "four good" and "five good" movements, the PLA's "revolutionary work style" and so on were to be observed. The *People's Daily* editorial observed :

> Created and led by the Chinese Communist Party and Comrade Mao Tse-tung, the Chinese PLA is a highly proletarianized, highly militant army of workers and peasants ....During the past decades, the PLA has carried on the excellent traditions and working style of the Party. This is due fundamentally to the guidance of all its work by the thinking of Mao Tse-tung. The PLA is an invincible army because it has laid great emphasis on political and ideological work, maintains the excellent traditions and working style of China's revolutionary army and attaches importance to strengthening work at the basic level. This valuable experience of the PLA should be studied widely in order to bring into fuller play the proletarian, militant, revolutionary spirit in the socialist revolution and all fields of socialist construction.[82]

Soon after the launching of the "Learn from the PLA" campaign, individuals as well as military collectives came to be singled out as shining examples for the rest of society. Thus, military heroes, such as Lei Feng, Wang Chieh, Mai Hsien-teh, Liu Ying-chun, etc. or the "good eight company" were presented before the people as models of self-sacrifice and heroism and people in all walks of life were asked to emulate them. In retrospect, one can say that this call to emulate the army's methods and style of work was apparently an indirect rebuke to the Party apparatus, controlled by Liu Shao-chi, for not doing its job properly. Parris H. Chang observes :

> Opposed and obstructed by his colleagues who controlled the Party organization, Mao was compelled to find a new power base outside the Party organization to project his will, and he subsequently turned to the PLA [and particularly, the GPD], which had, in his eyes, evolved into the foremost revolutionary organization in China....The GPD of the PLA, under Lin Piao's stewardship, became the Party's first competitive institution, becoming the object of national emulation after 1963 and rivaling the Party in prestige and political/ideological correctness. It also became Mao's instrument of power, used first to apply pressure on and then to attack the Party bureaucracy.[83]

The strengthening of political work, based on Mao Tse-tung Thought, afforded an opportunity for the commissars to embark on their political duties with youthful zeal while the "Learn from the PLA" movement greatly facilitated the extension of their activities into the civil sphere. A number of military men were transferred to civilian departments and financial and business enterprises, primarily with a view to prevent corruption and waste. According to the *People's Daily* of 18 May 1965 about 200,000 ex-PLA officers and men were working in various government, trade and financial institutions. The transfer of PLA personnel to civilian duties was sought to be counter-balanced, to a certain extent, by despatching many civilian economic officials and political cadres for political "referesher courses" to PLA units and training schools.

Abolition of Ranks

The abolition of all formal ranks and insignia in the PLA

by a decree, promulgated by the State Council on 24th May 1965, was part of the national campaign to strengthen ideological and socialist education, to enforce new discipline in the armed forces and to reinstate politics in a commanding position. The abolition of distinction between the officer corps and the general body of cadres weakened the claim of the officers to a monopoly of technical expertise. It also had the effect of increasing the power of the political cadres, who needed no insignia to exercise control over their units in the army. It might be recalled that the system of uniforms and insignia (instituted on 8 February 1955 alongwith the introduction of compulsory military service in the country) took into account the lessons of the Korean War on the need for a definite organizational structure in running a modern army. The creation of military ranks, the *People's Daily* editorial declared on 28 September 1955, would "facilitate the raising of the organizational and disciplinary spirit of military units."

During the ten years of existence of the military ranks, professionalism in the armed forces was seen coming into prominence and raising its ugly head. The development of "rank consciousness and ideas to gain fame and wealth" were undermining the "spirit of collectivism, revolutionary zeal and whole-hearted service to the people." The virus of "professionalism" was eating into the vitals of the established dogma "politics in command" and was weakening the mass base of the armed forces.

According to the Army's secret military journal *Kung-tso T'ung hsun* (*Bulletin of Activities*) more than 1,200 Party members and 940 probationery Party members had been dropped from the Party during the campaign launched by Lin Piao in 1960 for the reconstitution of the PLA Party branches.[84] However, the purge of Peng Teh-huai, Huang K'o-ch'eng etc. and the subsequent attempts of Lin Piao did not materially reduce the number of those harbouring "professional" views. Since veteran cadres were much less amenable to indoctrination than younger recruits, Lin Piao's "army-building" campaigns of the 1960s failed to win over many of the "professionally"-oriented cadres that remained in the PLA. The purge of PLA Chief of Staff, Lo Jui-ching, in 1965 invited speculation that the issue of "professionalism" was still far from resolved.[85]

The move to abolish ranks, Ralph L. Powell states, was an attempt to revive "in a vast, conscript garrison force the 'glorious traditions' of the Red Army : the elan, comraderie and revolutionary spirit of the years of revolutionary warfare" and "to reinforce political control even at the expense of professional competence, if necessary". An external objective, Powell adds, was "to remove another symbol of Soviet influence, for the system of organisation of ranks, adopted in 1955, had been closely patterned after that of the Soviet Union." Commenting on "other political motives" behind the decision to abolish military ranks, Powell observes as follows :

> The abolition of personnel ranks reduced the prestige of professional officers. Authority would no longer arise from conventional military seniority or ranks, but rather from the position to which the Party leaders assigned an officer. This could simplify the rapid promotion of commissars or politically active younger officers at the expense of veteran commanders. Finally, the abolition of ranks would facilitate the purge of some senior officers.[86]

The abolition of ranks did not signify that military commanders had ceased to be an important factor in Chinese politics. "Regardless of protestations to the contrary," W. W. Whitson points out, "professionalism and the *bourgeois* military line were the prevalent values within the PLA." In the sphere of ideology and indoctrination, the authority of the commissars still remained carefully circumscribed by military professionals.[87] During Peng Teh-huai's leadership, when "professionalism" and modernization were on the ascendancy, the tradition of political control had not altogether disappeared. Likewise, Lin Piao's politico-military campaigns of the early 1960s could not wholly root out the poisonous seed of professionalism from the army. In a way, the injunction in the *People's Daily* of 21 September 1965 that "Party organizations of all levels must *further* implement the principles of placing the armed forces under Party control and firmly grasp the militia work programme" lent support to the view that the absolute leadership of the Party over the army was far from established.

On 15 November 1965, Lin Piao issued five "important instructions" to the PLA as its guiding principles for 1966.

These five principles were :

1. creatively study and apply Chairman Mao's works, regard them as the highest instructions on all aspects of the work of the army ;
2. persist in giving first place to man as compared with weapons, to political work as against other work, to ideological work as against routine tasks in political work, and to living ideas as against ideas in books ;
3. leading cadres must go to the basic units and give energetic leadership in the campaign to produce out-standing companies and ensure that the basic units do their work effectively ;
4. boldly promote really good commanders and fighters to key posts of responsibility ;
5. train hard and master the finest techniques and close-range and night-fighting tactics.[88]

PLA Political Work Conference, January 1966

The 20-day PLA Political Work Conference of January 1966 was held at a time when "US aggression against Vietnam" was continuing and the first salvoes of the Cultural Revolution were being launched behind-the-scenes. That period—the first phase of the Cultural Revolution—was largely free of disorder and the Conference proceedings gave an appearance of a facade of unity between different contending groups within the political leadership.

The Conference discussed the instructions given by the CC of the CCP and Chairman Mao on building up the army, political work in the army and Lin Piao's five-point principle on keeping politics in the forefront. The Conference undertook a review of political work in 1964 and 1965, and finalized arrangements for political work in 1966. The Conference was addressed by Chou En-lai, Teng Hsiao-ping, Peng Chen, Hsiao Hua and Yang Cheng-wu. The consensus at the Conference was obviously the result of a compromise arrived at between diffe-rent viewpoints. Thus, the Conference stressed the importance of creative study and application of Mao's works and imple-mentation of Lin Piao's five-point principle of putting politics first (which was said to be in conformity with Mao's teachings). At the same time, it recognized that "the decisive factor in putting politics first was Party leadership." The army, it was stated, must come under the absolute leadership of the Party and the supervision of the masses in order to ensure that the principles, policies and programmes of the Party were resolutely implemented within the PLA. At the same time, the viewpoint of the military commanders and professionals was also not lost sight of. In the face of US imperialism wanting to impose war on the Chinese people and desiring to have a contest of strength with China, the PLA Conference declared : "To increase our combat readiness is not a temporary measure but a long-term strategic task. All our work must be put on a footing of readiness to fight." The strengthening of both revolutionization and modernization of the army was considered necessary and particular emphasis was laid on strengthening the work of building the Party organization in the army.[89]

While the *Hsinhua* press release on the *People's Daily* coverage of the PLA Conference was more or less of a non-controversial nature, the report delivered at the Conference by Hsiao Hua, Director of the GPD of the PLA, left no doubt about the views held by the GPD in the matter. "Our army," the Chief of the GPD declared, "is a worker-peasant army led by the Party and Chairman Mao and is *an instrument of class struggle.*" He laid great stress on studying Mao's ideas on people's war and on strengthening "political and ideological work in order to raise the level of the people's proletarian consciousness." By carrying out Lin Piao's five-point principle, Hsiao Hua explained, "we are able to use Chairman Mao's theory and line of army building" to overcome the *bourgeois* theory and line, to further purify and consolidate the Army politically, ideologically and organizationally, and to enable it to make great strides forward "toward becoming a highly proletarian and militant army."

He criticized those persons who asserted that "military affairs are politics" and/or that "military affairs and politics are of equal importance." Such views, Hsiao Hua observed, were "absolutely wrong...most harmful and run counter to what Chairman Mao has always taught." Furthermore, such views, he added, represented the purely military point of view and either confused politics with military affairs or substituted military affairs for politics. Military affairs, he emphasized, were the part and politics the whole. "Politics commands military affairs, and military affairs serve politics," he declared.

The Army, Hsiao Hua stated, must be "under the absolute leadership of the Party and the supervision of the people." It must be "the most faithful and responsive instrument of the Party." The system of dual leadership by the military command and the local Party Committees, under the unified leadership of the Party's Central Committee, he said, must be resolutely enforced, collective leadership by the Party Committees strengthened and the principle of democratic centralism adhered to. Party Committees and political departments at all levels, Hsiao Hua remarked, must put politics first. In all preparations, the first and foremost place should be assigned to political and ideological work.

"To meet the needs of the situation and of our Army building," Hsiao Hua observed, "we must boldly promote really good commanders and fighters to key posts of responsibility, in accordance with the teachings of Chairman Mao and the instructions of Comrade Lin Piao." This, he said, was an important organizational measure for guaranteeing the implementation of the five-point principle of putting politics first. According to Hsiao Hua, the standard of selecting cadres must be : faithful adherence to Mao Tse-tung's thinking ; wholehearted service to the great majority of the people of China and the world ; ability to unite and work with the overwhelming majority ; a democratic style of work ; and a self-critical spirit. Old cadres, Hsiao Hua stated, should welcome new cadres with great warmth. Basic-level cadres, he said, were the foundation of the ranks of the cadres. He declared : "We must boldly break with accepted conventions and really promote commanders and fighters who are politically reliable, young, capable and full of drive, and who have a good style to work."[90]

The *Liberation Army Daily*, in its comment on the PLA Conference, also reflected, the viewpoint of the GPD. It laid stress on three erroneous beliefs : that doing a military job well was the same as placing politics in the forefront ; that military affairs and politics are equally important ; and that the sole objective of political work was the improvement of military skill. Lin Piao's speech writers in the GPD, out of concern for their own power within the PLA, again stressed the inviolability of the PLA's dual leadership : the command line and the Party Committee system (under which commissars occupied most Party secretary posts at all levels). The five-point directive, issued by Lin Piao on 15 November 1965, emphasized the value of Mao Tse-tung Thought as a guide to the solution of the problem. However, by February 1966, the directive had become the point of reference for rectifying and purging leading Party cadres at the county level. A few PLA commissars were, at the same time, involved in the important propaganda "front."[91]

PART TWO

The Cultural Revolution and After

6 Cultural Revolution and Ninth Party Congress

In the face of "US aggression in Vietnam," the Chief of General Staff, Lo Jui-ching, emphasized (in 1965) the professional viewpoint "on all questions of military role, commander-commissar authority, organization, strategy and tactics." He also appealed for a *rapprochement* with the Soviet Union and called for serious preparations for war with the USA, and a forward defence in North Vietnam. Lo, it appeared, enjoyed the support of high Party functionaries, such as Liu Shao-chi and others. To counter such a viewpoint, the strategy of "people's war" was officially sanctioned in Lin Piao's 3 September 1965 article "Long Live the Victory of People's War." Judging by hindsight, we may say that Lin Piao was motivated more by political expediency than by honest conviction.

Continued opposition to Maoist values, strategy and organizational concepts (which persisted among many senior Party administrators and professional commanders), doubts about the correct strategy in the highest echelons, political bargaining among elites, and Mao's dissatisfaction with the huge Party bureaucracy—all these factors "contributed to Mao's personal determination to rectify the Party by employing his allies—the military commissars." During the first phase of the Cultural Revolution, these commissars were probably instrumental in organizing the Red Guards and inspiring them with the Maoist call to struggle against the "capitalist roaders" and finally to "seize power." Commenting on this aspect, W.W. Whitson observes :

> By the spring of 1966, it had become evident that, once again, the priesthood of military commissars would play a crucial role in applying the Maoist concepts of civil-military relations to an ever-widening circle of Party, government and, finally in 1967, military leaders. From Mao's viewpoint, the commissars were ideally trained for the task. Frustrated since 1944 by increasingly hardware-oriented commanders and an expanding civil Party bureau-cracy, commissars had found it difficult to play the part accorded to them in military and civil spheres by the Maoist scenario. Only after 1959 could they experiment with Maoist notions of the politicized soldier. Until late 1963, however, their efforts remained confined to a recti-fication movement within the PLA. Then, from early 1964 until late 1965, during the "Learn from the PLA" cam-paign, they moved cautiously into civil administration, clearly threatening civil Party power and privilege. With the spring 1966 attack on the Party Propaganda Depart-ment and the vital Peking Municipal Party Committee under P'eng Chen, they moved directly onto the political stage, aiming at the Party ideologues, whose willingness to compromise revolutionary principles after the failure of the Great Leap Forward in order to revive the economy and encourage production must have been tantamount in Mao's mind to a betrayal of the revolution.[92]

As the Cultural Revolution progressed, the Red Guards' excesses, factional infighting, incompetence and disorder came to the forefront. In such a situation, there appeared no other alternative except to rely on the help of the only organized and disciplined force in the country—the PLA—in order to save the country from chaos and confusion and restore peace and order in the land. It was in these circumstances that, sometime in early August 1967, Mao agreed to the proposals about granting additional authority to the commanders at the national and military-regional levels.

On 14 August 1967, in a gesture to assure professional military commanders, the Party Central Committee published a list of fifty-five persons who could be publicly condemned, and the only professional military names on the list were those of Peng Teh-huai and Lo Jui-ching. Even Chen Tsai-tao, the commander who had defiantly detained Wang Li and Hsieh

Fu-chih at Wuhan from 19 to 21 July 1967, was not punished. On the other hand, Wang Li was purged on 20 August 1967 because he had publicly attacked power-holders in the PLA three days earlier. Kuan Feng, Lin Chieh, and Mu Hsin, who had all been closely identified with Chiang Ch'ing on the Cultural Revolution Group, also suffered disgrace. Hsiao Hua, Director of the General Political Department, and several Deputy Directors were also subjected to poster attacks, followed by the disappearance of Hsiao Hua and the dismissal of the Deputy Directors of the GPD. Thus, commissars and Maoists at all levels suffered. On 19 August 1967, the *Red Flag* praised the PLA for its major contributions. On 25 August 1967, Mao personally led a new campaign with the old slogan, "Support the PLA and Cherish the People." This was, indeed, a bowdown, on the part of Chairman Mao in the face of a crisis of confidence, that confronted the Maoist-commissars alliance in Peking after the July 1967 Wuhan incident. However, as W. W. Whitson points out, that was not the first time that Mao had been forced to defer to the values and priorities of professional commanders.[93]

Thus, in the wake of the deteriorating internal situation the professional military values of order, stability, and "due process" came to be reaffirmed. Soon after the Wuhan Incident of July 1967, the general disenchantment of commanders with the GPD was reflected in a directive which demanded that Party Committees engage in a completely "free debate," unhampered by any presuppositions of commissar superiority. The directive enhanced the already considerable professional military prestige of commanders within the Party Committee at the expense of commissars.[94]

By 1966-68, the commanders' enhanced influence at division and regimental levels enabled them to lay greater emphasis on professional rather than political values. In February 1968, the supervision of PLA's political work was shifted directly from the General Political Department to the Military Affairs Committee, with Yang Ch'eng-wu, the acting Chief of General Staff, apparently acquiring responsibility for the latter's policy statements and directions to commissars throughout the PLA.[95] Although Yang was subsequently condemned, his fall, it appeared, was the outcome of Chiang Ch'ing's personal dislike for the man and her suspicion of his broader significance as the key symbol of career commander authority, which was then on the ascendancy at all levels of the Party-military hierarchy. To a certain extent, the powerful regional commanders were also responsible for Yang's downfall. Presumably, they were suspicious of his earlier collaboration with the Maoists, particularly Lin Piao, who had installed Yang as acting Chief of General Staff after the fall of Lo Jui-ching in late 1965. Mao and Lin probably sacrificed Yang as a scapegoat under pressure from both the Left (Chiang Ch'ing) and the Right (regional commanders).[96] If this explanation of events relating to the purge of Yang is correct, it brings out several things in sharp focus : firstly, the fact that regional commanders possessed tremendous power ; secondly, it indicated the existence of old quarrels and jealousies among them; and thirdly, the fact that the Leftist group still retained a modicum of influence.

The attempt at organizing a Cultural Revolution Group within the armed forces was short-lived. Although, for a while, it instilled the elan of revolution amongst soldiers, it did not altogether succeed in bringing the PLA under the complete control and subordination of that Group. The efforts at tightening the Maoist grip over the PLA by bringing about changes in the Military Affairs Committee, of which Mao had always assumed personal leadership, was also not very successful. While Ho Lung and Lo Jui-ching were dropped earlier, Hsiao Hua, who was temporarily made Secretary-General, and Yang Ch'eng-wu, his Deputy in 1967, were both dropped in 1968 from the Committee. They were replaced by Huang Yung-sheng, Commander of Canton Military Region and Acting Chief of General Staff; Hsieh Fu-chih, Minister of Public Security and Deputy Premier; and Su Yu, Vice-Minister of National Defence. Some of these leading figures were subsequently purged at the time of Lin Piao's fall.

The assumption of civilian (non-military) functions by the PLA during and immediately after the Cultural Revolution had been quite unprecedented in Chinese history. Moreover, it was on such a massive scale never experienced by the Chinese before. According to one estimate as many as 33 government ministries were at one time headed by men transferred from the PLA.[97]

Possibly, the extensive PLA involvement in the affairs of the country was not planned at the inception of the Cultural Revolution. It also appeared that the commanding officers of the PLA were not inclined to participate in what they regarded an intra-party dispute. Thus, power could be said to have gravitated in the hands of the PLA in the course of a protracted process, "which was neither planned nor predicted by the army high command."[98] However, as a result of the attacks by the inexperienced and disorderly Red Guard teenagers, the civilian Party and government bureaucracies were virtually paralyzed. Consequently, the army emerged as the dominant force in China's domestic politics.

Edgar Snow described this situation in the following words :

Mao Tse-tung had hoped that during the purge and cultural revolution a younger generation of "successors" would emerge to replace the "capitalist roaders" entrenched in the administrative bureaucracy. When millions of students and workers were "turned on" in 1966 they did rise to express long-repressed grievances against the Party elite. But the "rebels" failed to unite in a choice of new leaders and forms, they fell into many factions, fighting broke out, and near anarchy prevailed. The army was the only experienced Party organisation still intact. Events obliged Mao reluctantly to call upon the army to end the chaos and support industry, support agriculture, support the broad masses of the left, establish military control, and lead ideological and military training. Casualties ran into hundreds of thousands before the army took up weapons to restore order.[99]

Thus, in the latter part of the Cultural Revolution, the Army emerged as the most powerful force in China—controlling the apparatus of State power and the Revolutionary Committees that came to be established in place of the Party set-up. The army was explicitly entrusted with political tasks. As a result, instead of the Party controlling the army, the latter came to control the former. The PLA, which previously had devoted its attention exclusively to military functions, now became a military-cum-political institution.

The "Cultural Revolution" (November 1965-68) can be variously described as a conflict over ideology and policy, a power struggle, a pseudo-revolution, and an intra-party struggle over domestic and foreign policies. It was, one can say, a combination of all these. In this great internal political turmoil, Whitson points out, the main actors were the three major elites who had shared power within China ever since the beginning of the Chinese Communist movement, *viz.* civil Party cadres (*chi-kuan kan-pu*), career military commissars (*chen-kung jen-yuan*), and career military commanders. By 1954, each of these elites came to have a distinct formal chain of command, a distinct channel of career mobility for its members, and a distinct function. There was also a fourth elite, the so-called "Maoists," which sometimes functioned as a super-elite. Besides Mao Tse-tung himself, this elite had, at different times, included various representatives of the three major functional elites who supported Mao personally and/or his policies. Historically, the Maoists had controlled the levers required to mediate, if not to manipulate, the distribution of power among the three main elites. In effect, the function of the Maoists between 1927 and 1969 was to maintain a balance among the other three elite systems. Commenting on the so-called cyclical nature of power in the Chinese Communist hierarchy, W. W. Whitson observes :

> In the late 1920's field commanders were briefly dominant, only to be succeeded by civil Party cadres. During World War II, commanders regained certain initiatives, but were increasingly circumscribed by both Party cadres and commissars. Although commanders enjoyed extra power during the Civil and Korean Wars, commissars began to recover power within the PLA between 1959 and 1963, and, after the launching of the "Learn from the PLA" movement in February 1964, they commenced a broader invasion of the Party and governmental bureaucracies. Thus, the Cultural Revolution came as a violent climax to a period of increasing commissar participation in nonmilitary political and administrative affairs. Curiously, the trend toward involving military commissars in civil Party functions received a set back in January 1967, when the PLA was ordered to "support the left" on a wide front. Thereafter, until September 1968, commanders at all levels also became involved in the greatest internal political crisis to confront the Chinese Communist regime since the Civil War. By April 1969, evidence had emerged of a new balance of power among the three major elites on the new Ninth

Politburo and Central Committee, as well as on the twenty-nine provincial revolutionary committees.[100]

PLA Dominance and Ninth Party Congress

The Revolutionary Committees, established in 1967-68 in the different administrative areas of China, replaced the old Party Committees. They became the official ruling Party organs controlling the destiny of the Chinese people at provincial and municipal levels. These Revolutionary Committees were ostensibly composed of the PLA (commanders and commissars), the "revolutionary," *i.e.* reliable, Party cadres (old and new), and representatives of "revolutionary masses." However, the real power or controlling authority remained in the hands of the military representatives, who were apparently nominated by the army and were not elected by the masses. Commenting on the genesis of this triple or "three-way alliance," W. W. Whitson observes as follows :

> The problem confronting Party officials, Maoists, commissars, commanders, and pragmatic governmental administrators like Chou En-lai was to find a way to restore order and production without either damaging their own public images or altering the basic distribution of power. The solution, which has been attributed variously to Chou En-lai and to P'an Fu-sheng, was the concept of the "three-way alliance"—a new example of the Chinese genius for political compromise, in that it offered all major elites a means for camouflaging a conservative victory with a radical name.[101]

Whatever may have been the motives behind the establishment of the Revolutionary Committees, the fact remained that the PLA had been primarily responsible for the imposition of the new order. These Committees, therefore, were merely a facade, a face-saving formula and a cover for the continued domination of the country by the military. Before the establishment of Revolutionary Committees, the PLA was ruling the country directly, and thereafter, in the name of those Committees. Of the 29 Chairmen of provincial Revolutionary Committees, that had all been formed by September 1968, as many as 22 (over 75%) were military men (13 commanders and 9 commissars). Even 20 out of the 29 Vice-Chairmen of these

Committees were also military men. Seen from the stand-
point of Party-military power distribution among Field Army
(FA) loyalty systems, 2 of the 29 Chairmen belonged to the 1st
FA, 8 to the 2nd, 6 to the 3rd, 8 to the 4th, and 4 to the 5th
FA and 1 unknown.

At the centre, 11 out of 21 full members of the Ninth
Politburo were active military men. Of these, five (Lin Piao;
Huang Yung-sheng, Chief of Staff; Chiu Hui-tso, the PLA's
Logistics chief; Wu Fa-hsien, the air force commander; and
Li Tso-peng, the top commissar in the navy) were leaders in
the central organs of the national military establishment; three
were powerful regional or local commanders—Chen Hsi-lien
(Shenyang), Hsu Shih-yu (Nanking), and Li Teh-sheng
(Anhwei military district); the remaining three (Chu Teh, Liu
Po-cheng and Yeh Chien-ying) were survivors of the older
generation of military leaders.

Of the 279 members of the Ninth Central Committee, elected
in April 1969, more than 45% were active military officers and
only a quarter were men whose careers had been primarily in
civilian Party and government posts. As many as 80 senior
officers from the military regions or military districts, including
all known commanders, were elected as full or alternate members
of the Central Committee. The two most important features
of the Ninth Central Committee, as compared with the Eighth
CC, had been a significant increase in the representation of the
military as also of regions. The share of both regional and
central civilian representation, Jurgen Domes states, dropped
from 75% in the Eighth CC to 52% in the Ninth CC, while
that of the military rose from 25% to 47%. At the same time,
the share of the Centre, both military and civilian, declined
from 69% to 41%, while that of the regions increased from 31%
to 58%. This change was more clearly indicated by the fact
that the central civilian systems were represented by 46% of the
members of the Eighth CC, but only 20% in the Ninth. Regional military machines or organs, on the other hand, increased
their share from 2% in the Eighth CC to 27% in the Ninth.
The representation of central military organs remained approximately the same. The increase in regional representation,
Domes asserts, reflected a definite rise of regional autonomy
towards the centre. That, he adds, had usually happened in

Chinese history whenever the central authorities were torn by internal strife.[102]

The dominance of the Ninth Central Committee by professional military men, W. W. Whitson remarks, was reflected in their occupation of about 65 per cent of the full member seats, very nearly double their representation on the Eighth Central Committee and larger than their 50 per cent representation on the Seventh Central Committee at the end of World War II, when strong military representation might have been expected. The size of the military representation on the Ninth Central Committee, he adds, reflected the resurgence of professional military influence in China's political and decision-making process.[103] The commanders held more than twice as many full memberships on the Central Committee in 1969 as the commissars, whose representation was considerably reduced. Roughly one-third of the members of the Eighth Central Committee were re-elected to the Ninth CC.

Chairman Mao had relied heavily on the system of commissars from his first plea for its equality with commanders at Kutien in 1929 until his selection of its leadership to guide the Cultural Revolution in 1965. However, Premier Chou En-lai was never enthusiastic about the system of commissars. He had, in fact, expressed his personal disdain for these "Party soldiers" in the past and must have been a bitter witness to the temporary invasion ("Learn from the PLA Movement") of civil administrative units, under his State Council's authority, by amateurs from the GPD. The control of the GPD by the Party Military Affairs Committee (dominated by career commanders) seemed likely to insure that "a separatist, independent, institution, driven by its own blend of political and professional values, would not again challenge and annoy the now dominant junta of commanders and State planners under Chou En-lai."[104]

Following the break-up of the Party bureaucracy during the Cultural Revolution, the GPD, through which the Party used to exercise control and ensure loyalty of the military, had practically ceased to function. Its Director, Hsiao Hua, was under attack throughout 1967-68 and forced to appear at "struggle rallies," at one of which he had to submit a "written confession." The political commissars within the PLA regional commands (holding as they did in nearly every case, local civilian Party posts as well) could hardly escape the attacks on the former Party regional bureaux and provincial Party Committees. Consequently, they too were disgraced and dismissed from their Party posts.

Thus, after the fateful events of 1965-68, the system of commissars, it seemed, was destined never to regain its former glory or role. Thus, the only Party system (Communism's traditional institutional conscience, the GPD and the system of commissars) that had survived the Cultural Revolution, no longer seemed to have the status that it had gradually revived under Lin Piao's encouragement from 1959 to 1967. In 1969, the GPD high command was revived. However, Whitson observes, the late 1969 appointment of Li Teh-sheng, a close associate of Hsu Shih-yu and Su Yu (senior long-term members of the Third Field Army elite with its power base in Nanking), to command the General Political Department placed a veteran *commander* in the vital seat of "Military Grand Inquisitor." It might be recalled that no professional military commander had commanded the GPD since at least 1950. Thus, a critical new ingredient in the distribution of power between commanders and commissars was a probable shift in the priorities of military ethic and style from commissar (Maoist) to commander (professional) orientations.[105] The cadres, that were mainly based in the civilian Party machine, were squeezed out of the political commissar systems in the military areas and districts. They were replaced by men with a military career background. In 1965, 41 of 53 political commissars were—in this sense—civilians. However, by July 1970, of the 43, whose names were known by that time, as many as 36 were basically military men.[106]

7 Fall of Lin Piao

Mao could not be happy at the spectacle of the emergence of the PLA as the dominant force in Chinese politics after the Cultural Revolution. Throughout his life, he had fought against the principle of the army commanding the Party and had sought to ward off the possibility of a military dictatorship in China. He had not forgotten the chaotic warlords period of the 1920s, and the upsurge of professionalism in the PLA in the wake of the Korean War. Therefore, as soon as the situation in the country stabilized and peace and order was restored, Mao began to give thought to rebuilding the Party organization on a secure basis. At the Ninth Party Congress, convened in April 1969, Mao could not succeed in dethroning the military from the dominant position which it had acquired in the wake of the Cultural Revolution. The military, therefore, continued to retain its primacy in the Party set-up. Defence Minister Lin Piao delivered the main address—the Political Report of the CCP Central Committee—before the Party Congress and the new Party Constitution formally designated him as Mao's successor.

The institution of Revolutionary Committee, that had sprouted during the Cultural Revolution, had never been formally legalized. In order to do away with the Cultural Revolution heritage, provincial Party Committees came to be formed in place of Revolutionary Committees. This process began in December 1970 and was completed by August 1971. The preponderance of the military in the new Committees persisted

(21 of the 29 Committees were headed by PLA men who also dominated the lower ranks) (See Table 18). Nevertheless, the revival of the Party mechanism, and the rehabilitation of old, veteran and, for that matter, experienced cadres threatened the Army's political ascendancy.

The PLA had undoubtedly done a remarkable job in saving the country from relapsing into anarchy and chaos, but that did not mean that it had no shortcomings. Thus, the army was criticized for abuse of privileges and indifference to combat preparedness. For the economic recovery of the country, the Maoist leadership (in which Chou En-lai occupied a prominent position) planned a massive programme of mechanization of agriculture in the Fourth Five-Year Plan, which was to be financed by reducing expenditure on the armed forces. This was resented by PLA officers and gave rise to the so-called tractor *vs.* tank controversy, in which Chief of Army Staff, Huang Yung-sheng, a close associate of Lin Piao, sided with the military.

The task of rebuilding the decimated State and Party administrative apparatus fell on the shoulders of Premier Chou En-lai, who had all along kept close to Mao Tse-tung. However, it was not politic to ignore Lin Piao, who had been designated as the chosen successor to Mao in the Ninth Party Constitution and had emerged as the most powerful military overlord ever known in Chinese history. In fact, the slogan that the PLA was created, led and commanded by Chairman Mao came to be modified. The Chinese armed forces were now said to be commanded by Vice-Chairman Lin.[107]

In these circumstances, Mao was unmistakably concerned about the tendency among high military officers to become overlords of the Party. Mao had seen the performance of Peng Teh-huai, a former Minister of National Defence, who was as close an associate of the great helmsman as Lin Piao. Lo Jui-ching, a former Chief of General Staff of the PLA, was associated with Peng and both had to be denounced for promoting the "bourgeois military line." Ho Lung, another high ranking leader in the PLA, was found guilty of conspiring against Mao and attempting to stage a *coup d' etat* in February 1966. He was considered to be the moving spirit of an anti-Maoist clique, and was therefore disgraced. Hsiao Hua, the head of the GPD, was noticed to be following too independent a line and, hence, had to be dispensed with.

After the Cultural Revolution, Lin Piao had become so powerful that he could have easily taken an independent line, defied Mao and established a military dictatorship in the country. Since the idea of army dictatorship or military overlordship of the country contravened the principle "Party commands the gun," Chairman Mao was expected to oppose it. Chou En-lai, the close confidant and collaborator of Mao, called such an idea "absurd" when asked to comment on the matter. "How could that be?" he observed. During his conversations with Edgar Snow in the beginning of 1971, when the process of rebuilding of Party apparatus was in full swing, Chou remarked that the PLA was "an instrument of the Party" and the servant of the proletariat. "The army," Chou added, "is loyal to the Party. The Party within the army has always held leadership through its organizations right down to the company level." The army cadres, being less than one tenth of the former Party membership, Edgar Snow points out, could not run the country alone—plus all their production and defence tasks.[108]

Chou En-lai's remarks reflected the Maoist leadership's keen desire and determination to assert Party supremacy over the army. However, the military leaders seemed in no mood to give up their predominant position and meekly submit to Party dictates again. In these circumstances, a clash between the advocates of Party leadership and the main citadel of army leadership (represented by Lin Piao) was inevitable. Such a showdown occurred towards the middle of 1971 when Lin Piao and Huang Yung-sheng, realizing their weak position, reportedly tried to escape from the country and became victims of an aircrash (in September 1971) over Outer Mongolia.

In order to understand the fall of Lin Piao, one must take into account the distribution of power between the Party and the military as well as the relationship and the interaction between the central military elite and the regional military elites. After Lin had replaced Peng Teh-huai, as Minister of Defence, he continuously endeavoured to build for himself a position of pre-eminence in the country. In this endeavour, he sought to make full use of his position as *de facto* chief of the Party's powerful Military Affairs Committee, his professional background as well as the mantle he put on himself of promoting the Thought of Mao Tse-tung. According to one estimate, 11 out of the 22 known members of the Military Affairs Committee had historic ties with Lin, while at the military-region level, the careers of nine of the "fourteen" regional commanders were closely linked to Lin Piao. The purge of over 300 senior military figures at central, military-region and provincial levels gave Lin the opportunity to make the army in his own image.[109] Lin spared no effort to install men of his choice in key military posts throughout the mainland at the expense of the First Field Army elite and the suppression of the Second and Third Field Army elites.

However, during the six years of his Defence Ministership before the Cultural Revolution, *i.e.* from 1959 to 1966, Lin could replace only 5 out of 13 regional commanders and 5 to 7 political commissars. New deputy commanders had been named in only five regions. During the Cultural Revolution (1966-68), it was not possible for Lin to remove any regional commander, though about five more political commissars lost their positions in the military regions. (See Table 11) As regards Military Districts, of a total of 22 Military Districts, the commanders of only two had been removed while the political commissars in 13 had been dismissed or severely criticized by November 1968.

In many large military regions, including Tibet, the power of regional commanders and commissars, long entrenched in their strongholds, remained undisturbed. It was probably too risky for Lin Piao to encroach on their position by dethroning them from their citadels of power. Thus, in the important border regions of Sinkiang, Inner Mongolia and Fukien, even the old system, whereby the commander had been concurrently his own chief commissar, was retained.[110] W.W. Whitson observes :

The continued control of the most powerful military regions by traditional commanders (Ch'en Hsi-lien in Shenyang; Hsu Shih-yu in Nanking; Yang Te-chih in Tsinan; Han Hsien-ch'u in Foochow; Huang Yung-sheng, perhaps through Ting Sheng in Canton; and Chang Kuo-hua in Chengtu and possibly Tibet) suggested that even the massive conventional and nuclear threat posed by the

Russians on the northern border had not provided the Maoists with adequate arguments for shifting such key leaders in quite the same way that the Korean War had rationalized major transfers. For a multitude of reasons, it appeared in January 1970 that these military regional leaders were firmly entrenched in their regional strongholds of bureaucratic power and were collaborating with their representative in Peking to sustain the balance-of-power among field army elites—the process by which the mainland had been ruled since the creation of the People's Republic of China in October 1949.

Thus, at the end of the Cultural Revolution, Lin Piao did not emerge as the unchallenged military leader of China though he undoubtedly wielded considerable power and influence. He used this power to strengthen the position of his own 4th Field Army and endeavoured to tilt the balance-of-power among various Field Army elites in his favour. Nevertheless, the regional military leaders, who were firmly entrenched in the bastions of their power and had the backing of their troops and people, still remained a force to be reckoned with and the other Field Armies retained their group affiliations. After dealing extensively with Field Army institutional and elite histories, the prevailing formal system of military regional competition and the informal system of Field Army loyalties, W.W. Whitson comes to the conclusion that while even in late 1971 the Air Force and the Navy *probably were* more generally responsive to the centre than the ground forces, "control of most military power, seemed to remain as regionally oriented as ever." He states :

Regionalism in China since 1950 seems to have involved a political dynamic among fourteen military elites, thirteen of them based in their own military regions and the four-teenth based in Peking...these military regional loyalties have to some extent qualified the obligations derived from older field army associations. Because there were relatively few shifts of key leaders from military regions to Peking between 1950 and 1970, the thirteen regional elites have undoubtedly tended to acquire parochial viewpoints in their perception of priorities among local, regional, and national security values and goals.[111]

It appears quite obvious that without the assistance of the majority of regional military leaders it would not have been possible for the Mao-Chou group to bring about the fall of Lin Piao. Lin, a dedicated professional commander, often endeavoured to prove himself a true defender of the faith—a staunch supporter of Mao and Maoist military and political ideas. He often sought to reconcile the professional and the Maoist viewpoints. But in this venture, he did not, it seems, fully succeed. At the end of the Cultural Revolution, he could neither have the full confidence of Mao nor the absolute trust of the majority of regional military commanders and the professionals in the PLA. He obviously fell between two stools.

Mao was greatly concerned and quite apprehensive about the concentration of tremendous power at the Centre in the hands of Lin Piao and his men. Lin was the visible symbol of military power in the country and the man responsible for opposing, or rather reversing, Mao's well-known principle about the Party commanding the gun. Mao, Ellis Joffe states, "presumably held Lin and his colleagues on the General Staff responsible for the entrenchment of the PLA in the political arena" and probably viewed the assertiveness of the army and its leaders as a serious threat to his own position and authority. In his attempt to curb the power of the army, Chairman Mao enjoyed support both of the remnants of the radical wing (Chiang Ching, Chang Chun-chiao, Yao Wen-yuan, etc.) and of the veteran civilian leaders at the Centre, led by Chou-En-lai, who had deep personal and political differences with Lin and were apprehensive about the power of the PLA and the Lin Piao group at the Centre.[112] The resuscitated Party officials also joined hands with them since they also believed that the Party should command the gun.

In so far as the majority of regional military leaders and professionals were concerned, they too had their misgivings about the politicization of the PLA—the "Learn from the PLA" movement of 1964—and Lin Piao's seeming tilt towards the Left during the Cultural Revolution. Thus, Lin was criticized for his attempts to pay attention to the demands of radical leaders, for not raising his voice "forcefully and frequently enough to protect them [local commanders and some central leaders] from attacks by the Red Guards, especially...after the Wuhan incident." When Lin appeared to be "drawn or driven, more and more to the left" it is not clear "to what extent he was motivated by the profound loyalty to Mao, personal convictions, power considerations, or the pressure of events."[113] It is pertinent to recall that in the eyes of local commanders, Lin came to be identified as favouring radical elements, laying excessive emphasis on politics and undermining professional values. Moreover, the majority of regional commanders must have been apprehensive about the excessive concentration of political and military power in the hands of the central military leadership. They suspected erosion of their own power position in regional and local theatres and the tilting of balance-of-power in favour of one Field Army, *viz.* the Fourth Field Army. The rise of Lin as the most powerful military and political force at the Centre represented a threat to the positions of both the regional and local commanders as well as the civilian leaders (Mao and Chou).

Thus, the necessity of self-preservation brought the diverse elements together, and the unity thus forged resulted in the downfall of Lin Piao. In this context, Ellis Joffe observes :

> At first glance, the regional leaders could have been expected to back Lin on the crucial issue of Party control over the army, for it is plain that they had no desire to give up their political power. Nevertheless, it is clear that the institutional identification between the regional commanders and the Lin Piao group turned out to be weaker than the personal, factional, and political rivalries which separated them, and which obviously moved many regional leaders to throw in their support behind Mao and Chou. Greatly easing, if not facilitating, this move was the price paid by the Mao-Chou forces for such support : most of the regional commanders retained their position of power in the post-Lin period. The second group of anti-Lin officers consisted of professional commanders who had opposed the military's political involvement and who favoured its reduction so that the army could concentrate its energies on military tasks. These officers, moreover, undoubtedly also had a personal grudge against the central military leaders for not protecting them during the height of radical attacks against professionalism. This then appears to have been the composition of the coalition that confronted the Lin Piao group. To what extent it was deliberately put together by Mao and Chou and to what extent it crystallized in response to circum-

stances is not clear. But one thing is clear : the anti-Lin coalition contained disparate groups which came together for different reasons. The basis of this coalition thus was— and remains—extremely fragile.[114]

After Lin Piao's Fall

Since the officer corps of the PLA had been subjected to Lin Piao's influence for a long time, it was deemed necessary to weed out the "poison" of Lin Piao in the army. An important feature of the anti-Lin Piao campaign was the purging of military personnel who had served under Lin Piao and Huang Yung-sheng in the Fourth Field Army and who, during the Cultural Revolution, were promoted to important offices in the central military machine, as well as in the regional and provincial military districts.

The first casualty were the Party and military leaders closely associated with Lin in the Politburo : the Chief of General Staff, Huang Yung-sheng; the Commander-in-Chief of the Air Force, Wu Fa-hsien; the Director of the PLA General Rear Services Department, Chiu Hui-tso; and the First Political Commissar of the Navy, Li Tso-peng. All four belonged to Lin Piao's 4th Field Army and were dismissed, along with Lin Piao, in September 1971 itself. A large number of other top-ranking officers of the PLA who were considered as supporters, proteges or in some way connected with Lin Piao, were also disgraced and replaced. Among these were : three Deputy Chiefs of General Staff (Yen Chung-chuan, Wen Yu-cheng, and Cheng Tsi-teh), six Deputy Directors of the General Rear Services (Logistics) Department (Han Chen-tsi, Chang Ming-yuan, Yan Tsiun, Wang Hsi-ko, Chen Pang and Chou Yu-cheng), two Vice Commanders of the Navy, four Vice Commanders, including Tseng Kuo-hua and Wang Ping-chang, and three Vice Political Commissars of the Air Force, the Vice Commander of the Artillery and the Deputy Director of the GPD (Huang Chih-yung). About 56 military figures were purged in the immediate context of Lin's fall. Of these, 19 belonged to the Air Force.[115]

The regional military leadership, however, was not so much affected by the purge that accompanied Lin Piao's fall. Of the eleven Military Regions, only three commanders—that of Peking, Chengtu and Sinkiang—and about six First Political Commissars disappeared. (See Table 11) Out of the 26 Provincial Military District and City Garrison Commanders, three, *viz.* Hsiung Ying-tang (Chekiang), Yang Tung-liang (Kiangsi), and Lung Pin-chu (Kansu), disappeared. The conclusion that the regional leadership was not as severely affected, Jurgen Domes points out, was further substantiated by the fact that of the 29 Provincial Party First Secretaries, only four were removed—Lung Shu-chin (Sinkiang), Nan Ping (Chekiang), Cheng Shih-chih (Kiangsi), and Lan Yi-nung (Kweichow)—while one (Chang Kuo-hua of Szechuan) died in February 1972. Three of these were replaced by military men—Generals She Chi-te in Kiangsi, Liu Hsing-yuan in Szechuan and Lu Jui-lin in Kweichow—and two by civilian cadres, T'an chi-lung in Chekiang and Saifudin in Sinkiang. Thus, of the 29 administrative units on the provincial level, 19 were still headed by representatives of the PLA and only ten by civilian cadres. (See Table 18)

These facts, Jurgen Domes states, seemed to contradict the theory that the Lin Piao crisis was the result of a confrontation between "*the* Party" and "*the* Army" in the course of which the "Party" successfully reasserted its control over the "Army". This, he says, would appear much too simple an analysis. Domes points out that one could only assume a re-establishment of "Party" leadership over the military, if there really was a separate sub-system consisting of a civilian Party machine, as, in fact, existed between the early 1950s and 1966. Yet even after the impact of the Lin Piao crisis, leadership of the Party machine, at least on the provincial and county (*hsien*) level, remained strongly dominated by, if not in many cases almost identical with, that of the PLA. Inspite of a number of new appointments, Domes observes, by the end of May 1973, 85 (51.5%) of the 169 Provincial Party Secretariats were held by military men. Of the 14 appointments of ministers and commission-Chairmen, made in the post-Cultural Revolution period, ten had gone to military men, and this figure included five out of seven appointed *after* the demise of Lin Piao. Basing himself on this data, Jurgen Domes concluded in the summer of 1973 : "The PLA still plays a very important, if not decisive, role in political decision-making."[116]

In the field of personnel developments, the two dominant trends visible in the wake of the Lin Piao crisis were : a distinct increase in the spheres of influence of the Second and Third Field Army loyalty groups, in particular that of the Third, and the rehabilitation of a number of civilian cadres and generals who were purged or at least severely attacked during the Cultural Revolution. The trend to give new regional and central appointments to former members of the Second and Third Field Army, Jurgen Domes points out, had already started in 1970, when General Li Teh-sheng from the Second Field Army became Director of the PLA General Political Department. It continued through spring and summer 1971 with the appointments of Generals Wang Pi-ch'eng and P'i Ting-chun from the Third Field Army group as Commanders of the Kunming and Lanchow Military Regions respectively. In addition to these, Domes states, new appointments which became known outside China since mid-1971 included the following positions : the Ministers of First Machine Building, Metallurgical Industry, Public Security, and Commerce, and one Deputy Chief of General Staff were drawn from the Second Field Army/Shenyang Military Region Loyalty Combine, while the Minister of Water Conservancy and Power, one Deputy Chief of General Staff, and probably the Acting Commander of the Peking Military Region, the new First Political Commissar of the Wuhan Military Region, Deputy Commanders of Shansi and Inner Mongolia, and a Vice Political Commissar of the Tsinan Military Region were from the Third Field Army/ Nanking Military Region Loyalty Combine. In this connection, Jurgen Domes also draws our attention to the obvious rise in importance of another Third Field Army man, General Su Yu, in the central military machine, and to the rather unusual lavishness of the funeral ceremonies for the Third Field Army's former commander, Marshal Chen Yi, who died in Peking on 6 January 1972.

About 80% of the leading military cadres who disappeared after Lin Piao's demise were from the Fourth Field Army.[117] However, the Fourth Field Army leadership in the Canton Military Region remained basically intact. The principle of "Four Firsts," advocated by Lin, was criticized as "the setting off of military affairs against politics," leading to a weakening in the fighting capacity of troops. Lin Piao was denounced for following a *bourgeois* military line and for disguising himself as a "military genius" in his vain attempt to "have everything under his command and everything at his disposal," to plot for the usurpation of leadership and seizure of power in the Party and to create counter—revolutionary public opinion for restoring capitalism. Lin Piao's "six tactical principles"—"one spot, two sides," "four fast and one slow operations," "three methods of fighting under three kinds of situation," "fierceness in three respects," "three-three system," and "four groups in one team"—were all criticized and Lin accused of opposing Chairman Mao's proletarian military line.[118]

8 Tenth Party Congress

The fall of Lin Piao in 1971 did not lead to the immediate subordination of the PLA to the Party leadership. It is worth recalling that it was only after the enlarged Politburo meeting of June 1972, when five Politburo members were eliminated, that the Mao-Chou group felt confident enough to denounce Lin Piao as a traitor and rebel and openly accuse him of trying to stage a coup and of attempting to assassinate Mao. The attacks on Lin Piao, however, were by no means aimed at the PLA as a whole. Furthermore, while the power of the military elite in the Politburo had been somewhat weakened as a result of the purge of the army high command, the importance of regional military commanders not only remained undiminished but might even have increased. Therefore, in calling upon the army to display modesty, the Central leadership deemed it necessary not to tamper with the prestige of the army.

Nevertheless, there were repeated calls about obedience of the PLA to the Party Central Committee after Lin Piao's fall. Rigid adherence to Party discipline was considered an indispensable factor to ensure the successful implemention of Chairman Mao's Thought. All institutions of society were subjected to Party control. Particular stress was laid on the subordination of the Army by calling upon the PLA to learn from the people of the whole country. Although the army was recognized as the pillar of the proletariat, it was asked to eschew arrogance and complaceny and to increase its combat readiness. As part of the yearly "Support the Army" movement, a circular was issued in January 1972, by the Party's Military Affairs Committee to the effect that the army keep the Party's line and policies in mind and learn from the people. Even when the principle that "the Party should command the gun and the gun should never be allowed to command the Party" was not directly referred to, it was implicit in the Party's call that the armed forces lay stress on military training rather than ideological function and in the assumption of militia responsibility by the Party.

In the joint editorial of the *People's Daily, the Liberation Army Daily* and the *Red Flag,* on the occasion of the 45th anniversary of the founding of the PLA (1 August 1972), the main emphasis was laid on the question of internal unity. As it was the first Army Day since the fall of Lin Piao, it was considered necessary to assert the determined control of the Party Centre over the Army. While extolling the achievements of the PLA over the years and the manifold functions it continued to perform in the body politic, the army was stated to have been "founded and commanded by the great leader Chairman Mao and the Communist Party of China." The significance of this phrase can be understood by recalling that when the star of Lin Piao was at its peak the PLA was said to have been created by Chairman Mao but commanded by Lin Piao. It was only after the disappearance of Lin Piao in September 1971 that the formula —Mao created and commands the Army—became common once again.

After the Party was reconstituted in the post-Cultural Revolution period, there was practically no difference between the Mao line and the Party line. The name of the Chinese Communist Party, therefore, came to be added, alongwith Mao, while referring to the creation, command and leadership of the Army. This was done partly to refurbish the image of the Party and partly to create confidence in the collective leadership at the Centre in order to strengthen civilian Party control over the military.

It is pertinent to mention here that a salient feature of the earlier slogan "politics in command" had been that the Party leadership composed of Liu Shao-chi and Teng Hsiao-ping tried to bring the PLA under their control. Later on, this actuated supporters of Mao to complain that "the Liu Shao-chi-type swindler intended to grab the leading power of our army" by speaking only of "the predominance of politics." It was also asserted that the PLA should never again fall into the trap of "sham Marxists."[119] Likewise, the Maoists must also have been concerned about the exploitation of the slogan—"The PLA was Created by Mao and Commaded by Lin"—by Lin Piao in his bid to "grab the leading power of the army" in his own hands. It was only after the purge of Liu Shao-chi and the fall of Lin Piao that the theme of Party leadership of the army and of the Party commanding the PLA could be re-emphasized with greater confidence.

The *Red Flag* article on army-party relationship in July 1972 declared "the absolute leadership of the proletarian vanguard, the Chinese Communist Party, over the army, which was directed to take "the realization of the Party programme and line as the aim of its own struggle." According to Mao's precepts "military affairs" were only one means of accomplishing political tasks. The article, therefore, declared : "The Party must actively attend to and discuss military work. All the work must be discussed and decided upon by the Party before being carried out by the rank and file." The principle that "the Party commands the gun and the gun must never be allowed to command the Party"[120] was proclaimed unhesitatingly and unreservedly.

On 1 August 1972, the joint editorial of the three main papers of China—*People's Daily*, *Liberation Army Daily* and *Red Flag*—unequivocally reaffirmed the absolute leadership of the Party over the army and, indeed, over all institutions of society, the State organs, the youth corps, the workers, peasants, Red Guards or other mass organizations. The editorial criticized the "careerists or conspirators" for undermining the strength of the army. It laid stress on the maintenance of a stern discipline, a spirit of complete obedience to the Party and a consciousness of revolutionary traditions, which, it stated, characterized the Red Army of pre-Liberation days.[121]

Subsequently, the necessity of learning from the experience of Comrade Lei Feng (the outstanding Communist Party member and squad leader in a transport company of the PLA in Shenyang who died in the course of duty on 15 August 1962) was emphasized. It is significant to note that unlike the early 1960s (when Lei Feng was presented as a military hero before the public), his Party membership was placed first and he was admired for the "splendid example" he put before the Chinese people by "his utter devotion to the Party and to the socialist cause."[122]

China experienced a vacuum in its political and military leadership as a result of the Cultural Revolution and the dismissal of Lin Piao and his colleagues. Many of the old stalwarts in the Party and the army had been criticized, disgraced, purged or killed in the internal upheaval and the anti-Lin campaign. In order to fill this vacuum and to establish a stable and centralized Party leadership in the country, it was felt necessary to forge unity among the moderates (the veteran civil leaders, headed by Chou En-lai) and the leftists (the radical group comprising Chiang Ch'ing and Yao Wen-yuan, etc.). To that end, it was also deemed essential to rehabilitate the old guards, who had organizational talent, economic expertise or military experience. It was only then that the Party leadership at the centre could hope to re-assert its absolute control over the army, the regional commanders in particular.

Chou En-lai enunciated his policy of "seeking common ground on major issues while reserving minor differences." The need for centralized Party leadership and for unity was regularly emphasized in the Chinese news media. The central theme of the Political Report delivered by Chou at the Tenth Party Congress in August 1973 was "unity." He endeavoured to convey this message by clothing it in elegant dialectics and revolutionary catchwords. In his report to the Congress on the revision of the Party Constitution, Wang Hung-wen reiterated the success of the Cultural Revolution and declared that both the political and organizational lines of the Ninth Party Congress were "correct" A denial of the success of the Cultural Revolution, as incorporated in the Ninth Party Congress, would have amounted to questioning the infallibility of Chairman Mao and the Party. Moreover, it would have made more difficult a compromise with the leftist group (which was closely associated with the Party). Another consideration which must have weighed with the Chinese leadership in emphasizing its continuity and legality was its desire to bolster

China's internal and external image.

Mao, at first, made use of the army in his bid to suppress his opponents in the Party apparatus. After he succeeded in defaming and defeating the ruling Liu Shao-chi faction in the Party, it was realized that he would not have to face the challenging pre-dominance of the PLA in the various components of state power, including the Party and administration, had the Party apparatus remained intact and powerful. It was also recognized that the rise of the PLA as a pre-dominant force in China's domestic politics in the immediate aftermath of the Cultural Revolution was not so much due to the inherent strength of the army itself as it was due to the weakness of the Party. Therefore, more and more emphasis was laid on Party rebuilding, both at the Centre and in the provinces. Thus, before the Tenth Party Congress was held in August 1973, the Provincial Party Committees had been restructured.

Chiang Huang's article in the *Red Flag* (No. 7, 1972) made a strong plea for constantly strengthening the revolutionary unity between new and old cadres so as to strengthen centralized Party leadership.[123] This facilitated the rehabilitation of experienced cadres and the old guards (*e. g.* Teng Hsiao-ping, Ulanfu, Tan Chen-lin, Li Ching-chuan, Yang Cheng-wu, etc.) who had been criticized and disgraced during the Cultural Revolution. Of particular significance was the restoration of Teng Hsiao-ping, No. 2 in the defunct Party hierarchy. He had been a top level Party organizer, being the Secretary-General of the CCP Central Committee from 1954 to 1956 and the General Secretary thereof from 1956 to 1966; a Vice-Premier in the government from 1952 to 1966; and a top level military leader upto the mid 1950s; a well-known political commissar who knew how to deal with ambitious commanders. Therefore, it was felt that his organizational talent and administrative experience could be put to good use in mobilizing and reinvigorating the Party apparatus and to pressurize military leaders. Accordingly, Teng was included in the Central Committee of the Tenth Party Congress in 1973 and elevated to the Politburo in January 1974. In January 1975, he was not only promoted as Vice-Chairman of the Party Central Committee and a member of the powerful Standing Committee of the Politburo but was also confirmed as the senior-most Vice-Premier in the State

Council and appointed Chief of Staff of China's armed forces.

In order to fill the vacuum in the army leadership at the Centre, it was also deemed prudent to rehabilitate experienced military officers, particularly those who had either been disgraced during the Cultural Revolution or suffered at the hands of Lin Piao (and, thus, had convincing anti-Lin credentials). Prominent among such rehabilitees were : Yang Cheng-wu, Acting Chief of General Staff before his dismissal in March 1968; Air Force Commander Yu Li-chin, one of Yang's principal supporters; Wang Shang-jung and Hu Wei—both of which were named as Deputy Chiefs of General Staff; and Liu Chih-chien, a former Deputy Director of the GPD. Although the names of Minister of National Defence and Chief of General Staff were not announced till January 1975, an attempt was, nonetheless, made to fill certain vacancies created by the dismissal of Lin Piao's associates in the Defence Ministry hierarchy. Thus, on 1 June 1974, Ma Ning, previously Acting Commander, was officially designated as Commander of the Air Force to take the post of Wu Fa-hsien, that was lying vacant since the latter's disappearance in September 1971.

In order to establish the supremacy of the Party in the country, a conscious attempt was made in August 1973 to strengthen the Party position and to reduce military representation in the Tenth Central Committee and its Politburo. Of the total of 319 members (195 regular members and 124 non-voting alternates) in the Central Committee, approximately 100 cadres belonged to Party and State bureaucracies, roughly 80 had backgrounds primarily as active military leaders while about 100 were worker-peasant representatives. Thus, army representation was reduced from about 45% in the Ninth Central Committee to a little more than 30% in the Tenth. Of the 45 regular members of the Ninth Central Committee who were dropped from the Tenth Committee (including 10 members who had died), 30 were military leaders belonging to the Lin Piao faction, 13 cadres, 2 masses; of 28 alternates who were dropped, 22 were military men, 4 cadres and 2 masses. On the other hand, of the 55 newly-elected members to the Tenth Central Committee, 15 were military, 25 cadres, 12 masses and

3 unknown; of the 58 new alternates, 13 military, 11 cadres, 16 masses and 18 unknown.[124] (See also Appendix 12 and Table 15)

The over-all military representation declined both in absolute numbers and percentage. In contrast to a sharp decline in the representation of the Central military leadership there was some gain by Central Party and government officials. Likewise, there was a change in the civilian/military ratio among the provincial-based members. However, as Richard Wich points out, at this level, the shift was accomplished by keeping the military total static while substantially adding the number of provincial civilian members. Moreover, nearly all of the re-elected provincial military figures who were alternate members remained at the same level, whereas over a dozen provincial civilian alternate members were elevated to full membership. Wich further observes :

> These changes in the composition of the Central Committee reflects not only the fact of the erosion of military influence in the power structure, but also the manner in which this has been pursued. The purge of Lin and his high-level associates meant a sharp reduction in central military representation, but the process of civilianizing the provincial power structure has taken place mainly through the influx of new civilian leaders. This trend was particularly pronounced in the changing composition of the Central Committee, with three times as many provincial civilian as military figures added to that body at the 10th Congress. The Congress thus strongly reinforced the trend towards reducing the military role in provincial politics.[125]

Party cadres in the provinces thus benefitted the most by the reduction in military representation. This strengthening of the civilian position was followed by the appointment of more and more civilian Party cadres to the important posts of Provincial Party First Secretaries. However, it is pertinent to recall that even after the reconstitution of Provincial Party Committees in 1970-71, most of these top Party leadership posts in the provinces had remained in the hands of military men. Despite the sharp reduction in military representation, PLA officers still remained a sizable group within the Tenth Central Committee and practically all the military leaders who occupied key military positions in China either at the centre or in the regions were included in the Central Committee. (See Tables 11 and 15)

In the Politburo too, the military representation was reduced to seven (Yeh Chien-ying, Li Teh-sheng, Chen Hsi-lien, Hsu Shih-yu, Su Chen-hua, a relatively minor naval leader appointed new as alternate, Chu Teh and Liu Po-cheng), as compared to eleven in the Ninth Politburo. Moreover, 9 out of 10 new members, that were added to the Tenth Politburo, were civilians. Of the seven military men on the Tenth Politburo, the first two were members of the Politburo Standing Committee. Of these two, Li Teh-sheng (Director of the GPD) was also Vice-Chairman of the Party Central Committee. (See Table 14) Thus, although the Tenth Party Congress resulted in the strengthening of the hold of civilians in the top Party leadership, the military leaders continued to maintain a strong position in the Politburo. These military leaders might not act as a cohesive group, but they still remained a force to be reckoned with not only in the prevailing situation but also in determining the post-Mao leadership.

9 Reshuffle of Regional Commanders

An obvious result of the Cultural Revolution, which decimated the Party apparatus, and the fall of Lin Piao, which
paralyzed the PLA high command, had been that the leadership at the Centre was considerably weakened and the influence
of regional military commanders was greatly increased. The
provincial authorities, dominated as they were by military
personnel, also acquired a substantial degree of political and
economic autonomy. The most important features of the internal political scene in China, after the Cultural Revolution,
were the dominance of administrative organs by professional
military men and a resurgence of regionalism.

During 1971-72, there was a great deal of speculation in
Western political circles about the PLA ceasing to be "a highly
politicized force devoutly loyal and responsive to Mao." It was
felt that the Chinese army would become "a congeries of conflicting loyalties and uneven skills, responsive principally to
eleven military-region commanders." It was believed that the
central authority in China over the next five years "must rest
on the fortuitous whim of regional commanders' collective
compromises plus the loyalties of the military Party system, the
GRSD [General Rear Services Department] and the air and
naval force elites."[126] Another keen observer of the military-
Party interactions and the role of the PLA in Chinese politics
observed as follows:

Politics in any social system usually reflects the conflicts among the groups that wield power. Prior to the Cultural Revolution, Chinese politics to a large extent centered around the groups within the Party, as it was then the locus of power. Since the Cultural Revolution, the locus of power has shifted to the military, and national politics will most likely come to involve conflicts between central headquarters and regional commands, interservice rivalries, and disputes among the field-army systems.[127]

How to curb the execessive power concentrated in the hands of military satraps had long been one of the main preoccupations of the Chinese leadership. In 1973-74 this preoccupation was reflected in the lengthy articles written in praise of the First Chin Emperor for his contribution to the unity of China and in attacks on neo-Confucianists for their attempts to carve up China into principalities.

With a view to curb the power of the regional commanders, the Central Party leadership had sought to consolidate its base by seeking common ground between the moderate and radical wings of the Party and by emphasizing the need for rebuilding the Party. It also endeavoured to diminish military influence in general and that of the regional commanders in particular by the following methods :

1. by reducing the political role of the army in the top leadership organs, such as the cut-back in military representation on the Tenth Central Committee and Politburo (this has been discussed in the preceding chapter);

2. by removing or demoting military men from the high positions they occupied in the Party or administrative organs. Thus, the removal of Pai Hsiang-kuo from his post of Minister of Foreign Trade in October 1973 and his reversion to the PLA was probably motivated by the desire to reduce the presence of the army in the Party and administrative organs, although the possibility that his links with Lin Piao and Huang Yung-sheng and disagreement over trade policy were also factors in his removal could not be completely ruled out;

3. by reinstituting and reinvigorating the system of checks and controls on the authority of commanders by the appointment of political commissars of comparable, if not greater, stature and influence;

4. by strengthening the provincial Party apparatus; and

5. by shifting the regional and local commanders from the strongholds of their power.

By the end of 1973, the Central leadership in Peking felt confident enough to order a reshuffle of commanders in eight out of China's eleven principal military regions. The two-way switches involved such prominent personalities as Li Teh-sheng, Vice-Chairman of the Party Central Committee, and Chen Hsi-lien and Hsu Shih-yu—both senior Politburo members and powerful regional military commanders. The reshuffle of eight regional military commanders was an important step in paring down the political power of the PLA because in their new posts these commanders were not given concurrent political power. The reshuffle was also aimed at reinforcing Central authority and overcoming separatism and parochialism in the provinces. Thus, the reshuffle sought to weaken the regional military leaders' power and influence, to strengthen political control over the army and to assert the Central Party and civilian leadership over the provinces and the regional military bosses.

The transfer of commanders from their military and political bases, built up assiduously over a number of years, was obviously intended to reduce their over-all political influence. The move was ostensibly justified on the ground that it mitigated the opposition of radical elements against the commanders and contributed to stabilizing the situation. It might be recalled that, since November 1973, the forces of the Cultural Revolutionary-Left had been pressing for a curtailment of the regional commanders' power. They had formulated their demand into praises for Chin Chih-huang's system of periodical rotation of the provincial governors.[128]

The announcement regarding the reshuffle was made by way of a seemingly casual description of the attendance at the New Year celebrations in China in 1974. The Central Party leadership took this calculated and rather bold decision about the reshuffle of commanders for a variety of reasons. In the first place, the change in commandership was expected to increase the amenability of the provinces to Central influence and secondly, it facilitated the appointment of civilian Party cadres to the posts of Party First Secretaries in the provinces and as commissars in the PLA.

In some cases, the pre-Cultural Revolution Provincial Party bosses were restored to their positions of power as Party First Secretaries either in their old province (*e.g.* Chao Tzu-yang in Kwangtung) or in new ones (*e. g.* Tan Chi-lung, formerly of Shantung, became First Secretary of Chekiang; Liao Chih-kao, the former First Secretary of Szechuan, was appointed First Secretary of Fukien; and Chiang Wei-ching, Party chief of Kiangsu in 1966, was made First Secretary of Kiangsi). In other cases, new appointments indicated both rehabilitation and promotion. Thus, Peng Chung and Pai Ju-ping were appointed First Secretaries of the Provincial Party Committees of Kiangsu and Shantung respectively. (See Table 18) Both of them were civilian Party cadres and, therefore, their appointments were significant steps in the process of discouraging concurrent holding of civilian and military power. Of all the new appointments of Provincial Party First Secretaries that were disclosed during 1974, only one (in Kweichow) went to the local military commander. All others went to civilian Party cadres.

It might be recalled that the commanders of military regions had acquired provincial political authority as a result of the flow of power into military hands during the Cultural Revolution. Thus, a large number of military commanders simultaneously occupied the posts of Secretaries of Provincial or local Party Committees or the positions of political commissars in the PLA. In fact, commanders of all the eleven military regions and at least 27 out of 29 military district commanders were Secretaries or higher on the Party Committees that were established during 1970-71. Six military region commanders—those of Foochow, Wuhan, Nanking, Canton, Shenyang and Tsinan—were simultaneously Party First Secretaries in the principal province of their military region, *viz.* Fukien, Hupeh, Kiangsu, Kwangtung, Liaoning and Shantung respectively. (See Tables 11 and 18) This concentration of military, governmental and Party power in the hands of a single man in 1971 and upto the end of 1973, *i. e.* before the large-scale transfer of regional commanders, was, indeed, quite unprecedented and was fraught with the dangers of warlordism, disintegration and army dictatorship.

Commenting on the decentralization of power in China since the Cultural Revolution, the strengthening of the position of the provincial authorities *vis-a-vis* the Central leadership, and the dominant role of the PLA in Chinese politics, Parris H. Chang observed:

> Whereas the provincial authorities in the late 1950s were led by civilian Party officials (except in outlying regions like Sinkiang and Tibet), local PLA commanders or professional political commissars now head the Party and government organization in most provinces, and the PLA leaders actually provide the backbone of the leadership in virtually every province. Whereas in the 1950s and prior to the Cultural Revolution in 1966, senior provincial or regional Party bureau secretaries served concurrently as first political commissars in the provincial military districts or military regions and thus provided Party control over the local PLA, today in most provinces this practice has been discontinued. Instead, local PLA commanders or professional political commissars are concurrently top provincial Party secretaries. The inter-locking Party, Government, and military leadership positions and the concentration of political, military, and financial power in the same hands have generated new power equations in Chinese politics. It seems very likely that the new provincial forces may ultimately prove more intractable and difficult to control by the central leadership, whoever they may be.[129]

After the fall of Lin Piao, a vigorous attempt was made to strengthen Party leadership over the army, to curb the political role of the military leaders, and to discourage the practice of the concurrent holding of civilian and military power. Provincial directives for the Army Day (1 August 1974) enjoined on the PLA to check up its "record in respecting and obeying the centralized leadership of the local CCP Committees." In other words, the PLA was required not to become a tool of individual careerists in the Party but, instead, to submit itself to the centralized leadership of the Party as a whole. It meant that, in the whole country, the PLA should obey the leadership of the Party Centre, while, in a region, it must obey the centralized leadership of the local Party Committee. In order to assert the Party's leadership over the army, even the PLA Party Committees and the political commissars were asked to place themselves under the supervision of the corresponding local

Party units.

In most cases, there was no question of the regional commanders being demoted. However, they were removed from the command of their troops and from their local power bases where they had established themselves for many years (in one case nearly twenty). Moreover, the transfers had been arranged in such a manner that no commander was permitted to take with him the political commissars he had worked with. Thus, in their new headquarters the military commanders found themselves at a disadvantage in their dealings with the new political commissars and with the provincial Party Committees under them. For instance, in their new postings to Peking and Canton, Chen Hsi-lien and Hsu Shih-yu were saddled with political commissars of comparable prominence. The two powerful regional military leaders (who were also members of the Politburo) were displaced from the bastions of their power and subjected to a greater degree of restraint and limitations. In many cases, the political power of the military commanders was sought to be curtailed by the presence of civilian First Political Commissars who held senior positions in the Central or Provincial Party hierarchy.

Lin Piao's stronghold in Canton had decidedly been broken by the removal of Ting Sheng. His successor, Hsu Shih-yu, originally regarded as having been neutral in the Lin Piao affair, also lost his stronghold in the Nanking region, where he had been in control for nearly two decades. Yang Teh-chih was uprooted from the Tsinan region, possibly because of his soft attitude towards the Leftists but more so because of his connections with Lin Piao. Tseng Ssu-yu, who replaced Yang, was removed from his base in Wuhan to which he had been assigned in 1967 when Lin Piao's power was at its height.

Chen Hsi-lien was probably brought to Peking—the sensitive area around the capital, vital both for national defence and in the domestic power game—partly because of his association with Chou En-lai and partly to compensate him adequately for relinquishing his "independent Kingdom" in the important Shenyang military region. In is worth recalling that the Liaoning Provincial Party Committee under Chen's leadership was the first in the country to openly attack Lin Piao in early

November 1971. Possibly Chen's transfer to Peking was intended to guarantee the safety and freedom of action of the moderate leadership. However, the First and the Second Political Commissars (Chi Teng-kuei and Wu Teh respectively) associated with Chen are leftists and they owe their prominence to the Cultural Revolution.

Likewise, it is difficult to say, with any certainty, how far the removal of Li Teh-sheng from Peking to Shenyang had the effect of weakening the Leftists in the Party Centre. It might be recalled that besides Yeh Chien-ying (who is senior to Li and close to Premier Chou), Li is the only other military figure occupying a seat in the powerful nine-man Standing Committee of the Party Politburo. Li's pro-Left leaning could be inferred from his unusual promotion during and after the Cultural Revolution. At the time of his induction in the Ninth Politburo in 1969, Li was a relatively low-ranking military leader commanding the Anhwei provincial military district (his status was not at all comparable with that of Chen Hsi-lien and Hsu Shih-yu, both Politburo members who commanded the principal military regions of Shenyang and Nanking respectively). That Li belonged to the Leftist group was also obvious from the way in which the province under his control responded to the results of the Tenth Party Congress. Anhwei alone, among the 29 administrative units at provincial level, advocated the radical view that new cadres, who had been promoted since the Cultural Revolution should take one-third of the seats in leadership groups at all levels. Li was no doubt assigned a very important military region, charged with the duty of defending the border with the USSR, but he was not only moved out of Peking but removed from the important post of Director of the GPD of the PLA as well in January 1975, when Chang Chun-chiao was appointed to that post. However, as commander of an important military region, he is likely to wield considerable influence in internal power-politics.

Even after the reshuffle, several military commanders continued to be subjected to poster attacks and criticism, in some cases in the areas of their previous postings. Among these were: Li Teh-sheng, Chen Hsi-lien, Tseng Ssu-yu, Han Hsien-chu, Wang Pi-cheng, Hsieh Chen-hua (the PLA Commander and Party First Secretary in Shansi), and Chou Chih-ping, the author of a pro-Lin pamphlet and Political Commissar of the Fukien Front PLA. The anti-Lin and anti-Confucius campaign was primarily utilized to curb the political power of the PLA in the provinces. Thus, the campaign helped, to a great extent, in restoring Party leadership that was largely destroyed during the Cultural Revolution. Criticism of Lin Piao's military line had been accompanied by an assertion of Party authority and control over the army. Occasionally, however, emphasis was also laid on combat readiness and military training as well.

Although the large-scale reshuffle of regional military commanders was carried out peacefully and without any untoward incident, it could not but have created a certain amount of heart burning or misgiving in the minds of military leaders affected by the reshuffle. They might have felt that the principle of seniority was not adhered to or given due consideration in effecting those transfers. While no visible signs of commanders' defiance or Party-PLA tension had immediately come to surface, it was reported that the regional commanders later refused to participate in a meeting which was to be held in Peking in the fall of 1974. As a consequence, the meeting was reportedly convened in Wuhan and efforts were made to soothe the feelings of the disgruntled commanders. The paring down of the political role of the PLA was sought to be compensated by agreeing to divert larger resources for military purposes. With a view to reassure the commanders, it was stated that the campaign to criticize Lin Piao and his *bourgeois* military line was by no means aimed at the individual's personal responsibility.

On 26 December 1974, Hung Chou-wen wrote an article entitled "The Absolute Leadership of the Party is the Basic Guarantee for the Victory of Our Army" in *Kuang-ming Jih-pao*. The whole thrust of the article was that the Party should exercise absolute leadership over everything, the army included. Hung recalled the resolution of the Kutien Conference when Chairman Mao had criticized those mistaken ideas that advocated "letting Army Headquarters handle outside matters" and "giving military affairs a leading position over politics." In that resolution, Hung pointed out, Chairman Mao had repeatedly asserted: "If allowed to develop, this idea would involve the danger of estrangement from the masses, control of the government by the army and departure from proletarian leadership—it would be to take the path of warlordism like the Kuomintang army."[130]

The New Year Joint editorial, carried by the *Peoples' Daily*, *Red Flag* and the *Liberation Army Daily* on 1 January 1975, laid considerable emphasis on the centralized leadership and Party discipline. It called upon the nation to learn from the army. At the same time, it asked the army to learn from the people of the whole country. The PLA, it said, had made great contributions in the struggle to defend "our socialist motherland and consolidate the dictatorship of the proletariat." In the coming year, it stated, "we should apply Chairman Mao's proletarian military thinking and military line...and strengthen the unity between the army and the government and between the army and the people." The editorial then emphasized : "We must continue to strengthen Party building (at all levels) and the Party's centralized leadership." Party branches, it said, should play their proper role as the vanguard of the proletariat, and Party members should strive to fulfil the five requirements set for them in Article 12 of the Party Constitution (See Appendix 9), strengthen their Party spirit and observe Party discipline. The role of Revolutionary Committees and that of organizations of workers, peasants, women and youths and other mass organizations, the editorial observed, "should be given full scope under the unified leadership of the Party."[131] No department or organization was permitted to disrupt the centralized leadership of the Party. The need to obey the unified leadership of the Party was particularly impressed upon the PLA.

10 Fourth National People's Congress

The convening of the Fourth National People's Congress (NPC) in January 1975 was an important step towards normalcy in China and went a long way in strengthening Party control over the State apparatus and the Army. The appointments to ministerial posts indicated the emergence of the so-called moderate group led by Chou En-lai in the dominant position. Teng Hsiao-ping, with his appointment as the senior-most Vice-Premier, Vice-Chairman of the Party Central Committee, and Chief of Staff of the PLA, acquired the best credentials to succeed to the top leadership post in the country after Chou En-lai.

The last session of the NPC was held in 1964. Therefore, the convening of the NPC session in early 1975 proved the validity of the general saying that it is easier to destroy than to construct. It took less than three years to smash the Liu Shao-chi-controlled Party and State mechanism. However, the process of rebuilding of the Party apparatus and the reassertion of its supremacy over the administration and the army took nearly twice that long. This is likely to have a dampening effect on the revolutionary zeal of those radicals who advocate a series of "Cultural Revolutions" or intermittent upheavals to keep the elan of Maoism alive.

After the Tenth Party Congress, the convening of the NPC was very much in the air. However, it could be convened only in January 1975. This delay was partly due to the fact that the radical and moderate wings of the ruling coalition at the Centre could not come to an agreement earlier about the reallocation of offices, and partly because of the time taken in further consolidating the leadership of the Party over the army. It was, therefore, between August 1973 and January 1975 that a broad consensus was reached on the distribution of administrative offices, including the significant posts of Vice-Premiers, Minister of Defence, Chief of Staff and Director of GPD in the PLA. Bold steps were simultaneously taken to dislodge the powerful regional commanders from their bastions of power and thereby preclude any active resistance on their part to the proposed arrangements.

The most significant changes introduced in the new Constitution, adopted by the NPC in January 1975, were the abolition of the post of Chairman of the State and the establishment of the absolute, open leadership of the Party over the Central Government organs. The Draft Revised Constitution of the State, the Report on its Revision, the "Report on the Work of the Government," and the lists of nominees for the membership of the Standing Committee of the NPC and the State Council were first considered by the Second Plenary Session of the Tenth Central Committee, (from 8 to 10 January 1975), before they were presented before the NPC. While presenting his "Report on the Work of the Government" to the NPC on behalf of the State Council, Chou En-lai prefaced his statement by saying that he was making that report "in accordance with the decision of the Central Committee of the Communist Party of China."[132]

Mao himself was the Chairman of State from 1949 to 1958. From 1959 onwards, Liu Shao-chi had occupied that post. After his disgrace and dismissal during the Cultural Revolution, the post of the Chairman of State had remained vacant and there were indications that the post might even be abolished. The actual abolition of the post in the new Constitution was obviously intended to eliminate a power base that could, from its vantage position, possibly challenge in the future (as it had done in the past) the Chairman of the Chinese Communist Party.

Under the old Constitution of 1954, the Chairman of the State was also the supreme Commander of the Chinese armed forces. Under the new Constitution, however, the PLA has been placed under the direct command of the Chairman of the Central Committee of the Communist Party of China. Consequently, the Party chief emerges as the embodiment of all power and the symbol of the Party's control and authority over the army. Article 15 of the new Constitution further declares that the PLA and the people's militia "are the workers and peasants' own armed forces led by the Communist Party of China." It, thus, seeks to assert the validity of Mao's proletarian military thinking. The PLA, it is further stated, "is at all times a fighting force, and simultaneously a working force and a production force." The tasks of the armed forces were stated to be "to safeguard the achievements of the socialist revolution and socialist construction, to defend the sovereignty, territorial integrity and security of the state, and to guard against subversion and aggression by imperialism, social-imperialism and their lackeys."

Under the new Constitution, the formal (*i.e.* ceremonial) functions of the Chinese Head of State apparently will henceforth be performed by Chu Teh, the Chairman of the NPC Standing Committee. In case he is somehow incapacitated or unable to discharge the protocol functions of the Head of State, two Vice-Chairmen, *viz.* Tung Pi-wu (he died in April 1975) and Madame Soong Ching-ling, were appointed to perform the ceremonial functions of State.

The Preamble of the new Constitution sanctifies the Maoist thesis that classes and class struggle continue to exist in the "entire historical period of socialism" and reaffirms the "theory of continued revolution under the dictatorship of the proletariat." China, it states, would always advance along the road indicated by Marxism-Leninism-Mao Tse-tung Thought. The Constitution, it must be pointed out, not only asserts the main tenets of political radicalism in order to satisfy Mao and/or the radicals but also displays a sense of moderation and pragmatism in the economic field. While declaring the state sector to be "the leading force in the national economy" and ensuring the predominant position of the collective economy of the people's communes, the Constitution allows Chinese artisans and craftsmen to engage in private labour so long as it involves "no exploitation of others." It also guarantees peasants the right to cultivate private plots (which Mao had abolished, for a short period, during the Great Leap Forward) and "to keep a small number of livestock for their personal needs." It might be recalled that during the Cultural Revolution the concepts of small farming for personal use and "limited household side-line production" (now permitted under the new Constitution) were considered "revisionist" and vehemently criticized. In his report on the revision of the Constitution, Wang Hung-wen justified its liberal provisions regarding cultivation of small plots for personal needs and the right to engage in limited household side-line production by saying that they "integrate the principle of adherence to socialism with the necessary flexibility."[133]

The so-called *necessary flexibility* in regard to private farming and limited side-line production reflected the pragmatic viewpoint and the moderate line of thinking. However, the freedom to strike, Chang Chun-chiao stated, had been added to the list of Fundamental Rights and Duties in Article 28 of the new Constitution at Chairman Mao's suggestion. This provision, which permitted industrial workers to indulge in "rebellious" behaviour, could hardly be regarded as being in consonance with the current moderate emphasis on Party leadership and industrial order. But it was probably included to satisfy the radicals who wished to keep bureaucratic tendencies and evils under control.

Premier Chou En-lai made full use of Mao's authority in support of his moderate policies and ideas. Revolution, he stated in his Report on the Work of the Government, must aim at increasing production. He even quoted Chairman Mao on the need for "external assistance" as a subsidiary means to self-reliance and for learning from both the good and bad experiences of other countries.[134]

The abolition of the post of Chairman of State and related changes, Chang Chun-chiao, the new Vice-Premier, asserted, "will certainly help strengthen the Party's centralized leadership over the structure of the State and meet the desire of the people of the whole country."[135] Accordingly, under the new Constitution, the National People's Congress was declared to be the "highest organ of State power *under the leadership of the Communist Party.*" This was a clear confirmation of Party control over State legislation and administration. The Party, in the past, had no doubt exercised unchallenged control over the Government—in the formulation of policies and in the selection of officials—but it had all along remained a behind-the-scenes force. Nominally, the NPC had the exclusive right to nominate and elect the Chairman of the State (who then nominated the Premier of the State Council for approval by the NPC), its Standing Committee and to approve officials of the State Council, upon recommendation by the Premier. Apparently, the framers of the Chinese Constitution in 1954 were keen to create an impression that the NPC and the Government under its control were a self-ruling entity not subject to Party domination. However, in its anxiety to assert and strengthen Party leadership over all sections of society, the army in particular, the Chinese leadership in 1975 deemed it necessary to make a clear-cut affirmation about Party control over the government in the new Constitution. Therefore, Article 17 thereof unreservedly stipulates that the NPC could appoint and dismiss the Premier of the State Council and members of the State Council only "on the proposal of the Central Committee of the Communist Party of China." (See Appendix 10)

The dominating role of the Party in the political structure of China was also evident from the fact that 8 of the 12 Vice-Premiers are members of the powerful Politburo of the Communist Party. (See Table 20) The number of the Vice-Premiers has been increased from 5 to 12 in order to accommodate the radical elements in the Party and to effect necessary compromises within the collective leadership now ruling the country.

The Chairman of the NPC Standing Committee, Marshal Chu Teh, is a member of the Standing Committee of the Party Politburo. Of the 22 Vice-Chairmen of the NPC Standing Committee, 17 are members or alternate members of the Party Central Committee. (See Table 19) Among these, six—Tung pi-wu, Kang Sheng, Liu Po-cheng, Wu Teh, Wei Kuo-ching and Saifudin—are members of the Politburo; four—Chen Yun, Tan Chen-lin, Marshal Nieh Jung-chen and Ulanfu—are former Vice-Premiers; one (Li Ching-chuan) is former Party Chief of Southwest China; one (Chang Ting-cheng) is former Procurator-General of the Supreme People's Procuratorate. Only two (Li Wu-wen and Yao Lien-wei, member and alternate member respectively of the Central Committee) are newcomers since the Cultural Revolution. Three of the 17 Vice-Chairmen of the NPC Standing Committee (Tan Chen-lin, Li Ching-chuan and Ulanfu) had been severely attacked by the radicals during the Cultural Revolution but were rehabilitated in 1973.

Chou En-lai was re-appointed as Premier of the State Council by the NPC. The post of Defence Minister, which had been lying vacant since Lin Piao's disappearance, went to Yeh Chien-ying—a close associate of Chou. In other appointments too, the veteran cadres, who had experience of working in the ministries and commissions of the State Council and, for that matter, had been close to Chou were given preference over others. Thus, a number of veteran government, Party and Army leaders, were either promoted or re-appointed to ministerial posts in the newly-constituted State Council. It appeared that the pragmatists, who were attacked by the radical left during the 1974 thought-purification campaign, ostensibly directed against Lin Piao and the ideas of Confucius, had weathered the storm. They were, therefore, reinstated in governmental posts. On the other hand, the stalwarts of the radical group—Chiang Ching, Yao Wen-yuan and Wang Hung-wen—were not given any posts in the State Council. According to a Taiwanese intelligence report, quoted by Chiang Ching-kuo, Premier of Taiwan in the Legislative Yuan on 21 February 1975, a proposal to make Chiang Ching a Vice-Premier was vetoed by veteran Party regulars.[136]

Thus, the NPC session seemed to confirm the dominant position of the moderate group under Chou's leadership. This tilt in favour of the moderates was generally believed to enhance China's image as a peace-loving country and facilitate economic stability and progress in the country. It also reflected the growing strength of the moderate group, who enjoyed the support of the government, Party and military leaders subjected to criticism by the radicals. However, the emergence of the moderates as a dominant force in China did not mean that the radicals ceased to exercise any influence in Chinese politics. Although, the latter had been reduced to a minority in both the Party and State organs, they had nevertheless managed to control two important posts, *viz.* that of Minister of Public Security and Minister of Culture. Five Vice-Premiers also belonged to the radical group.

A significant development of the NPC session has been the rise of Teng Hsiao-ping to No. 2 position in the State apparatus, next only to Chou. Hardly a week before the convening of the NPC, Teng was elevated to the post of Vice-Chairman of the Party Central Committee and became a member of the Standing Committee of the Politburo. This was somewhat comparable to his own earlier rise from 24th position in the Seventh Central Committee to 6th position in the Eighth CC and that of Chou En-lai from 24th place in the Sixth Central Committee to 3rd place in Seventh Central Committee. Lest the radical elements in the Party felt unhappy about the spectacular rise of Teng as the senior-most Vice-Premier, Chang Chun-chiao, a leading Cultural Revolution activist from Shanghai, was included in the State Council as the second ranking Vice-Premier, *i.e.* next to Teng. Soon after the NPC session was over, Teng Hsiao-ping was appointed Chief of Staff, while Chang Chun-chiao was made Director of the GPD. It is difficult to say as to what extent Chang Chun-chiao has become a new convert to the moderate group and/or can play a key role in reconciling the differences between the radicals and the moderates. The fact remained that Chang, like Teng Hsiao-ping, also concurrently holds effective power positions (though slightly lower in rank as compared with Teng) in the Party, state and the PLA.

Although Teng Hsiao-ping has emerged with the best credentials to succeed to the top leadership position in China, he is still outranked by one or more persons in all the three pillars of the political system, *viz.* Party, Army and Administration. Within the Party, Wang Hung-wen holds No. 3 position after Mao and Chou and both Yeh Chien-ying and Kang Sheng are probably senior to Teng because they were appointed Vice-Chairmen of the Party Central Committee prior to Teng's elevation as Vice-Chairman. In the PLA, as Minister of Defence, Yeh Chien-ying has a superior status as compared to Teng, though, unlike Teng, he is not a Vice-Premier in the State Council. In the Administration, Teng is the senior-most Vice-Premier next to Premier Chou En-lai. In the Chinese political system, the state apparatus has been effectively subordinated to Party control. Therefore, Teng's senior position in the State Council does not matter much, though it can confer on him a certain degree of legitimacy in case he otherwise succeeds to the top leadership post in China.

Yeh Chien-ying has been made Defence Minister, but the incumbents of the important offices of Chief of Staff and Director of General Political Department of the PLA are both Vice-Premiers and, therefore, senior to Yeh in the State Council. Evidently, they are not amenable to control by Yeh and this is derogatory to the prestige of the Minister of Defence. This incongruous arrangement, to a certain extent, also hampers the effective functioning of the Defence Minister as the leader of the Army. However, keeping in view the special circumstances through which China had passed, such an arrangement or a system of checks and balances (as the present writer prefers to call it and discusses in detail in chapter 12) appears to be most suitable for China's domestic politics in the post-Mao era. With Liu Shao-chi's example before them, the present Chinese leadership—a coalition of different groups now ruling China—could not possibly permit the Head of State, who enjoyed immense patronage, to hold the concurrent post of the Commander-in-Chief of the PLA as well. Similarly, with the vivid memory of Lin Piao's misdeeds of seeking to establish military dictatorship in the country, the concentration of effective military power in the hands of a Defence Minister was considered too hazardous. Yeh Chien-ying, the present Minister of Defence, shares the belief that the army must always be subordinated to the Party but that was hardly convincing partly because Lin Piao too had claimed himself to be a faithful exponent of Maoist Thought and partly because there was no guarantee that Yeh's successor would hold similar views in the matter. Therefore, with a view to effectively ensure that Party control would never again be challenged by military leaders, two powerful civilian leaders—Teng Hsiao-ping and Chang Chun-chiao—were appointed to the vital posts of Chief of Staff and Director of GPD in the PLA. Moreover, it was felt that Teng's leading position in the PLA would facilitate his task of undertaking a thorough reorganization of the armed forces in order to eliminate any actual or potential dangers to the authority of the Party high command.

In non-communist countries, a civilian is generally appointed as Defence Minister and a military man holds the post of Chief of Staff. In communist countries, on the other hand, both these posts are held by military leaders. Thus, in both communist and non-communist countries, a military person invariably holds the post of Chief of Staff. In China, however, while Marshal Yeh Chien-ying was appointed Defence Minister the post of Chief of Staff had gone to Teng Hsiao-ping. Since Teng had served as political commissar in the Second Field Army and the South-west Military Region, with Marshals Liu Po-cheng and Ho Lung respectively as military commanders, during and after the victory of the Chinese revolution, and organized and led some guerilla units in the Red Army, he could be said to have had a certain degree of military background. But he was never a professional soldier and is not known to have ever commanded any regular military units in his life time. Thus, the appointments of Yeh and Teng as Defence Minister and Chief of Staff respectively were in marked contrast to the practice followed in both Communist and non-communist countries of the world and at variance with the practice in vogue in China itself in the 50s and 60s. In particular, the appointment of Teng as Chief of Staff was an innovation of the highest order. Commenting on this anomalous situation, S. K. Ghosh, an Indian commentator, has observed as follows :

A professional Army leader, Marshal Yeh Chien-ying, is holding the essentially political post of Defence Minister, responsible for laying down the general policy lines for the PLA, while a non-professional non-military political leader is holding the essentially military and technical post of the Chief of the General Staff, responsible for executing the political decisions handed down to him by his Minister. Had it been the other way round, that is Teng working as Defence Minister and Yeh as Chief of the General Staff, it would have fitted in with the accepted military pattern, because the Defence Ministers generally laying down policy lines keeping in view the Party mandate, are normally civilian Party leaders, whereas the Chief of the General Staff, who actually plans for and coordinates the forces in combat, is a professional officer on active military list;

although in Communist countries both these posts are normally held by military men, who, by and large, are also
ranking Party members. Many previous PLA Chiefs of
the General Staff including Lo Jui-ch'ing and Huang Yung-
sheng, held senior Party posts (Lo was a Central Committee
member while Huang was a Politburo member between the
9th and 10th Party Congress; but the criterion of the
selection was usually the "reddest" among the available
experts. The expertise required was never completely
overlooked as seems to have been done now.[137]

According to Ghosh, the appointment of Teng Hsiao-ping
as Chief of Staff of the PLA "is only a temporary, stop gap
arrangement, pending the availability of a military man, with
the necessary professional and technical qualifications, who
will at the same time be amenable to Party discipline." Ghosh
admits that it was not unnatural that the mind of the Party
leadership would be haunted by the apparitions of Huang
K'o-ch'eng, Lo Jui-ching and Huang Yung-sheng, the three
successive Chiefs of the General Staff holding ranks of Army
Generals, who allegedly flouted Party mandates to achieve
their military goals. However, he yet seems to overlook the
importance or the immediate relevance of asserting Party
supremacy and leadership over the army in the prevalent
situation in China. Accordingly, Ghosh comes to the conclusion that "whatever may be the reasons which have com-
pelled the Peking leadership to take this incongruous step" of
appointing Teng as Chief of Staff, "if the arrangement continues too long, it is bound to have its repercussions felt on the
efficiency and morale of the PLA forces, particularly the
officer cadre." This appointment, he states, was bound to be
regarded as displaying want of confidence in the professional
military men and their loyalty to the Party. Instead of serving
to increase the control of the Party on the PLA, Ghosh asserts,
"this may well alienate them" because "Stalin, even when he
executed Marshal Tukachevsky and other military leaders did
not slight the Red Army by appointing a non-professional
Party leader at the head of the More Army."[138]

If Taiwanese intelligence sources, which have often
proved correct in so far as developments in China
are concerned, are to be believed the veteran military
leaders of the PLA had insisted that both the posts of Defence

Minister and Chief of Staff must be filled by men with military background. It was thought, at the same time, that a compromise solution of appointing a civilian to the post of Defence Minister and a military man to the post of Chief of Staff would be acceptable. Accordingly, the name of Chang Chun-chiao was suggested for the post of Defence Minister and that of Yang Cheng-wu, who had the experience of acting Chief of Staff and had been rehabilitated and appointed as Deputy Chief of Staff, was said to have been proposed for the post of the Chief of Staff. It is reported, that Liu Po-cheng, the veteran military leader, pounded the table with his hand to voice his opposition to the proposal of making Chang Chun-chiao Defence Minister and that Mao's wife, Chiang Ch'ing, in turn, opposed the appointment of Yang Ch'eng-wu as Chief of Staff.[139]

In the circumstances obtaining in China in 1974-75, neither civilians nor military leaders could possibly be appointed to both the posts of Defence Minister and Chief of Staff without giving rise to serious misgivings or apprehensions in the minds of either the army or the Party. A *via media* was found by selecting Marshal Yeh Chien-ying for the post of Defence Minister and Teng Hsiao-ping for the office of Chief of Staff. To have reversed this order, *i. e.* Teng as Minister of Defence and Yeh as Chief of Staff, might have fitted in with the so-called "accepted military pattern," but it was hardly feasible or practicable in the prevalent situation in China. Yeh was too senior a man to be appointed as Chief of Staff under Teng. It would have been considered damaging to the prestige of the army and degrading to Yeh's stature. Besides, the appointment of Teng to the post of Chief of Staff was deemed essential for bending the military commanders to Party leadership. Lest the Leftists feel dissatisfied and ignored, Chang Chun-chiao was appointed as Director of GPD in the PLA. Thus, the PLA appointments, that were announced in January 1975, were probably the best in the circumstances and, therefore, acceptable to the military leaders as well as to the contending groups within the Party. They also reflected the existing balance of forces among different groups within the top leadership echelons.

The appointment of regional military leaders (the potential candidates being Chen Hsi-lien, the only Vice-Premier among regional commanders, and Li Teh-sheng) to the post of Defence Minister or Chief of Staff was not without risks. Although both Chen and Li belonged to the Second Field Army, the former was closely associated with the moderates while the latter belonged to the radical group. Besides, there was the need of striking a balance among Field Armies and the question of inter-service rivalries. Therefore, the promotion of any one of them was fraught with the danger of causing discontent and dissatisfaction among others, including Hsu Shih-yu. For that matter, the simultaneous promotion of the two was also not considered prudent. The arrangement that was eventually worked out was somewhat favourable to the moderates as both Yeh Chien-ying and Teng Hsiao-ping had more in common with them than with the radicals. But this probably reflected the prevailing power equation between the two groups at the Centre. However, the radicals had to be satisfied with the appointment of Chang Chun-chiao as Director of GPD in the PLA. Since both the posts of Defence Minister and Chief of Staff could not possibly be given to the civilians, the aged Yeh Chien-ying was chosen to occupy one of the two posts so that the arrangement could be acceptable to the military as well. Whatever may have been the considerations and the circumstances in the matter, the arrangement may not last long, particularly as Teng moves into positions now occupied by Mao, Chou or both. Yeh Chien-ying is also not likely to live long and a successor will have to be found for him too. In the post-Mao and post-Chou era, much would depend on the relative strengths of the two groups (the moderates and the radicals) and the support they manage to get from the army. One can speculate that Teng's further rise will be matched by Chang Chunchiao's elevation and that Chen Hsi-lien will most probably be inducted in the Central military leadership.

PART THREE

The Future

11 Group Rivalries

Ever since Mao Tse-tung established himself as the undisputed leader of the Chinese Communist Party at the Tsunyi Conference in 1935, he has persistently endeavoured to retain his supremacy and power. Often he has had to face several serious challenges to his authority and, at times, even set-backs and reverses in the last forty years. A salient feature of the Chinese political system has been that the Chinese leadership, both within the Party and in the Army, has never been monolithic. The purge of Jao Shu-shih and Kao Kang in 1954-55, the fall of Peng Teh-huai in 1959, the dismissal of Liu Shao-chi in 1966-67 and the disappearance of Lin Piao in September 1971 are cases in point.

The Cultural Revolution, in fact, was a power struggle waged under an ideological garb, the outcome of the open rift between the Liu Shao-chi-controlled Party bureaucracy and Mao Tse-tung and his supporters. The disappearance of Lin Piao, likewise, resulted from the subsequent clash between clearly distinguishable factions. The different constituent elements of the anti-Lin coalition, that brought about the downfall of Lin Piao, appeared to be united against what they perceived to be a common danger to their own positions. However, they can hardly be said to share in common a unified approach on all issues. As a result of certain calculated moves, the Party has, to a great extent, succeeded in paring down the political role of the PLA and asserting its "centralized leadership" over the army. But, even today, it cannot be regarded as being a monolithic structure. True, the convocation of the Fourth National People's Congress in January 1975 apparently stabilized the internal situation in China and signified that a certain degree of consensus, based on compromises, had been reached among the Chinese leadership. But that did not imply that the factional disputes or group rivalries have ceased to exist in China.

"One-divides-into-two" and struggle-unity-struggle are the very essence of the Maoist dialectic. According to Chairman Mao, contradictions and struggles continue to exist even in a "socialist society." There are always possibilities of capitalism re-asserting itself in a socialist society and, therefore, one must continue to lay emphasis on asserting and strengthening the dictatorship of the proletariat. Writing in the Chinese communist theoretical journal, *Red Flag* (January 1975), Kao Li laid stress on the theory of continued revolution. He emphatically asserted that there was no such thing as "a state without differences," that it to say, without contradictions. One should, he pointed out, see the existence of a struggle during the period of changes. Similarly, one should not forget the existence of struggle during the period of relative tranquility. The passing from the state of relative tranquility to the state of conspicuous changes, Kao Li stated, meant going forward and developing. The passing from the state of conspicuous changes to that of tranquility, he asserted, also meant going forward and developing. Thus, "revolutionary struggle goes through the continuous process of interchanges between the states of relative tranquility and conspicuous changes." Furthermore, Kao Li pointed out, those individuals whose thinking went beyond a certain stage of development and who pursued "adventurism" in action were "Leftist Opportunists." On the other hand, those who did not think that the struggle between contradictions had pushed forward development and whose thinking still lingered on the old period, trying by every means to turn back the wheel of history, were "Rightist Opportunists."[140]

In these circumstances, it is hardly surprising that soon after the First Session of the Fourth National People's Congress came to an end, a new ideological campaign for the study of the dictatorship of the proletariat was launched. The *People's Daily* editorial of 9 February 1975 observed that Chairman

Mao had "recently" issued an "important instruction" (published in *People's Daily* on 8 February) calling upon the people of the whole country to correctly handle the question of the dictatorship of the proletariat failing which the country might go revisionist. In this connection, reference was made to the retention of the so-called "bourgeois rights"—the existence in China *even now* of the unequal eight-grade wage system, a commodity economy, the use of currency, and payment according to work—all of which were said to be scarcely different from the practice prevailing in pre-liberation China. Only the ownership of the means of production had changed. In this situation, the possibility of the country "changing colour," *i.e.* deviating to the path of revisionism, and the emergence of "newly engendered" *bourgeois* elements, could not be completely ruled out.

The fight against revisionism, the *People's Daily* editorial remarked, "is a protracted struggle, not one or two trials of strength." "Our tasks," it stated, were, as Lenin put it, "to work ceaselessly to dig up the soil that breeds revisionism," and to create conditions in which it would be impossible for the *bourgeoisie* to exist or for a new *bourgeoisie* to arise. Small production, which existed in China and was permitted under the new Constitution, was considered as engendering capitalism and the new *bourgeois* elements "continuously, daily, hourly, spontaneously and on a mass scale." Sections of the workers as well as Party members, both within the ranks of the proletariat and among office staff, were believed to be susceptible to the corrupting influence of *bourgeois* tendencies, which were manifest in the "bourgeois style of life."[141]

On 22 February 1975, the *People's Daily* published three and a half pages of quotations from Marx, Engels and Lenin, that had been jointly compiled by the editorial boards of the *People's Daily* and the *Red Flag*. The theme of these quotations was the danger of a restoration of capitalism and the need of an intensive study of the dictatorship of the proletariat.[142] Another important article by Yao Wen-yuan, a prominent radical leftist leader, a close associate of Mao and a Politburo member, appeared in the March 1975 issue of the theoretical journal of the Party, *Red Flag*. Entitled "On the Social Basis of The Lin Piao Anti-Party Clique," the article was critical of the resurgence of the *bourgeois* life-style and it appeared to be intended more as an attack on "people like Lin Piao" than a mere continuation of "Pi-lin Pi-kung" ("Criticise Lin, Criticise Confucius") campaign of 1974.

The article directed the readers' attention to the "social basis," which was said to have engendered the Lin Piao clique and "people like Lin Piao," who were "representatives of the *bourgeoisie*" within the Party and in society and "who will try to turn their hope for restoration of capitalism into attempts at restoration." Yao particularly warned against the corruption of youth by "material inducements," which had been revived in China since 1972. The article also warned against the counter-revolutionary double-dealers—those who opposed red flag while flying a red flag and waved "Chairman Mao's banner to strike at Chairman Mao's forces." In criticizing capitalist tendencies, the article stated, it was necessary "to create public opinion, win over the majority, awaken consciousness and give active guidance." This was apparently the voice of a spokesman of a minority group. However, in order to conclude with an optimistic note, Yao Wen-yuan observed : "As for the few who have sunk deep into the quagmire of capitalism, they must be told sharply : 'Comrades, mend your ways right now'."

The last paragraph of the article was a "summing-up" by Chairman Mao. It stated : "No reactionary has been able to stay long in power...If the right stages an anti-communist *coup d' etat* in China, I am sure they will know no peace either and their rule will most probably be short-lived."[143] Thus, the *People's Daily* article not only held out a threat against those who were asking for higher material rewards and greater improvement in standard of living but also appeared to warn factory managers and cadres at the enterprise and provincial levels who had not been particularly circumspect in the use of material incentives to make up for production shortfalls that occurred as a result of the "Pi-lin Pi-kung" campaign of 1974.

The new ideological campaign was apparently directed towards dispelling any hopes about higher wages and better style of life, etc. following the acceptance of private ownership of small plots and limited side-line production in the new constitution and striking the right balance between economic

development and the development of revolutionary consciousness. It sought to combat the normal human instinct to work
for personal gain and the inherent acquisitive tendencies in
man. For the first time, the new campaign also contained an
attack on "empiricism" and thereby criticized pragmatism.
It, thus, reflected the concern of "ideologues" that the wealth
generated by the social effort did not produce disparities, thereby disturbing the classless structure of the society. According
to Gerd Ruge, a West German writer, Chou En-lai's report
to the first session of the Fourth NPC was, for the most part, a
catalogue of economic successes and an exhortation to keep up
the good work, with the result that the call to maintain revolutionary vigilance seemed to be relegated to a secondary role.
Moreover, the new Chinese Constitution allowed material
inducements to remain in certain sectors. The new political
campaign was, therefore, aimed at forestalling a reversion to
bourgeois, capitalist tendencies in the Chinese economy and
among the ranks of officialdom.

Gerd Ruge believes that this ideological offensive "seems
to be strictly limited in scope and unlikely to wreak havoc with
the government's course of economic consolidation." Calls to
eliminate *bourgeois* capitalist thinking, he states, must not be
taken as an invitation to exterminate entire sections of society
suspected of subscribing to such views. He further remarks :
"They need not be taken to presage suicidal in-fighting either.
What they amount to is a warning not to allow revisionist
deviations to re-establish themselves." However, the German
writer does not rule out "many a dispute over economic and
political priorities" which are likely to occur before the next
five-year plan—due to start in 1976—is finally approved.[144]

It is possible that the new ideological campaign was merely
in the nature of ideological rectification, aimed at sharpening
the political consciousness of the people and Party members by
laying emphasis on theoretical study of the dictatorship of the
proletariat, and therefore unlikely to disturb the prospects of
stability in the country. However, one cannot altogether rule
out the possibility of the campaign being used by different
groups for political in-fighting. In fact, the articles by Nan yü
and Li Hsin—both of which appeared on page two of the
People's Daily on 16 March and 21 March 1975 respectively—

presented differing or rather conflicting interpretations of the concept of "proletarian dictatorship." Thus, it appeared that different political forces inside the Party were using the same Party organ to serve their own ends. The article by Nan yü entitled "The Vast Masses of People Must be Relied Upon to Consolidate Proletarian Dictatorship" emphasized the role of the "masses" in "exposing the dark side from the lower level upwards" so as to consolidate the dictatorship. In the past 20-odd years since the establishment of New China (the People's Republic of China), the article by Nan yü stated, all the successive political campaigns personally launched and led by Chairman Mao had invariably entrusted the Party's line to the vast numbers of the masses, inspired the masses to struggle against the *bourgeoisie*, thereby crushing the various conspiracies of *bourgeois* restoration, steeling the masses and continuously consolidating proletarian dictatorship. To rely on the masses to consolidate proletarian dictatorship, Nan declared, was a fundamental experience of New China.[145]

The other article by Li Hsin entitled "The Proletarian Dictatorship is Led by the Communist Party" stressed the role of the Party Centre in exercising leadership over all other organizations, including the government, army, mass organizations, and criticized those who attempted to "abolish or undermine the Party Centre's unified leadership." The entire political, economic, cultural and educational work of the country, Li Hsin declared, must be led by the Party—the vanguard of the proletariat. The working class, which is susceptible to *bourgeois* influence, must necessarily remain under the Party's leadership. Only the Party can overcome *bourgeois* influence and the effect of *bourgeois* rights, struggle against newly engendered *bourgeois* elements, and create conditions under which the *bourgeoisie* could neither exist nor be regenerated. The authority of Chairman Mao was invoked and even the victory of the Cultural Revolution was stated to have been won under the Party Centre's unified leadership.

Lin Piao was accused of setting up *bourgeois* headquarters in an attempt to antagonize the Party Centre and to usurp the supreme power of the Party and State and of splitting the Party, the Army and the people. "Engaging in splitting," the article by Li Hsin warned, "is always directly linked with engaging in revisionism." To abolish or undermine the Party Centre's unified leadership, it added, was bound to abolish and undermine proletarian dictatorship. That was "a fundamental feature of revisionism." In conclusion, the article issued an appeal for strengthening Party leadership and emphasized the need for unity.[146] It is interesting to note that Li Hsin's article did not use the term "the vast masses of people" and mentioned the term "masses" only ten times, whereas Nan yü's article did not mention either the Party Centre or leadership by the Party, but referred to the "masses" 67 times,

In some articles appearing in the Chinese press one sees a deliberate attempt at reconciling the moderate and the radical points of view. Thus, in a report by its own provincial correspondent published on 12 March 1975, the *People's Daily*, pointed out that although the cultivation of private plots was permitted, the peasants should not look after their private plots *exclusively*, and thereby ignore collective production.[147] The *People's Daily* editorial of 11 March 1975 criticized tendencies towards capitalism and demanded that the enterprises should stick to the socialist orietation. However, the editorial in the Party paper, at the same time, observed : "We must carry out the Party's various proletarian policies, promote nation-wide stability and unity."[148]

Chang Chun-chiao's article entitled "On Exercising All Round Dictatorship Over the Bourgeoisie" in the April 1975 issue of the *Red Flag* seemed to be directed at veteran cadres. He referred to the "bourgeois" wind among "leading cadres" and the importance of "leadership" in units and enterprises. He emphasized that capitalist restoration and all other important changes in social systems in history were made possible only through a "seizure of political power." He laid stress on ideological purity and denounced in stong terms corruption, speculation and profiteering.[149] Thus, Chang seemed to provide the extreme Left of the Party with a weapon against the local "power holders." Chang's article completly ignored the need for "stability and unity" which appeared to have been the theme of a central directive issued about 1 March 1975 and which had been emphasized in all provincial broadcasts since then.

Lest Chang's article, together with the campaign against

"bourgeois rights" and the warning against "people like Lin Piao" coming to power give rise to any doubts about the continuance of official policies, a short commentary was issued by the Central authorities—the Party and government leadership at the Centre—in the April 1975 issue of *Red Flag* itself and reported by *New China News Agency* on 3 April 1975. The commentary entitled "Study Well and Understand Thoroughly on the Plane of Integrating Theory with Practice" declared : "When it comes to questions of policies and systems, we should act prudently and, where specific policies have been laid down, do accordingly and refrain from making indiscreet alterations." The commentary sought to turn the study of the "theory of proletarian dictatorship" as well as the attack on "empiricism" against the radical Leftists—"opportunists flying the colours of Marxism-Leninism." The commentary laid emphasis on "stability and unity" and on the role of "leading cadres," who, it said, "must take the lead in studying well, in reading conscientiously and in getting a good grasp on the plane of integrating theory with practice, and must give effective leadership to the study by the Party membership and the masses."[150]

Another article in the same April 1975 issue of *Red Flag* by Chi Yen was also aimed at discouraging any hasty changes in current policies. Chi called for the restriction of "bourgeois rights." But, at the same time, he stressed that anyone who advocated an outright abolition of such "rights"—the policy of distribution according to work, rural private plots, sideline production and free markets—would be making the mistake of ultra-leftism. Basing himself on Chairman Mao's report to the Second Plenary Session of the Seventh CCP Central Committee of 5 March 1949, Chi Yen advocated the adoption of "well-measured and flexible policies" for restricting "private capitalist elements," which, he said, were beneficial to the national economy. The three major differences between workers and peasants, town and country and mental and physical labour, Chi observed, could be reduced only "step by step," and that it required a long period of time to create material and moral conditions for it. It was impossible, he added, to solve the problem overnight, and that attention must be paid to preventing such an attempt. Chi concluded by emphasizing the need to adhere to the Party's line and policies and to prevent and overcome various erroneous tendencies" in carrying out the struggle to restrict *bourgeois* rights to the end.[151]   Thus, both the groups—the proponents of economic progress based on material incentives and the keepers of the Marxist conscience—appeared to be using the Party media, the *People's Daily* and the theoretical monthly *Red Flag*, for propagating their own viewpoints.

The compromises effected in the new Constitution to accommodate the points of view of both the "pragmatists" and the "ideologues," Denzil Peiris observes, "hold within it contradictory pulls."   On the one hand, there is the pragmatists' concern not to disturb the "bourgeois rights" unduly lest production suffer a setback.   On the other hand, there is the compulsion to work towards their elimination, which drives the "ideologues."   Their inter-play, Denzil Peiris remarks, "can easily upset the equilibrium that has been institutionalized in the new Constitution."   Already, some of the "bourgeois rights" were in the process of being withdrawn in some areas. For instance, the decision of the Party leadership to pay over-time for extra work to the workers of a cotton mill in Wuhan was objected to, allegedly by a large number of workers.   A big character poster was put up saying that "one should work hard and aim at raising output quickly but not for monetary incentives" and the bonus decision was revoked. These were, indeed, pointers to future tension.   In any region where the "pragmatists" were outnumbered, Denzil Peiris points out, the state's repressive apparatus could be used against them.[152] Similarly, in other areas where the "ideologues" are in a minority, the possibility of the state apparatus being used, in some manner, against them could not be totally ruled out.

The very fact that the session of the Fourth National People's Congress and the filling of the important vacancies in the Party, army, and Government hierarchies, *e.g.* that of the Minister of National Defence, Chief of Staff and the appointment of several provincial Party First Secretaries (who concurrently hold the posts of Chairmen of Revolutionary Committees, which have now been reduced to mass organizations), had to be deferred for nearly a year and a half, after the holding of the Tenth Party Congress, signified that the interests of various groups had to be accommodated, differences reconciled and a consensus reached. By the middle of 1975, First Secretaries of two Provincial Party Committees—Anhwei, and Liaoning—have yet to be appointed. That showed that the positional struggles among the various groups for top leadership positions in the provinces was not yet over.

Possibly the differences of opinion had not, thus far hardened and the various groupings had not yet crystallized into clear-out factions. To use the Maoist phraseology, the contradictions are as yet of "non-antagonistic nature," which could, under certain situations and conditions, become antagonistic in nature. These contradictions seem to be "a series of confrontations between ever-changing, mostly issue-based alignments of functional and opinion groups." The *Far Eastern Economic Review* (Hong Kong) therefore pointed out that China's domestic politics "were back to a stage of a still indistinct, gradually evolving factionalisation rather than open factionalism." The campaigns to criticize Lin Piao and Confucius did not gain the momentum of a Second Cultural Revolution for that reason, the magazine asserted.

Chinese domestic politics in 1974, the Hong Kong magazine stated, cannot be analysed by the simplistic formula of two factions in battle. The paper identifies at least six groups "which are partly based on opinions and partly on their functional character." These are :

1. Those leaders of the State administrative and diplomatic machine who were not purged during the Cultural Revolution, such as Chou En-lai, Li Hsien-nien, Tung Pi-wu, Nieh Jung-chen, Chi Peng-fei and Chiao Kuan-hua;

2. A group of Party and administrative cadres who were purged during the Cultural Revolution but later reinstated, probably rallying around Teng Hsiao-ping;

3. The Cultural Revolutionary-Left around Chiang Ching, Yao Wen-yuan and possibly Chang Chun-chiao;

4. An emerging Secret police Left-wing, whose members had gained considerable influence since the Tenth Party Congress;

5. The regional military leaders who, despite the setback which they suffered in late 1973, were still a force to be reckoned with in future conflicts;

6. A newly emerging, obviously highly professionalised central military elite, which was represented in the Politburo by Yeh Chien-ying and Su Chen-hua, and which had gained strength with the rehabilitation of Yang Cheng-wu.

According to the Hong Kong magazine, cited above, the alignments in the Party were not clearly distinguishable and that concise sets of divergent opinions on major areas of conflict had not yet developed. But behind the screen of compromise, it adds, alliances might have already been formed between groups which had found themselves repeatedly on the same side during conflicts. Once they stabilized into factions, the magazine warns, "the stage would be set for the next major domestic crisis : the conflict over long-range decisions on development policies and over generational, rather than personal, succession."[153]

The enumeration of six groups by the Hong Kong magazine obviously represented only the broad trends in the wide spectrum of the Chinese political scene. It did not suggest the existence of a six-pronged struggle for power waged by half a dozen independent and clearly distinguishable entities. Moreover, the *Far Eastern Economic Review* assessment (quoted above) was made prior to the convening of the Fourth NPC session. It, therefore, took into account the situation obtaining in China in 1974. The subsequent devolopments, especially the convocation of the NPC session, represented substantial progress towards normalcy and signified that a broad consensus had been reached between the two contending groups—the so-called moderates and the radicals within the Party. These two groups seemed to be united on the question of asserting and establishing the over-all leadership of the Party over all sectors, including the army. However, the fact that they appeared to be united at present on certain issues did not necessarily mean that there were no differences of opinion between them in their basic approaches and style of work.

In his report on the Party Constitution to the Tenth Party Congress, Wang Hung-wen laid much emphasis on the concept of "collective leadership." Both the moderates and the radicals appear to be quite conscious of the danger inherent in split-ism factionalism and stronghold-ism. Nevertheless, neither of the two groups can possibly be expected to easily give up the positions they hold on matters of policy and the allocation of posts in administrative and Party hierarchy. Therefore, the contest of wills is likely to continue, sometimes in a low key, and, at other times, at a high pitch.

It is not quite possible to sort out all individuals, military and civilian, one by one and to say who is associated with whom. However, one can discern certain groupings—groupings that represent different interests and different styles of life and work. Among such groupings, one can easily speak of the so-called moderate group, composed of veteran Party and government functionaries led by Premier Chou En-lai, and the radical group, led by Chiang Ch'ing (Mao's wife) and Yao Wen-yuan, said to be Chiang Ch'ing's son-in-law. Besides, one can certainly speak of the army as a group. But the present writer does not, in the immediate context, regard the army to be an independent entity or a clearly distinguishable third group struggling for power and/or top leadership positions for two main reasons. In the first place, the military leaders are so much divided among themselves that they do not, as of yet, constitute a coherent and united group at the Centre. They are, therefore, unable to stake an independent claim, in their own right, to the position of supremacy in the whole country though, in certain circumstances, they may act as king-makers or wire-pullers. Secondly, although their political affiliations, in many cases, may be hard to define, they can be said to be associated with or found in sympathy with one or the other political groupings mentioned above, *i.e.* either the moderates or the radicals.

Of the two main groups, the pragmatists or the moderates are at present on the ascendancy, partly because they enjoy the support of the veteran cadres in the Party, administration and the army. Many of these veteran leaders had been vehemently criticized during the Cultural Revolution and afterwards by the extremist left but now they have been rehabilitated and reinstalled in positions of responsibility and power. The country has not yet fully recovered from the violent shake-up and the serious upheavals of the late 60s and the early 70s. Consequently, the people at large are in no mood to either entertain any fresh wave of the so-called cultural upsurge or relish the idea of continued revolution. The moderates represent a force for sanity, stability, and economic progress, which seems to be very much in accord with the present mood of the nation. Accordingly, the radicals, at present, seem to be lying low. The moderates also occupy a dominant position in the newly-constituted State Council partly because state management is considered to be the business of experienced administrators or bureaucrats and not of revolutionary cadres. It is also worth recalling that 9 out of 26 members of the Politburo, *viz.* Mao Tse-tung, Wang Hung-wen, Chiang Ch'ing, Hsu Shih-yu, Wang Tung-hsing, Li Teh-sheng, Yao Wen-yuan, Su Chen-hua and Ni Chih-fu, had not been appointed to any post in either the Standing Committee of the NPC or the State Council. Most of these leading personalities, it is worth noting, are prominent members of the radical group. Of these nine dignitaries, two, namely Chairman Mao and Wang Tung-hsing, who rose to prominence during the Cultural Revolution, were absent from the NPC Session. That gave rise to much speculation. It was rumoured that their absence indicated a decline in Chairman Mao's influence. Wang, Director of the General Office of the Party Central Committee, had been Mao's bodyguard for several decades and was believed to have controlled a secret service watching over all Party, Army and Government leaders. His absence from the NPC session may have been accidental due to the nature of his duty.

Mao's conspicuous absence from the Second Plenum of the Party Central Committee (held from 8 to 10 January 1975) seems to have been even more intriguing than his absence from the NPC Session. Grounds of ill-health and indisposition of the great helmsman cannot be regarded proper explanation for his absence because he had received West German Opposition leader Strauss only on 16 January 1975. It was, therefore, believed in certain circles that although Mao disapproved of the arrangements for the NPC Session and the appointments made by the leadership at the Centre, he was hardly in a position to prevent their confirmation at the Party plenum and the NPC Session. It was speculated that relations between Mao and the moderates—the dominant group in Party leadership—had deteriorated. According to one report, Mao had to stay away from the NPC session because the veterans otherwise threatened to boycott the Congress. Some went to the extent of asserting that the great helmsman had been ousted.

In the opinion of the present writer, there appears no substance in such conjectures or wild speculations as the ouster of Chairman Mao or his taking *sanyas* (renunciation) from power politics. Similarly, not much credence can be given to the view that Mao was opposed to the elevation of Teng Hsiao-ping in the Party hierarchy as Vice-Chairman of the Central Committee and member of the Politburo Standing Committee. Had that been the case, Teng would not have, in the first place, been described as a "responsible person" and his promotion as Politburo member would not have taken place in January 1974. It is quite probable that after having ensured the abolition of the post of Chairman of State and the establishment of Party supremacy over the highest State organs, Mao deemed it necessary to remain aloof from the NPC Session.

In fact, Mao's absence from the NPC Session and the Party plenum may well have served a two-fold purpose : firstly, it appeared to ensure recognition of the fact that not much importance was to be attached to the government or the administrative sector ; and, secondly, it indicated that the physical presence of Chairman Mao was not necessary for the continued functioning of a coalition in Chinese politics. The latter, it could be said, was desirable for asserting Party, rather than personal, leadership over all sectors of the nation's life. This could perhaps, give the impression that one should not be unduly worried about the question—who after Mao ?—that things have settled down, and that there should be no fear about the country relapsing into chaos or anarchy after the death of the great helmsman. It is quite likely that the decisions of the Party Plenum, *viz.* Teng's promotion and approval of the arrangements in regard to the revision of the Constitution and the NPC Session, were made with Mao's concurrence and *not in defiance* or opposition to his wishes.

The dominant position of the moderates in the administrative apparatus was evident by the number of posts held by them in the State Council. There appeared a considerable strengthening of the moderate position (since the convocation of the Tenth Party Congress) even in the Party hierarchy—the real locus of power. Much importance in this regard had been attached to the rise of Teng Hsiao-ping and the decline in the position of Li Teh-sheng. Li rose to prominence, apparently with the support of the radicals, during the Tenth Party Congress. His decline was indicated in the Press Communique of the First Session of the Fourth NPC, which listed 16 Party leaders seated in the front row of the rostrum. Li was placed among ordinary Politburo members, not among the Vice-Chairmen of the Central Committee or among the members of the Politburo Standing Committee. Li Teh-sheng was also deprived of the post of Director of General Political Department of the PLA, which was entrusted to Chang Chun-chiao.

Teng's rise and Li's decline had significantly tilted the balance of power (that had prevailed since the Tenth Party Congress) in favour of the moderates. As a result, moderates came to occupy five out of the total of nine seats in the Politburo Standing Committee—Chou En-lai, Yeh Chien-ying, Teng Hsiao-ping, Chu Teh and Tung Pi-wu (his death on 2 April 1975 reduced the moderate strength to four). Three of the five Vice-Chairmen of the Party Central Committee, *viz.* Chou, Yeh and Teng, were also moderates. As for the remaining two Vice-Chairmen—Wang Hung-wen and Kang Sheng—one may not be quite sure about Kang Sheng—whether he would be inclined to support the radicals in opposition to the Chou-led moderate group. Again, of the remaining four Standing Committee members, including Chairman Mao, it is not quite certain whether Chang Chun-chiao is irrevocably committed to the radical group. There is much speculation about the adoption of a neutral stance by him, if not switching over to the side of the moderates.

In the Party Central Committee also, the moderates appear to be in a majority position, partly because quite a few neutrals, and even some radicals, seemed to have joined the ranks of the moderates since August 1973. Evidently, this trend is likely to be accelerated with the increased prestige and strengthened position of the moderates in both the administration and the highest echelons of Party organs. Within the PLA too, the moderate position appeared to be considerably improved with the appointment of Yeh Chien-ying as Defence Minister and Teng Hsiao-ping as Chief of Staff and the transfer of Li Teh-sheng from Peking to Shenyang.

In view of the enhanced position and stature of the moderate group in the three components of China's political system—the Party, the government and the army—there can hardly be any doubt that Chou En-lai will succeed Mao to the highest position of Chairman of the Party Central Committee. He is No. 2 after Mao and has a stature comparable to the previous two claimants to the throne. Like Liu Shao-chi at the Eighth Party Congress and Lin Piao at the Ninth, it was Chou En-lai who had delivered the official Political Report, on behalf of the Central Committee, to the Tenth Party Congress in August 1973.

Even if Chou does not live long, the moderates are likely to remain in a dominant position because Teng Hsiao-ping has emerged as the most powerful candidate for top leadership in the country. Teng has now superseded Wang Hung-wen. Theoretically, the latter might still be rated No. 3 in the Party hierarchy. In 1973, he *was* believed to be the heir-apparent with Chou as regent. Although Wang continues to be Vice-Chairman of the Central Committee and listed as such. not much is heard about him these days. Morever, unlike Teng, he has no *locus standi* in either the government or the army. Teng, on the other hand, concurrently holds high positions in the Party, the PLA, and the Administration. He also has a distinguished revolutionary career in his own right and has a stature of a national leader of long-standing. Wang does not possess such credentials. He appears to lack the high personal, intellectual, administrative and organizational qualities of Teng and does not have a strong power base. Teng has, thus, apparently outstripped Wang and, in the present situation, he has, indeed, become the real heir-apparent to Chou. His image got a boost-up in April 1974 when he was selected leader of the Chinese delegation to the special session of the United Nations. In that capacity he put forward China's world view in the clearest terms before the world forum. Teng's position was considerably enhanced in January 1975, when he was elevated in the Party hierarchy, made No. 1 Vice-Premier in the government and appointed Chief of General Staff in the PLA.

What has been said in the preceding paragraphs does not, however, mean that the question of succession has been settled for good and for all time to come. There is no surety that

Chou, with his failing health, would outlive Mao. Even if he outlives Mao and succeeds him, it will only be a stop-gap or short-term arrangement for he is not expected to live very long. In so far as Teng Hsiao-ping is concerned, inspite of the highly significant concentration and combination of Party, Army and Governmental power in his hands, he is still outranked by one or more persons in all the three segments of the Chinese political system. His senior-most position in the State Council after Chou may be an indication about his succession to the top leadership position in China, but one must not forget that what matters most in China are the Party and the Army.

As one of the three key leaders of the former Second Field Army, Teng Hsiao-ping has, in the central military establishment, the assistance of such PLA veterans and former colleagues of the Second Field Army as Li Ta and Ho Cheng-wen, Deputy Chiefs of General Staff; Ma Ning, Commander of the PLA Air Force; Su Chen-hua, First Political Commissar of the PLA Navy; Kuo Lin-hsiang, First Political Commissar of the PLA General Logistics Department; and Tien Wei-hsin, Deputy Chief of General Logistics. Previously these key posts were all held by Lin Piao's "sworn supporters." Even in regional PLA commands, Teng's former colleagues in the Second Field Army now hold important posts. These veterans include Sinkiang Commander Yang Yung, Tibet Commander Chen Ming-yi, Shenyang Commander Li Teh-sheng, Shenyang Political Commissar Tseng Shao-shan, Peking Commander Chen Hsi-lien, Chengtu Commander Chin Chi-wei, Peking Garrison Commander Wu Chung and Peking Political Commissar Yang Chun-sheng. These PLA veterans are practically in control of two-thirds of the PLA. Teng's appointment to the PLA General Staff, therefore, stemmed from his position of strength and long years of association with Liu Po-cheng. Because of Liu's poor health, Teng had been selected by Mao to fill the key post in the central military establishment.[154]

It might be that with his organizational talent and administrative experience, Teng may succeed in outmanoeuvring his rivals, the most formidable of whom appears to be Chang Chun-chiao. Like Teng, and unlike Wang Hung-wen, Chang holds concurrent positions of power and influence in all the three pillars of the Chinese political system. In the State

Council, his position as Vice-Premier is only next to Teng; in the Party, he is a member of the all powerful Standing Committee of the Politburo, though not a Vice-Chairman; in the Army, he is not only the First Political Commissar of the important Nanking military region but also holds the very important post of Director of General Political Department of the PLA—a position which enables him to control the ideas of the soldiers and to exert a great deal of influence over the military through the political commissars attached to the regional and district commands. This parallel elevation of Chang, therefore, is a highly significant development from the point of view of post-Mao succession. It indicates a persistent duality in China's domestic politics which could, perhaps, lead to an intensification of group rivalries, and erupt in factional struggles.

12 Checks and Balances

A system of checks and balances has been a prominent feature of the political set-up of Imperial China as well as Communist China. Traditional Chinese governments maintained a checks and balances system between two or more state bureaucracies. After the establishment of the People's Republic of China in 1949, Chairman Mao Tse-tung, the astute politician that he is, sought to guarantee his supremacy and perpetuate himself in power by establishing a skillful counterpoise among the three compoments of state power, *viz.* the Army, the Party and the Government. At the same time, he maintained a people's militia and assiduously built up a unique institutional framework of political commissars as a last resort on which he could fall back, in times of need, with a view to face the challenge offered by a defiant bureaucracy of either the Party, the army or the state apparatus.

Within the PLA, the Central military leadership was, to a certain extent, kept in check by regional commanders, who had endeavoured to preserve their share of power, influence and prestige. There was also a certain amount of balancing as between troops belonging to the different Field Armies. This method of balancing, W.W. Whitson remarks, had been demonstrated in the allocations of units and in personnel assignments. In Mukden, he points out, while the 4th Field Army predominated with five Corps, the 2nd and 3rd Field Armies each had one Corps in the region. In Peking, while the 5th Field Army dominated with four Corps, the 3rd Field Army maintained two Corps. In Nanking, the dominance of the 3rd Field Army with three Corps was balanced against one from the 5th Field Army and one from the 2nd Field Army. Since the 1954 positioning of most of these units (some in each regions having been in position since 1950), Whitson observes, the official press had announced minimal movement of units within regions and almost no inter-regional movement. In part, the continuing preservation of 1950-56 unit allocations, he says, might have reflected mutual suspicion among "old comrades" then holding power on the Politburo and the Military Affairs Committee. In any case, Whitson adds, "the partial dispersion of military power must have reinforced the need for compromise on crucial issues and probably helped unify command opinion in those instances where opposition loomed from the party, the commissars or Mao."[155]

In personnel assignments too there existed a balancing of different systems, which also showed a remarkable stability "for the most tumultuous period of post-1950 Mainland politics." Between 1954 and 1968, Whitson points out, the four most powerful military systems (2nd, 3rd, 4th and 5th Field Armies) apparently exchanged certain elements as if to provide either hostages or observers to ensure that the dominant system in the region could not discriminate against the others. Thus the three crucial military regions of Mukden (industrial centre), Peking (political centre) and Nanking (with the commercial centre at Shanghai) each had elite representatives and units from other Field Armies, one having a preponderance of strength. In this search for a balance, Whitson states, the need for a relatively objective arbitrator might have been one factor contributing to the late March 1968 removal of Yang Ch'eng-wu, whose views and reported personal ambitions might have threatened the continued validity of a coalition which had managed to reach compromise agreements since 1954.[156]

Even when the star of Lin Piao was on the ascendancy, he could not install himself as the supreme ruler of China partly because his Fourth Field Army, though holding dominant positions in various departments, service arms, and regional commands, was not the only force in China. Although the General Staff and the General Rear Services (Logistics) Departments were under the control of men loyal to him, the General

Political Department, which was revived in late 1969, was placed under the charge of Li Teh-sheng, a military commander of the 2nd Field Army and believed to have leanings towards Mao rather than Lin. After the fall of Lin Piao and the subsequent purge of military leaders belonging to the 4th Field Army, some sort of a balance had been maintained between the 2nd, 3rd and the North China (5th) Field Armies.

The system of checks and balances is also a cardinal feature of the new political set-up that had emerged in the wake of the Tenth Party Congress and the First Session of the Fourth National People's Congress. The existence of such a system is apparent (See Chapters 10 and 11) in almost all branches of the Party, State and the Army apparatus. It is probably designed to forestall the emergence in future of a single individual as the supreme dictator, who might seek to further his own individual ambitions. So long as China remains under the one Party system and espouses the concept of the dictatorship of the proletariat, the possibility of a single person acquiring dictatorial powers cannot altogether be ruled out. Although the arrangements, that had been instituted in the wake of the 4th NPC, are not at all comparable to the American practice of separation of powers, they nevertheless seek to strengthen the base of collective leadership, facilitate adoption of decisions by consensus, and restrain tendencies towards one-man rule.

In the Party hierarchy, we witness the revival of the institution of multiple Vice-Chairmen. The practice of appointing only one Vice-Chairman of the Central Committee, as was done in case of Lin Piao's selection at the Ninth Party Congress, has now been discarded. The nomination of twelve Vice-Premiers in the State Council at the 4th NPC session is likewise intended to facilitate collective decision-making and accommodate the interests of various contending groups. The concurrent holding of Party, State and Army functions by Teng Hsiao-ping and Chang Chun-chiao seem to counter-balance each other. At the same time, both within the Party and the Army, Teng as well as Chang are outranked by others. Within the Party, at least Wang Hung-wen, Kang Sheng and Yeh Chien-ying are senior to them. In the Army, Marshal Yeh Chien-ying (who is Defence Minister) has a superior status though, unlike Teng and Chang, he is not a Vice-Premier. There are also others who could probably exercise a certain degree of check on the propensities of Teng and Chang to behave as overlords. Seven military leaders are members of the Party Politburo. Of these seven, three—Yeh Chien-ying, Li Teh-sheng and Chu Teh—are simultaneously members of the Politburo Standing Committee. Three military leaders (Chen Hsi-lien, Wang Chen and Yu Chiu-li) are also Vice-Premiers in the State Council.

The system of checks and balances, which is sought to be instituted among personalities, different groups and as between Party functionaries and army leaders, is not confined only to the central leadership organs. It is also at work in the regional military commands, the provincial Party Committees and as between the PLA and the Party at the provincial level. Li Teh-sheng, Chen Hsi-lien and Hsu Shih-yu seem to balance each other. During the Tenth Party Congress, Li, as Vice-Chairman and member of the Standing Committee, obviously enjoyed a higher status in the Party hierarchy, but with his decline now, all three have, more or less, an equal status in the Party Politburo, though Chen, at present, appears to have a slight edge over the other two by virtue of his position as Vice-Premier in the State Council and his command of the sensitive Peking region.

The military commanders of the Military Regions and Military Districts are kept in check by the institution of civilian Political Commissars. Besides, the commanders are required to comply with the instructions of the centralized leadership of the Party Centre, which is often stated to be identical with the local Party organizations in the provinces and at other levels. In many cases, the regional commanders are kept under check by powerful Party cadres holding senior positions in the Party leadership either at the centre or in the provinces. Thus, Chang Chun-chiao, Director of the GPD and member of the Politburo Standing Committee, is the First Political Commissar of the Nanking Military Region, commanded by Ting Sheng. Chen Hsi-lien (who is believed to be a close associate of Chou En-lai and a member of the moderate group) is saddled with Chi Teng-Kuei and Wu Teh as First and Second Political Commissars respectively. Both these commissars are leftists and Politburo members. Hsu Shih-yu, commander of the Canton Military Region, has to confront Chao Tzu-yang, the First Secretary of the Kwangtung Provincial Party Committee.

Just as the military commanders are kept in check by the Party functionaries, the Party bosses of the Provincial Committees in turn, are, to a certain extent, checkmated by the military leaders. For instance, Chao Tzu-yang's task in managing the affairs of the Kwangtung province cannot be all that smooth for he has to deal with Hsu Shih-yu, who is a Politburo member whereas Chao is only a member of the Central Committee. Likewise, Pai Ju-ping, First Secretary of the Shantung Province and concurrently First Political Commissar of the Tsinan Military Region has to face Teng Ssu-yü, commander of the same region, and *vice-versa*.

The system of checks and balances as between Party and the Army and the appointment of civilian Party secretaries as head of Provincial Party Committees in 1974-75 (as of late 1972, no military man in such a position had been replaced by a civilian, although some had been replaced by other military men) no doubt facilitated the reassertion of Party authority over the PLA. However, the manner in which the contest between the so-called moderate and radical groups within the Party hierarchy, both at the Centre and in the provinces, is carried and eventually resolved will determine the final outcome of the efforts to keep the gun subordinate to the Party. That the two groups are still jockeying for positions is evident from the fact that while some sort of a consensus had been reached in filling the vacant posts of Minister of Defence, Chief of Staff and Director of the GPD in the PLA, two provinces, *viz.* Anhwei, and Liaoning, are still (*i.e.* by the middle of 1975) without a First Secretary. It appears that so far there had been no agreement as regards the choice of candidates for the posts of First Secretaries of these provinces between the moderates and the radicals. The contest between these two groups about consolidating their positions and expanding their influence in the local Party committees and the PLA seems to be continuing. Apparently what had been achieved is only a shaky compromise and a temporary unity. The contradictions between the two lines of policy have only been institutionalized, not fully resolved, and they seem to have been deferred for a final settlement at a future date.

However, Chinese politics, at present, seem to be moving in the direction of coalition politics. The relationship between the moderates and the radicals is somewhat similar to the existing relationship between the USA and the USSR—a curious blend of collusion and competition. In China, one notices a certain degree of cooperation between the two contending groups for achieving certain common ends. At the same time, one finds competition in gathering support in the Party and the Army, and in the expansion of their influence.

With the restructuring and strengthening of the Party apparatus and the transfer of the regional military bosses from the seats of their power towards the end of 1973, the fears about the country relapsing into the chaotic era of "warlordism" no longer holds good. A centralized military dictatorship, which was conceivable under Lin Piao's ascendancy during 1967-71, is also out of question. The re-establishment of the dictatorship by the Party apparatus (which can be said to have ruled China from 1961 to 1965 under Liu Shao-chi's leadership) is also highly unlikely partly because the Party has ceased to be a monolithic structure, if at all it ever was, and partly because the military leaders (even though their political role had been on the decline ever since 1973) still wield a certain degree of influence which is not likely to disappear in the near future. Thus coalition politics appears to be the only feasible alternative in the immediate context of China's domestic scene. The moderates and the radicals, it seems, would try to avoid serious conflicts and adopt decisions by consensus and compromise. At the same time, they would seek to strengthen their respective positions of power and influence. Because of this competition and power rivalry, the arrangement of collective decision-making would, by its very nature, have to remain fragile and shaky.

The collective leadership at the Centre is likely to retain Marxism-Leninism-Mao Tse-tung Thought (which has been sanctified in the new Constitution) as the offical creed of the State. The presence of radicals in the ruling coalition will act as a deterrent to the establishment of a state governed by a non-ideological technocracy of administrators and bureaucrats and prevent the emergence of any "revisionist" communist system of the Yugoslav type. There is no likelihood of China becoming an "open" or pluralist society with a political system having legal freedom for opposition political parties and movements. However, the minority group within the ruling coalition, it seems, would continue to lay emphasis on intra-party democracy and oppose monopolistic and dictatorial tendencies on the part of the dominant group in order to preserve a satisfactory balance of power and communist orientation.

The unfolding of a "de-Maoisation" campaign in China on the pattern of the "de-Stalinization" movement in the USSR, seems improbable even after Mao's death since both the contending groups—the moderates as well as the radicals—would seek to justify their stands and wage their struggles for power under the cover of Marxism-Leninism-Mao Tse-tung Thought. Memories of the dislocation and havoc experienced during the Cultural Revolution, the outlook of the younger cadres (both within the PLA and the Party), and the compulsions and complexities of modern life—all would no doubt act as a constraint on putting a premium on some of the outworn and anarchist tendencies inherent in Maoism and strengthen the forces of stability and unity within the country.

13 Role of the Army

China has constantly been plagued by internal disorders
and dissensions and subjected to foreign pressures and intervention. Consequently, the government had come to increasingly rely on the armed forces to quell revolts, confront
foreign invaders, maintain unity, and establish law and order
within the country. Some people, therefore, naturally overesti-
mated the political role and influence of the Army in China's
domestic politics. Simultaneously, a distinct tendency not to
accept the army as the arbiters of Chinese society was also
apparent. Thus, writing in 1971, when the PLA had emerged
as the dominant force in the country, a discerning scholar of
Chinese affairs, Lucian W. Pye, observed as follows :

> In no country in the world have soldiers dominated politics
> as extensively or for so long as in China. Modern Chinese
> politics has revolved around armies and military figures.
> Yet the convention of Chinese historiography has been to
> minimize, if not ignore, the role of the military in Chinese
> history. In truth, at each stage of Chinese history, soldiers
> and armies have generally been more important than con-
> temporary observers or subsequent historians have allowed.
> Even though every dynasty was established by military
> force and the rule of all emperors depended ultimately upon
> their armies, the Confucian interpretation of government
> insisted that soldiers were insignificant and ranked near
> the bottom of the social scale. What was true in traditional
> China is still largely true today in Communist China. At
> a time when the People's Liberation Army has become

the key to government in China, the formal doctrines of Communism, while acknowledging the merits of martial qualities, continue to suggest that events are shaped more by peasants and workers than by soldiers.[157]

Lin Piao, in his report to the Ninth Party Congress, described the PLA as "the mighty pillar of the dictatorship of the Proletariat." This description helped him in legitimizing military dominance of the political life in China. According to Lin, the PLA was "the main component of the State."[158] After the Tenth Party Congress, however, the army is stated to be only one of the seven sectors of the nation's life. The overall leadership of the Party is now asserted over all social, economic, political and military institutions of Chinese society. The Party, it seems, had been quite successful in establishing its leadership, if not absolute supremacy, over the army. How long this situation will last and whether the PLA would continue for all time to remain under the subordination of the Party is, indeed, difficult to say, Evidently, much would depend on the conditions prevailing in China, particularly the extent to which the Party leadership at the Centre remains united and the coalition between the moderates and radicals survives after Mao.

Ever since its establishment in 1949, the People's Republic of China had been successively governed by the Army and the Party. From 1949 to 1954, military leaders directly ruled China through the Military Control Committee and Military and Administrative Committees (MAC)—the highest organs of authority in China's provinces and six major regions. By 1954, however, the last vestiges of military rule had largely disappeared and civilian authorities had replaced military bodies in the provinces. In subsequent years, there was a bifurcation of military and civilian functions and the military leaders were seen fighting for military priorities and resisting demands of civilian Party officials. However, almost on all issues, such as the degree of professionalization and politicization of the PLA, the degree of PLA participation in economic tasks, the build-up of militia, etc., the military leaders were overruled by the civilian Party leadership which had a clear majority in the Politburo and the Central Committee of the Party. Thus, in the first half of the 1960s, a strong body of Party officials, led by Liu Shao-chi, ruled the country and exercised effective control over the Army.

In the wake of the Cultural Revolution, however, the Chinese domestic scene once again came to be dominated by the PLA, its officers and personnel who assumed the top leadership positions in the provinces as Chairmen of the Revolutionary Committees and First Secretaries of the Provincial Party Committees. This military rule lasted for approximately five years, *i. e.* from 1967 to 1973. The programme of Party rebuilding, begun in 1970-71, was pushed ahead with renewed vigour with the rehabilitation of old cadres and the demise of Lin Piao.

Beginning with the Tenth Party Congress in August 1973, the Party made a determined attempt to regain and reassert its leadership over all sectors, including the army. In the Central Committee and the Politburo, military representation was drastically slashed. Towards the end of 1973, 8 of the 11 commanders of the Military Regions were transferred from the seats of their power. The prestige, the power and the dominating role of the regional military leaders, thus, received a severe set-back. These wholesale transfers dislodged regional commanders from their local power bases and weakened their positions in the Party and the Administration. However, these developments must not be construed as implying that the PLA had ceased to be a political force in the polity of China. Even today, it constitutes a sizable group in the Central Committee and its leaders still occupy important positions in the Politburo and its Standing Committee. In the State Council (appointed on the proposal of the Party Central Committee in January 1975) 3 out of the 12 Vice-Premiers and 10 out of 29 Ministers are military men. (See Table 20) Furthermore, despite the concerted attempt by the Party to replace military men by civilians in influential posts of First Secretaries of Provincial Party Committees, even by the middle of 1975, as many as 9 out of 29 provinces, *i.e.* nearly one third of the total, still remained under the leadership and control of military men. (See Table 18)

Thus, sufficient progress has been made, especially after the convocation of the Tenth Party Congress, towards establishing

Party supremacy and control over the army. Teng Hsiao-ping's appointment as Chief of Staff is a shrewd device to further strengthen and tighten Party control over the army. From the vaunted position of Chief of Staff, it would be quite easy for Teng to undertake a thorough reorganization of the PLA and, in the process, to eliminate any actual or potential dangers to the authority of the Party leadership at the Centre.

Owing to the recent changes in the leading organs of the State, the Party and the PLA, the regional commanders have, it seems, receded in the background. However, they still remain a force to be reckoned with. Evidently, they cannot be *completely* deprived of their power and influence over the troops, particularly in the military regions. True, the PLA, at present, has somewhat receded in the background, but it is still very much there. In case the country relapses into chaos or witnesses prolonged internecine struggles between contending groups, the PLA could again come very much to the forefront and resume its dominant role in the political life of the country.

The PLA's possible role in the battle of succession and/or the army being utilized by an "ambitionist" to further his own ends are matters of acute concern and a source of fear for the Party leadership. It was, therefore, not without reason that two articles in the *Jen-min Jih-pao* dealt with that problem. The articles published in the Party paper on 13 and 27 November 1974 accused Lin Piao of overstepping his mandate during the Cultural Revolution and laid considerable emphasis on absolute control of the Party over the PLA and total subordination of the PLA to the Party.[159]

14 Conclusions

The system of political control over the Chinese army, instituted with the establishment of the General Political Department of the PLA in 1931, had been effective only to a certain extent in bringing the gun under the command of the Party. The prestige and influence of the GPD and that of the commissars under its direction had fluctuated, depending on the exigencies of the situation, the degree of modernization in the army, and the use the central leadership chose to make of it. Under the peculiar circumstances of the Civil War, the commissars' management of guerillas tended to support, rather than interfere with, the unity of command. The commanders, therefore, did not mind sharing command authority with the political commissars. However, in the aftermath of the Korean War, there was an increasing trend towards professionalism and a scorn for the ideologues. As a result, the commanders began to ignore the requirement that commissars countersign operational orders. Party administrators and officials also became increasingly reluctant to share local political power with the military commissars. The former seemed to have lost all confidence in Mao's leadership during and after the Great Leap Forward. The failure of the Great Leap movement adversely affected the morale of the soldiers as well. In these circumstances, Mao probably began to think that his revolutionary ideals were being abandoned for rewards of "bureaucratic status, power and privilege." He, therefore, sought to revive the revolutionary elan of basic cadres by launching the Socialist Education Campaign and "Learn from the PLA" movement in the early 1960s. However, these efforts were only partly successful.

In the early phase of the Cultural Revolution, influence of commissars was probably at its peak. However, Red Guard excesses and the deterioration in the law and order situation in the country resulted in the commissars being forced to subordinate their political values to the commanders' combat values, which were a curious blend of Russian and earlier war-lord perspectives.[160] In view of the worsening internal situation, the army had to intervene and assume control of the political affairs of the nation. Thus, the power vacuum created in the domestic politics of China by the paralysis of the Party and administrative organs was filled by the military, which emerged as the most powerful force in the country. The predominance of professional military men was evident in all the major components of state power—the Party, the government and the army. The leading officers of the PLA acquired political and administrative authority in the provinces. They also had a powerful voice and considerable say in the national decision-making processes.

The dominant position of the military in the wake of the Cultural Revolution could well be compared to the 1949-52 Communist takeover and consolidation period, when military leaders ruled China through the "Military Control Committee" and the "Military and Administration Committees"—the highest organs of authority in China's provinces and six major regions. However, unlike the 1950s, when the military governors of the provinces rapidly "returned to the barracks" and transferred power to civilian Party/government hands, the military leaders in late 1960s seemed in no mood to forgo the power they had acquired during the Cultural Revolution.

Prior to the Cultural Revolution, senior provincial or regional Party bureau Secretaries concurrently served as the First Political Commissars in the Military Regions or Provincial Military Districts. This, in effect, ensured firm Party control over the local PLA units and was tantamount to civilian supervision over the military. However, in the wake of the Cultural Revolution, local PLA commanders were, in many cases, not only their own Commissars but also concurrently occupied the posts of Chairmen of Revolutionary Committees and First

Secretaries of the Provincial Party Committees. The inter-locking of the Party, government and military leadership positions in the hands of PLA representatives reflected the dominant political role of the military in the power structure of the provinces and the nation as a whole.

Both the composition of Revolutionary Committees of 1967-68, and the establishment of new Provincial Party Committees during 1970-71 confirmed the fact that professional military leaders controlled the strings of power at all levels of the governmental structure. In the State Council, 20 out of 29 (*i.e.* 70 per cent) ministers were, at one time, professional career commanders. Even after the fall of Lin Piao and his associates in September 1971, several influential military men were appointed (in 1972) to top ministerial posts like the posts of Minister of Public Security and Chairman of the State Planning Commission. Thus, at the end of 1972, as many as two-thirds of the known ministers in the central government were military men.[161] Evidently, Mao could not deny positions of considerable political influence to military leaders, especially those with whose support he had been able to subjugate his formidable rivals—Lin Piao and his associates.

General Political Department and Political Commissars

During 1965-67, as already stated, the role and influence of political commissars was at its height. Subsequently, the military commanders emerged as the dominant force in the country. Almost all the leading officers of the GPD were purged. The Department was, thus, paralyzed and the role and influence of commissars, who had often acted as rivals of professional commanders was considerably reduced. But with the spectre of military dictatorship or overlordship looming large on the horizon, the Maoist leadership soon realized the necessity of asserting civilian control over the Army. Accordingly, steps were taken to revive the system of political commissars within the PLA. In 1969 Li Teh-sheng, a military commander, was appointed as Director of the GPD. Evidently, this was not a very satisfactory arrangement because under the direction of a military commander, the commissars could possibly find encouragement in respect of keeping their options open *vis-a-vis* the Party leadership and military hierarchy. They could, at the same time, feel inhibited in faithfully executing the duties assigned to them by the Party leadership. Therefore, not long after the restructuring of the Party apparatus was completed and the dominant role of the army in the domestic politics of China disappeared following the Tenth Party Congress, Li Teh-sheng was replaced by a civilian (Chang Chun-chiao).

As things stand now, neither the GPD nor the system of political commissars are likely to regain their former status—a truly unique position in which they were subject to, and required to comply with, the instructions of the Military Commission of the Party Central Committee but retained a distinct institutional hierarchy or set up of their own that was seemingly independent of the regular Party apparatus. The political commissars could not hope to enjoy much discretionary authority and independent role in the future.

Even if the system of political commissars is not completely merged with the civilian Party set-up and thereby brought under the direct control of the Party mechanism, it appears quite evident that, in future, it will be subject to more stringent control and supervision by civilian Party leadership. Thus, the institution of political commissars would no longer remain an amorphous group owing allegiance to an individual or subserving its own vested interests rather than those of the Party. In future, no "ambitionist" person, intending to follow the footstep of Chairman Mao, can possibly hope to utilize political commissars for the purpose of confronting the Party leadership or subduing the powerful military commanders in order to enforce his own brand of communism or military style and assert his supremacy.

Civilian *vs.* Military Rule

The very idea of the substitution of the Party by the military as the principal agent of communism was antithetical to both Marxist precepts and Maoist military thinking. Accordingly, the greatest emphasis was laid on the absolute leadership of the Party—the vanguard and the organized conscience of the proletariat. Therefore, Mao, the radicals as well as the veteran civilian leaders and the old Party functionaries joined hands to subdue the Central military leadership which had grown very powerful in the wake of the Cultural Revolution. But they could succeed in accomplishing the downfall of Lin Piao and his group only with the help of the regional commanders, whose power and influence, therefore, remained undiminished.

Thus, the fall of Lin Piao did not resolve the issue of civilian *vs.* military control in China's political system. Apparently, "the task of regaining control over an Army-dominated political apparatus" seemed more formidable than the earlier task, undertaken in the Cultural Revolution, of "regaining control over a Party-dominated political apparatus."[162] The tendency towards regionalism and decentralization was much accentuated after the fall of Lin Piao. Therefore, as soon as the 29 Provincial Party Committees were reconstituted in August 1971, the *People's Daily* editorial (27 August 1971) called upon all Party members and all departments to place themselves "under the absolute leadership of the Party and reject the reactionary theory of many centres, that is, the theory of no centre."

The main beneficiaries of the collapse of the Party apparatus during the Cultural Revolution were the regional commanders. The Cultural Revolution had the effect of considerably loosening, if not altogether obiliterating, the control exercised by the Party hierarchy over the regional military leaders. The subsequent fall of Lin Piao and his close associates further enhanced the power and prestige of the regional commanders as it freed them from the strings of the central military high command as well. The fall of Lin Piao also demonstrated that the leadership at the Centre was disunited and weak.

The Maoist leadership felt deeply concerned about the growing power and influence of the regional military commanders. They took shrewd and calculated steps to curb their power and strengthen the base of Party leadership. As a result, the Wuhan Incident of July 1967 had remained the solitary instance of open defiance of the Central Party leadership on the part of regional commandres. Thereafter, both the large-scale reshuffle of regional military leaders (effected towards the end of 1973) and the drastic reduction in the military representation in the leading Tenth Party organs were accomplished peacefully, without any untoward incident. Predictions about the emergence of a new kind of "warlordism" on the Chinese domestic scene or internal instability have all been falsified. Despite their ambitions for power and prestige and the existence of inter-service rivalries, regional military leaders were found committed to the goal of national unity and subjected themselves to the control of the central Party leadership. This happened because the Party appeared united under the leadership of the Mao-Chou group while the regional commanders were divided amongst themselves. In fact, the military leadership, it might be recalled, had never been a closely-knit and cohesive group. Besides the extensive purging of the early 1960s following the downfall of Peng Teh-huai, nearly one-third of top military leaders were replaced during the Cultural Revolution. The fall of Lin Piao further undermined the image, the prestige and the position of the military leaders.

The total PLA strength of 2.5 million represented less than half of one per cent of the Chinese population, which in itself was highly organised, politically conscious and run on military lines. In fact, the PLA officers' ambitions and aspirations could, to a certain extent, be kept in check by increasing the scope of, and asserting Party control over, the militia. It is not without significance that a month after the convocation of the Tenth Party Congress, there was an extensive campaign (ostensibly pegged to the 15th anniversary of Mao's instruction of organiz-ing militia units) emphasizing the need for increased Party control over militia organizations in order to "maintain their proletarian nature." This campaign, Richard Wich points out, was marked by an emphasis on the role of urban workers in militia units and on the value of these units in public security and related activities. The use of the militia for such activities, Wich adds, would further supplant the army from the functions of social control and provide the Party with yet another auxi-liary instrument—like the Communist Youth League, and the trade union organizations, both in the process of being reconst-ructed in the months before the Tenth Congress—through which to assert its authority.[163] Besides, the imperatives of modernization, which required increased planning and coordi-nation of both military and military-industrial elements, tended to reinforce the hands of the Central leadership.

The national leadership has done creditably well during the last few years in rebuilding strong Party and government institutions. In January 1975, Yeh Chien-ying was named Minister of National Defence, Teng Hsiao-ping was appointed Chief of Staff, and Chang Chun-chiao was made Director of the GPD of the PLA. The long overdue session of the National People's Congress was also convened. All this further demonstrated to the people the end of a turbulent and uncertain period. These developments tended to strengthen the forces of peace and stability, further enhance the image of civilian Party and government leadership in the country, and pare down the political role of the military. If this trend towards normalcy is accelerated and the coalition of the collective leadership at the Centre remains united and stable and survives after Mao, it would certainly enable the Party leadership at the Centre to establish the effective supremacy of the civilian institutions over the military and to meet the challenges of the regional and provincial forces.

However, if the Central leadership is found to be weak and divided, the various factions engaged in an open struggle for power leading to the breakdown of civilian institutions, the military leaders could possibly be tempted to reassert the primacy of the PLA's political role and strive either to achieve top leadership positions for themselves, or seek to act as king-makers by backing civilian leaders of their choice. While the military establishment is expected to play a significant role in the post-Mao era, much would depend on the cohesiveness, the unity and strength of the Party leadership as also on the equation and relationship of the military leaders with the Party leadership, their own standing and influence within the Party, the internal conditions and external pressures, and the backing of their own troops.

Notes

1   *Selections from People's Republic of China Magazines*, No. 792 (7 October 1974), pp. 59-65.
2   W. W. Whitson with Chen Hsia-Huang, *The Chinese High Command : A History of Communist Military Politics 1927-71* (New York, 1973), pp. 478-9.
3   H. F. McNair, ed., *China* (California, 1951), pp. 522-3.
4   *Ibid.*, 27.
5   Mao Tse-tung, *Selected Military Writings* (Peking, 1963), p. 86.
6   Article by Hsiao Hua in *Hung Chi* (*Red Flag*) Nos. 15-16, as reproduced in *Extracts from Chinese Mainland Press*, No. 72 (30 October 1963).
7   Edward L. Dreyer, "Military Continuities : The PLA and Imperial China," in W. W. Whitson, ed., *The Military and Political Power in China in the 1970s* (New York, 1972), pp. 23-4.
8   Mao Tse-tung, n. 5, p. 88.
9   *Ibid.*, pp. 271 and 302-4.
10 See Sun Tzu, *The Art of War* as translated by Samuel B. Griffith (London, 1963), pp. 64-8 and also the translation of the same by Lionel Giles (Pennsylvania, 1949).
11 Mao Tse-tung, n. 5, pp. 300-1.
12 Edgar O. Ballance, *The Red Army of China* (London, 1962), pp. 204-5.
13 Article by Liu Yun-Ching in *Jen-min Jih-pao* (*People's Daily*) 28 June 1962, as translated in *Survey of China Mainland Press*, No. 2780 (18 July 1962), p. 1.
14 See *Extracts From China Mainland Press*, No. 72 (30 October 1963) p. 6.
15 See *Survey of China Mainland Press*, n. 13.
16 See *Extracts from China Mainland Press*, n. 14.
17 *Ibid.*
18 Whitson, n. 2, p. 450.
19 *Ibid.*, p 452.
20 *Ibid.*, p. 453.
21 John Gittings, *The Role of the Chinese Army*, (London, 1967), pp. 106-9.
22 Whitson, n. 2, p. 450.
23 A. Doak Barnett, *Uncertain Passage : China's Transition to the Post-Mao Era* (Washington, 1974), pp. 99-100.
24 Whitson, n 2, p. 451.

25 *Ibid.*, p. 452.
26 See *People's China* (16 August 1951), p. 7.
27 *Ibid.*, p. 6.
28 See *Ibid.* (1 August 1951), p. 6.
29 Mao Tse-tung, n, 5, p. 52.
30 See *People's China* (16 August 1951), p. 7.
31 Whitson, n. 2, pp. 441, 527, 437-8, and 440-2.
32 See *People's China* (16 August 1951), pp. 7-8.
33 *Ibid.*, pp. 5-6
34 *Ibid.*, (1 August 1951), p. 8.
35 *Ibid.*, (16 August 1952), p. 15.
36 Chu Teh's speech, 1 August 1951. *Ibid.*, (16 August 1951), p. 6.
37 Robert B. Rigg, *Red China's Fighting Hordes* (Harrisburg, Pennsylvania, 1951), p. 343.
38 *People's China* (1 August 1952), p. 29.
39 Chen Yi, "Thirty Glorious Years," *People's China* (1 August 1957), p. 19.
40 Liu Shao-chi, *Report on the Draft Constitution of the People's Republic of China and Constitution* (Peking, 1954), p. 77.
41 Ellis Joffe, "Contradiction in the Chinese Army," *Far Eastern Economic Review* (11 July 1963), p. 123.
42 O. Ballance, n. 12, p. 209.
43 Ellis Joffe, n. 41, p. 123. See also Edgar Snow, *The Other Side of the River : Red China Today* (New York, 1962), p. 289.
44 O. Ballance, n. 12, p. 209.
45 Whitson, n. 2, pp. 446-7.
46 Lin Piao's speech, 1 October 1959. *China Today* (Embassy of China, New Delhi), No. 46 (24 October 1959).
47 *Survey of China Mainland Press*, No. 1881 (24 October 1958), pp. 4 and 2.
48 *Ibid.*, No. 1874 (14 October 1958), p. 6.
49 *Ibid.*, No. 1882 (27 October 1958), p. 10.
50 James D. Jordan, "The Maoist vs. The Professional Vision of a People's Army," in Whitson, ed., n. 7, p. 32.
51 *Peking Review*, No. 33 (14 October 1958), p. 4.
52 Jordan, n. 50, p.32,
53 See David A. Charles, "The Dismissal of Marshal P'eng Teh-huai," *China Quarterly* (October-December 1961), p. 73.
54 *China Today*, No. 46 (24 October 1959), pp. 32 and 35.
55 *Kung-tso T'ung-hsun* (Bulletin of Activities), No. 3 (7 January 1961), see also J. Chester Cheng, ed., *The Politics of the Chinese Red Army* (Stanford, 1966), pp. 66-94.
56 *Peking Review* (18 October 1960), p. 7.
57 *Survey of China Mainland Press*, No. 2971 (3 May 1963), pp. 1-2.
58 This working style is generally summarized in three mottos and eight words. The three mottos are : keep firmly to the correct political direction; maintain an assiduous and simple working style; be flexible and mobile in strategy and tactics. The eight words are : be united; keep on your toes; be earnest; be lively.
59 See *Survey of China Mainland Press* (3 January 1961), pp. 1-10.
60 See *Ibid.*, No. 2433 (7 February 1961), pp. 4-6.
61 *Peking Review* (27 January 1961), p. 5.
62 See *Kung-tso T'ung-hsun* No. 23 (13 June 1961) and J. Chester Cheng, ed., n. 55, pp. 593-5.
63 *New York Times*, 5 August 1963, For details see *Kung-tso T'ung-hsun* and J. Chester Cheng, ed., n.55.
64 *Peking Review* (27 January 1961), p. 6.
65 *Survey of China Mainland Press*, No. 2439, (17 February 1961), pp. 4-5.
66 *Ibid.*, No. 2447 (2 March 1961), pp. 7-8.

67 *Peking Review* (14 July 1961), pp. 3-4. See also *Survey of China Mainland Press*, No. 2535 (12 July 1961), pp. 1-2 and No. 2540 (19 July 1961), pp. 1-3.
68 *Hsinhua* News Agency, 5 July 1961.
69 *Survey of China Mainland Press*, No. 2556 (11 August 1961), pp. 7-8 and 11.
70 See *Ibid.*, No. 2801 (17 August 1962), p. 6.
71 *Peking Review* (10 August 1962), p. 8.
72 See *Extracts from China Mainland Press*, No. 72 (30 October 1963) p. 5.
73 *Survey of China Mainland Press*, No. 2620 (16 November 1961), p.9.
74 See *Ibid.*, No. 2626 (27 November 1961), pp. 1-4.
75 See *Ibid.*, No. 2971 (3 May 1963), pp. 1-16.
76 *Huhehot Radio*, 26 July 1968.
77 See *Jen-min Jih-pao*, 29 April 1963, as translated in *Survey of China Mainland Press*, No. 2981 (17 May 1963), pp. 2-3. See also *Ibid.* No. 2984.
78 See *Peking Review* (21 June 1963), pp. 6-22.
79 Whitson, n. 2, pp. 442 and 449.
80 *Survey of China Mainland Press*, No. 3143 (21 January 1964), pp. 1-2.
81 *Ibid.*, No. 3154 (5 February 1964), pp. 5-19.
82 *Ibid.*, No. 3166 (26 February 1964), pp. 5-9.
83 Parris H. Chang, "Changing Patterns of Military Roles in Chinese Politics," in W. W. Whitson, ed., n. 7, pp. 50 and 62.
84 See *Kung-tso T'ung-hsun*, No. 23, n.62 and J. Chester Cheng, ed., n. 55, p, 595.
85 Stephen A. Sims, "The New Role of the Military," *Problems of Communism* (November-December 1969), p. 31.
86 Ralph L. Powell, "The Increasing Power of Lin Piao and the Party Soldiers 1959-1966," *China Quarterly* (April-June 1968), pp. 51-2.
87 Whison, n. 2, p. 384.
88 *Peking Review* (21 January 1966), p. 5.
89 *Ibid.*, pp. 5-6.
90 *Hsinhua* News Agency, 24 January 1966, as reproduced in *Survey of China Mainland Press*, No. 3627 (31 January 1966), pp. 6-20.
91 Whitson, n. 2, pp. 370-1.
92 *Ibid.*, pp. 529-30.
93 See *Ibid.*, pp. 398-9. See also Jurgen Domes, "The Cultural Revolution and the Army," *Asian Survey* (May 1968), p. 358 and *Survey of China Mainland Press*, No. 4015 and 4028.
94 See Whitson, n. 2, p. 448
95 *Ibid.*, p. 405. See also *Survey of China Mainland Press*, No. 4148 (28 March 1968), p. 10
96 Whitson, n. 2, p. 407
97 Parris Chang, "Mao's Great Purge : A Balance Sheet, " *Problems of Communism* (March-April 1969), Footnote 37.
98 Ellis Joffe, "The Chinese Army After the Cultural Revolution : the Effects of Intervention," *China Quarterly* (July-September 1973), p. 452.
99 Edgar Snow, "Report from China—IV : The Army and the Party," *The New Republic* (22 May 1971), p. 12.
100 Whitson, n. 2, pp. 365-6.
101 *Ibid.*, p. 386.
102 Jurgen Domes, "Some Aspects of the Cultural Revolution in China." *Asian Survey* (September 1971), p. 937.
103 Whitson, n. 2, pp. 412-3.
104 *Ibid.*, pp. 549-50.
105 *Ibid.*

106 Domes, n. 102, p. 936,
107 It is not without significance that the *Hung Chi* article of 1 September 1974 criticized Lin Piao, among other things, for asserting that "the founder [Mao] could not command and that he [Lin Piao] should be allowed to command and mobilize everything." Tien Chun's article in *Hung Chi*, No. 9 (1 September 1974), as translated in *Selections from People's Republic of China Magazines*, No. 792 (7 October 1974), p. 65.
108 Edgar Show, n. 99, p. 12.
109 See Thomas W. Robinson "Lin Piao : A Chinese Military Politician," in W.W. Whitson, ed., n. 7, pp. 85-6.
110 See Ralph. L. Powell, n. 86, p. 62.
111 Whitson, n. 2, pp. 415 and 540.
112 Ellis Joffe, n. 98, p. 472.
113 *Ibid.*, pp. 461-2.
114 *Ibid.*, p. 473.
115 For a list, see *Chung-kung yen-chiu* (Taipei), VI : 9 (10 September 1972) 6-7. Cited in Jurgen Domes "New Course in Chinese Domestic Politics : The Anatomy of Readjustment," *Asian Survey* 13 (July 1973), p. 636.
116 Domes, n. 115, pp. 636-7.
117 *Ibid.*, pp. 638-9.
118 See Hsüeh Chun-wen, "Criticism of the 'Six Tactical Principles'," *Kuang-ming Jih-pao* (Peking), 2 January 1975, as translated in *Survey of People's Republic of China Press*, No. 5776 (20 January 1975) p. 2.
119 See *China News Analysis*, No. 866 (7 January 1972).
120 *Hung Chi*, No. 7 (1972), as broadcast from *Peking Radio* on 17 July 1972 and reproduced in Foreign Broadcast Information Service, *Daily Report*, 18 July 1972.
121 *Jen-min Jih-pao*, 1 August 1972.
122 *China Pictorial*, No. 5. (1973).
123 *Hung Chi* No. 7 (1972), as reproduced in *Daily Report* (19 July 1972).
124 Ahn, Byung-joon, "The Cultural Revolution and China's Search for Political Order," *China Quarterly*, 58 (April-June 1974), p.281
125 Richard Wich, "The Tenth Party Congress : The Power Structure and the Succession Question," *China Quarterly* , 58 (April/June 1974), pp. 238-9.
126 W. W. Whitson, ed., n. 7, p. XXVIII.
127 See Parris H. Chang in *Ibid.*, p. 67.
128 Far Eastern Economic Review, *Asia 1975 Yearbook* (Hong Kong, 1975), p. 149.
129 Parris. H. Chang, n. 83, p. 63.
130 See *Survey of People's Republic of China Press*, No. 5772 (14 January 1975), pp. 41-5.
131 *Hsinhua* News Agency, 31 December 1974.
132 *Peking Review* (24 January 1975), p. 21.
133 *Ibid.*, 20.
134 *Ibid.*, p. 24.
135 *Ibid.*, p. 19.
136 *Central News Agency* (Taipei) 22 February 1975.
137 S.K. Ghosh, "Crisis in Military Leadership in China," *News Review on China, Mongolia & The Koreas* (New Delhi) (February 1975), pp. 81-2
138 *Ibid.*
139 *Central News Agency*, 22 February 1975.
140 *Hung Chi*, No. 1 (1975).
141 *Jen-min Jih-pao*, 9 February 1975.
142 *Ibid.*, 22 February 1975.

143 *Hung Chi*, No. 3 (1975).
144 See Gerd Ruge's article in *Die Welt,* as translated in *German Tribune* (Hamburg) (6 March 1975).
145 *Jen-min Jih-pao*, 16 March 1975.
146 *Ibid.*, 21 March 1975.
147 *Ibid.*, 12 March 1975.
148 *Ibid,.* 11 March 1975.
149 *Hung Chi*, No. 4 (1975).
150 See *Ibid.* and *Hsinhua* News Agency, 3 April 1975.
151 *Hung Chi*, No. 4 (1975).
152 See Denzil Peiris, "Pragmatists vs. Ideologues," *Times of India,* 13 March 1975.
153 Far Eastern Economic Review, n. 128, pp. 148-50.
154 See *Peking Informer* (Hong Kong), 30 (16 February 1975), p. 4.
155 William Whitson, "The Field Army in Chinese Communist Military Politics," *China Quarterly* (January-March 1969), pp. 23-4.
156 *Ibid.*, p. 24.
157 Lucian W. Pye, *Warlord Politics* (New York, 1971), p. 3.
158 See *Peking Review* (30 April 1960), p. 25.
159 See *Jen-min Jih-pao,* 13 and 27 November 1974.
160 See Whitson, n. 2, p. 539.
161 See Barnett, n. 23, p. 87.
162 Philip Bridgham, "The Fall of Lin Piao," *China Quarterly* (July-September 1973), p. 448.
163 Richard Wich, n. 125, p. 239.

Appendices

APPENDIX 1

Kutien Resolution of December 1929, Drawn by Mao Tse-tung for the Ninth Party Congress of the Fourth Red Army (Extracts)

The resolution enabled the Red Army to build itself entirely on a Marxist-Leninist basis and to eliminate all the influences of armies of the old type. In the last thirty and more years the Chinese people's armed forces have made tremendous developments and innovations in their Party activities and political work, which now present a very different picture, but the basic line remains the same as that laid down in this resolution.*

There are various non-proletarian ideas in the Communist Party organization in the Fourth Red Army which greatly hinder the application of the Party's correct line. Unless these ideas are thoroughly corrected, the Fourth Army cannot possibly shoulder the tasks assigned to it in China's great revolutionary struggle. The source of such incorrect ideas in this Party organization lies, of course, in the fact that its basic units are composed largely of peasants and other elements of petty-bourgeois origin; yet the failure of the Party's leading bodies to wage a concerted and determined struggle against the incorrect ideas and to educate the members in the Party's correct line is also an important cause of their existence and growth. In accordance with the spirit of the September letter of the Central Committee, this Congress hereby points out the manifestations of various non-proletarian ideas in the Party organization in the Fourth Army, their sources, and the methods of correcting them, and calls upon all comrades to eliminate them thoroughly.

ON THE PURELY MILITARY VIEWPOINT

The purely military viewpoint is very highly developed

---

* Footnote appearing in *Selected Military Writings of Mao Tse-tung* (Peking, 1963).

among a number of comrades in the Red Army. It manifests itself as follows :

1. These comrades regard military affairs and politics as opposed to each other and refuse to recognize that military affairs are only one means of accomplishing political tasks. Some even say, "If you are good militarily, naturally you are good politically, if you are not good militarily, you cannot be any good politically"—this is to go a step further and give military affairs a leading position over politics.

2. They think that the task of the Red Army, like that of the White army, is merely to fight. They do not understand that the Chinese Red Army is an armed body for carrying out the political tasks of the revolution. Especially at present, the Red Army should certainly not confine itself to fighting; besides fighting to destroy the enemy's military strength, it should shoulder such important tasks as doing propaganda among the masses, organizing the masses, arming them, helping them to establish revolutionary political power and setting up Party organizations. The Red Army fights not merely for the sake of fighting but in order to conduct propaganda among the masses, organize them, arm them, and help them to establish revolutionary political power. Without these objectives, fighting loses its meaning and the Red Army loses the reason for its existence.

3. Hence, organizationally, these comrades subordinate the departments of the Red Army doing political work to those doing military work, and put forward the slogan, "Let Army Headquarters handle outside matters". If allowed to develop, this idea would involve the danger of estrangement from the masses, control of the government by the army and departure from proletarian leadership—it would be to take the path of warlordism like the Kuomintang army.

4. At the same time, in propaganda work they overlook the importance of propaganda teams. On the question of mass organization, they neglect the organizing of soldiers' committees in the army and the organizing of the local workers and peasants. As a result, both propaganda and organizational work are abandoned.

5. They become conceited when a battle is won and dispirited when a battle is lost.

6. Selfish departmentalism—they think only of the Fourth Army and do not realize that it is an important task of the Red Army to arm the local masses. This is cliquism in a magnified form.

7. Unable to see beyond their limited environment in the Fourth Army, a few comrades believe that no other revolutionary forces exist. Hence their extreme addiction to the idea of conserving strength and avoiding action. This is a remnant of opportunism.

8. Some comrades, disregarding the subjective and objective conditions, suffer from the malady of revolutionary impetuosity; they will not take pains to do minute and detailed work among the masses, but, riddled with illusions, want only to do big things. This is a remnant of putschism.

The sources of the purely military viewpoint are :

1. A low political level. From this flows the failure to recognize the role of political leadership in the army and to recognize that the Red Army and the White army are fundamentally different.

2. The mentality of mercenaries. Many prisoners captured in past battles have joined the Red Army, and such elements bring with them a markedly mercenary outlook, thereby providing a basis in the lower ranks for the purely military viewpoint.

3. From the two preceding causes there arises a third, over-confidence in military strength and absence of confidence in the strength of the masses of the people.

4. The Party's failure actively to attend to and discuss military work is also a reason for the emergence of the purely military viewpoint among a number of comrades.

The methods of correction are as follows :

1. Raise the political level in the Party by means of education, destroy the theoretical roots of the purely military viewpoint, and be clear on the fundamental difference between the Red Army and the White army. At the same time, eliminate the remnants of opportunism and putschism and break down the selfish departmentalism of the Fourth Army.

2. Intensify the political training of officers and men and especially the education of ex-prisoners. At the same time, as far as possible let the local governments select workers and

peasants experienced in struggle to join the Red Army, thus organizationally weakening or even eradicating the purely military viewpoint.

3. Arouse the local Party organizations to criticize the Party organizations in the Red Army and the organs of mass political power to criticize the Red Army itself, in order to influence the Party organizations and the officers and men of the Red Army.

4. The Party must actively attend to and discuss military work. All the work must be discussed and decided upon by the Party before being carried out by the rank and file.

5. Draw up Red Army rules and regulations which clearly define its tasks, the relationship between its military and its political apparatus, the relationship between the Red Army and the masses of the people, and the powers and functions of the soldiers' committees and their relationship with the military and political organizations.

ON ULTRA-DEMOCRACY

Since the Fourth Army of the Red Army accepted the directives of the Central Committee, there has been a great decrease in the manifestations of ultra-democracy. For example, Party decisions are now carried out fairly well; and no longer does anyone bring up such erroneous demands as that the Red Army should apply "democratic centralism from the bottom to the top" or should "let the lower levels discuss all problems first, and then let the higher levels decide." Actually, however, this decrease is only temporary and superficial and does not yet mean that ultra-democractic ideas are eliminated. In other words, ultra-democracy is still deep-rooted in the minds of many comrades. Witness the various expressions of reluctance to carry out Party decisions.

The methods of correction are as follows :

1. In the sphere of theory, destroy the roots of ultra-democracy. First of all, it should be pointed out that the danger of ultra-democracy lies in the fact that it damages or even completely wrecks the Party organization and weakens or even completely undermines the Party's fighting capacity, rendering

the Party incapable of fulfilling its fighting tasks and thereby causing the defeat of the revolution. Next, it should be pointed out that the source of ultra-democracy consists in the petty bourgeoisie's individualistic aversion to discipline. When this characteristic is brought into the Party, it develops into ultra-democratic ideas, political and organizational. These ideas are utterly incompatible with the fighting tasks of the proletariat.

2. In the sphere of organization, ensure democracy under centralized guidance. It should be done on the following lines :

(1) The leading bodies of the Party must give a correct line of guidance and find solutions when problems arise, in order to establish themselves as centres of leadership.

(2) The higher bodies must be familiar with the situation in the lower bodies and with the life of the masses so as to have an objective basis for correct guidance.

(3) No Party organization at any level should make casual decisions in solving problems. Once a decision is reached, it must be firmly carried out.

(4) All decisions of any importance made by the Party's higher bodies must be promptly transmitted to the lower bodies and the Party rank and file. The method is to call meetings of activists or general membership meetings of the Party branches or even of the columns (when circumstances permit) and to assign people to make reports at such meetings.

(5) The lower bodies of the Party and the Party rank and file must discuss the higher bodies' directives in detail in order to understand their meaning thoroughly and decide on the methods of carrying them out.

ON THE DISREGARD OF ORGANIZATIONAL DISCIPLINE

Disregard of organizational discipline in the Party organization in the Fourth Army manifests itself as follows :

(a) Failure of the minority to submit to the majority. For example, when a minority finds its motion voted down, it does not sincerely carry out the Party decisions.

The methods of correction are as follows :

1.   At meetings, all participants should be encouraged to voice their opinions as fully as possible.   The rights and wrongs in any controversy should be clarified without compromise or glossing over.   In order to reach a clear-cut conclusion, what cannot be settled at one meeting should be discussed at another, provided there is no interference with the work.

2.   One requirement of Party discipline is that the minority should submit to the majority.   If the view of the minority has been rejected, it must support the decision passed by the majority. If necessary, it can bring up the matter for reconsideration at the next meeting, but apart from that it must not act against the decision in any way.

(b)   Criticism made without regard to organizational discipline :

1.   Inner-Party criticism is a weapon for strengthening the Party organization and increasing its fighting capacity.   In the Party organization of the Red Army, however, criticism is not always of this character, and turns into personal attack. As a result, it damages the Party organization as well as individuals.   This is a manifestation of petty-bourgeois individualism.   The method of correction is to help Party members understand that the purpose of criticism is to increase the Party's fighting capacity in order to achieve victory in the class struggle and that it should not be used as a means of personal attack....

ON ABSOLUTE EQUALITARIANISM

Absolute equalitarianism, like ultra-democracy in political matters, is the product of a handicraft and small peasant economy—the only difference being that the one manifests itself in material life, while the other manifests itself in political life.

The method of correction : We should point out that, before the abolition of capitalism, absolute equalitarianism is a mere illusion of peasants and small proprietors, and that even under socialism there can be no absolute equality, for material things will then be distributed on the principle of "from each according to his ability, to each according to his work" as well as on that of meeting the needs of the work. The distribution of material things in the Red Army must be more or less equal, as in the case of equal pay for officers and men, because this is required by the present circumstances of the struggle. But absolute equalitarianism beyond reason must be opposed because it is not required by the struggle; on the contrary, it hinders the struggle.

ON SUBJECTIVISM

Subjectivism exists to a serious degree among some Party members, causing great harm to the analysis of the political situation and the guidance of the work....

The method of correction is mainly to educate Party members so that a political and scientific spirit pervades their thinking and their Party life.

ON INDIVIDUALISM

The tendency towards individualism in the Red Army Party organization manifests itself as follows :
1. Retaliation.
2. Cliquism. Some comrades consider only the interests of their own small group and ignore the general interest. Although on the surface this does not seem to be the pursuit of personal interests, in reality it exemplifies the narrowest individualism and has a strong corrosive and centrifugal effect. Cliquism used to be rife in the Red Army, and although there has been some improvement as a result of criticism, there are still survivals and further effort is needed to overcome it.
3. The "employee" mentality, some comrades do not understand that the Party and the Red Army, of which they are members, are both instruments for carrying out the tasks of the revolution. They do not realize that they themselves are makers of the revolution, but think that their responsibility is merely to their individual superiors and not to the revolution.
4. Pleasure-seeking.
5. Passivity. Some comrades become passive and stop working whenever anything goes against their wishes.

6. The desire to leave the army.

The method of correction is primarily to strengthen education so as to rectify individualism ideologically. Next, it is to conduct affairs, make assignments and enforce discipline in a proper way. In addition, ways must be found to improve the material life of the Red Army, and every available opportunity must be utilized for rest and rehabilitation in order to improve material conditions. In our educational work we must explain that in its social origin individualism is a reflection within the Party of petty-bourgeois and bourgeois ideas.

Common Programme of the Chinese People's Political Consultative Conference, 29 September 1949 (Extracts)

Article 10

The Armed Forces of the People's Republic of China—that is, the People's Liberation Army—the people's public security forces and people's police, are armed forces belonging to the people. Their tasks are to defend the independence, integrity of territory and sovereignty of China, and the revolutionary fruits and all legitimate rights and interests of the Chinese people....

CHAPTER THREE—MILITARY SYSTEM

Article 20

The People's Republic of China shall build up a unified army; that is, the People's Liberation Army and the people's public security forces, which shall be under the command of the People's Revolutionary Military Council of the Central People's Government, and which shall institute a unified command, unified system, unified formation and unified discipline.

Article 21

The People's Liberation Army and the people's public security forces shall, in accordance with the principle of unity between the officers and rank and file, and unity between the army and the people, set up a political work system and educate the commanders and fighters of these troops in the revolutionary and patriotic spirit.

Article 22

The People's Republic of China shall strengthen the modernized land force and establish an air force and a navy to consolidate national defense.

Article 23

The People's Republic of China shall enforce the system of people's militia to maintain local order, lay the foundation for national mobilization, and prepare for the enforcement of an obligatory military service system at the appropriate moment.

Article 24

The armed forces of the People's Republic of China shall, during peace time, systematically take part in agricultural and industrial production, to assist in national construction work, on the condition of not hindering military tasks.

Article 25

Dependents of revolutionary mastyrs and revolutionary servicemen who suffer from privation, shall receive preferential treatment from the state and from the society. The People's Government shall appropriately provide the means of livelihood and settling down for disabled servicemen and retired servicemen who have participated in the revolutionary war.

APPENDIX 3

Constitution of the People's Republic of China, 20 September 1954 (Extracts)

Article 20

The armed forces of the People's Republic of China belong to the people; their duty is to safeguard the gains of the people's revolution and the achievements of national construction, and to defend the sovereignty, territorial integrity and security of the country...

Article 39

The Chairman of the People's Republic of China is elected by the National People's Congress. Any citizen of the People's Republic of China who has the right to vote and stand for election and has reached the age of thirty-five is eligible for election as Chairman of the People's Republic of China.

The term of office of the Chairman of the People's Republic of China is four years.

Article 40

The Chairman of the People's Republic of China, in pursuance of decisions of the National People's Congress or the Standing Committee of the National People's Congress, promulgates laws and decrees; appoints or removes the Premier, Vice-Premiers, Ministers, Head of Commissions and the Secretary-General of the State Council; appoints or removes the Vice-Chairmen and other members of the Council of National Defence; confers state orders, medals and titles of honour; proclaims general amnesties and grants pardons; proclaims martial law; proclaims a state of war; and orders mobilization.

Article 41

The Chairman of the People's Republic of China represents the People's Republic of China in its relations with foreign states, receives foreign diplomatic representatives and, in pursuance of the decisions of the Standing Committee of the National People's Congress, appoints or recalls plenipotentiary representatives to foreign states and ratifies treaties concluded with foreign states.

Article 42

The Chairman of the People's Republic of China commands the armed forces of the country, and is Chairman of the Council of National Defence.

APPENDIX 4

Speech by the Peng Teh-huai, Minister of Defence, at the Eighth Party Congress, September 1956 (Extracts)

Resolute obedience to the Party's correct leadership of the armed forces, formation of close ties with the masses of the people and preservation of the qualities of a people's revolutionary army—these have been the basic guarantees of victory for our army....

The founding of the Chinese People's Republic ushered in a new era of socialist construction and socialist transformation in our country. Our army's tasks in this new period are : to protect our country's socialist construction, to safeguard its sovereignty, territorial integrity and security, to maintain a state of readiness for the liberation of Taiwan; and to strengthen peace and order in our country.

Immediately after the liberation of the mainland, the Central Committee of our Party and our government clearly pointed out that the Chinese People's Liberation Army must build itself on its original basis into a fine, modernized revolutionary army.

Modernization of our army has not been proceeding for very long, and all our services and arms have not yet been fully modernized, but they have already been modernized on a scale unprecedented in our country. With the rapid development for our national economic construction, our army's modernization will certainly be further advanced. Here I must express our gratitude to our great ally the Soviet Union, because the Soviet Union has in a fraternal spirit provided us with military equipment and helped us to build up a national defence industry.

In addition to improving the technical equipment of the armed forces, regular training has been introduced throughout the army to enhance the capability of the commanders, to improve the use of equipment, and to raise the political consciousness and scientific and cultural levels of all ranks. This is because, although we have got modernized equipment and modernized organization, full use cannot be made of all this excellent equipment without able commanders and expert technicians. Thus in the past few years, the training of officers and troops has been the central routine work in our army. Various military academies and schools have now been established to give advanced training to large numbers of cadres with battle experience, and raise their knowledge of the principles and techniques of modern warfare to a much higher level. As was shown in recent tasks and manoeuvres, marked progress has been made in raising the standard of training of the troops.

An important condition of a modern army is a regular military system. It is especially important to emphasize regularization in the modernization of our army because in the past our army was long scattered in various places, and there was no uniform military system for all the units. Regularization means a unified command, and uniformity in military organizations, systems, training and discipline. Rules and regulations to this effect have already come into force throughout the army, and produced good results in the training, work and life of the armed forces....

The basic system of leadership of the Chinese People's Liberation Army is a system of individual responsibility of the leaders in the army under the collective leadership of the Party committee. This system of leadership has long proved effective in our army practice.

The Communist Party committees at all levels in the army are built upon the basis of democratic centralism. The Party committee exercises its collective leadership over the army according to Marxist-Leninist principles. Except in emergencies when the leaders of an armed unit can make decisions at their own discretion within their competence, all important matters, such as important directives and orders to be issued by higher organizations, plans and measures for military, political and logistics work, allocation of cadres, etc., should all be discussed in a democratic way at Party committee meetings so that the wisdom of all the members may be brought together and definite decisions made, which will then be given to the military and political leaders of the unit, whose responsibility it is to organize their implementation.

In our army both military commanders and political commissars are leaders; they are jointly responsible for leadership in the army. However, there is a division of work between them: military commanders are responsible for the implementation of order and directives issued by higher authorities and decisions made by the Party committees of the same level so far as they concern military affairs, while political commissars are responsible for the implementation of those concerning political work.

The system of collective leadership by the Party committee must be carried out in the army, because only by so doing can the Party's leadership over the army be better ensured, the carrying out of Party policies and state laws and decrees be guaranteed, and the tendency towards a purely military viewpoint and individualism among leading personnel be prevented. Only by so doing can we give full play to the collective wisdom to complement and supplement deficiencies in the abilities of each individual and guard against any individual's subjectivist and one-sided way of looking at things, so that all tasks, especially military operations, will be carried out on a sound basis and after careful deliberation. Only by so doing can the leaders of a unit grasp the whole situation and arrive at a unified understanding of an issue, and thus give better assurance that there is a centralized command and unified action of the forces and that problems can be correctly solved in a flexible way according to actual conditions.

To strengthen its collective leadership, the Party committee should promote a democratic style of work and keep to the mass line in practical work. The Party committee should strengthen and extend close relations with the broad mass of cadres and the rank and file, constantly go to the lower levels to check up on the progress of work, sum up and popularize the good experience gained by the masses, and correct defects and mistakes in our work by means of criticism and self-criticism. In this way, we can prevent the responsible cadres of the Party committee from committing mistakes of bureaucracy and pure commandism due to alienation from the masses and from reality. Once decision on a certain task has been reached, the Party committee must unhesitatingly let the leaders of the unit put it into execution, giving them full scope to use their initiative and creative ability and assume personal responsibility for their actions. It is wrong for the Party committee to interfere in routine work and to take everything into its own hands.

The system of individual responsibility of leaders must be maintained in the army, because our army is an armed revolutionary organization fulfilling fighting tasks. If, in the emergency of battle, the leaders of an armed unit fail to resolutely assume responsibility and issue firm and timely orders, their forces of combined arms will be plunged into confusion even to the point of losing the battle. In our work, too, failure of leaders to assume individual responsibility will lead to dilatoriness and a state of affairs in which nobody takes charge of anything. Hence leaders at all levels must, according to the division of work, do their duty energetically and resolutely under the collective leadership of the Party committee. It is also wrong to think and behave as if the Party committee's collective leadership lightened the leaders responsibility.

The system of leadership which combines the collective leadership exercised by the Party committee with individual responsibility borne by the leaders in the armed forces has been put on a fairly sound basis in our army in the course of long practice. So long as we grasp the full significance of this system, and so long as we correctly put it into practice without emphasizing collective leadership at the expense of individual responsibility or vice versa, this system, far from weakening, will make still more effective the centralized and unified leadership of the army and, far from impeding, will ensure necessary flexibility of action in an emergency.

With the modernization of our army, we shall have a greater variety of arms, and it will be all the more necessary to allow this system to develop its good points to the full and not to inhibit it.

The Communist Party of China established the system of political work in the Chinese People's Liberation Army from the very day of founding of the army. Thanks to the correct leadership of the Party and the efforts of all army political workers and officers and men, our army, in passing the test of a protracted war, gained a rich store of experience in political work; this played an important part in consolidating its internal unity, raising its fighting ability, mobilizing the broad masses of the people to support and take part in the revolutionary war, disintegrating the enemy ranks and winning over its men and thereby ensuring victory. Political work has become the lifeline of our army.

Political work in the army is in essence Party work in the army, and the political organs are the party's working organizations. Through the political organs, the Party directs the political and ideological education of the whole army, imbues all the fighters with patriotic spirit and communist ideology, corrects whatever wrong ideas are current as well as wrong ways of working, leads the army in carrying out the political line of the Central Committee of the Party and the laws and decrees of the state, and leads the Party and Youth League organisations in the army and the broad masses of officers and men to follow the orders and directives of the higher organizations and to fulfil the various tasks of the army conscientiously and resolutely.

Political work must serve the army's fighting tasks and other work. The tasks of the political organs in the army should be defined only in accordance with the basic and specific tasks of the army. The basic task of our army in the past was to win victory in the national democratic revolution; from now on it is to guard against imperialist aggression and protect the socialist construction of our country. Apart from fighting, the specific tasks of our army in peace time consist of building itself up, keeping in readiness in case of war and various kinds of routine work, all of which centre on training. At the present time the specific tasks of our political work in the army are to give adequate political and ideological education to the troops, to raise the political understanding of officers and men, to further strengthen unity in the army and unity of the army and the people, to bring into full play the initiative and creative ability of every revolutionary soldier, to develop the fighting capacity of the troops, and to maintain high vigilance against any surprise attacks the imperialists may spring on us, so as to ensure the complete fulfilment of both the basic and specific tasks of the army.

In order that political work may play its part correctly, any tendency to belittle or weaken the leading role of political work in our army should be brought to an end. At the same time a stop should also be put to the erroneous tendency to confer special position and prerogatives on the political organs in the army. Political organs should take the initiative to maintain harmonious co-operation with the military departments; they should know how to organize the entire body of officers and men to participate in political work. Only in this way can the political organs play their role to the full and accomplish their tasks.

Under the new historical circumstances of today, the political workers in our army must preserve and develop the working style of following the mass line and practising democracy, of going deep into realities and uniting with the masses, and of practising criticism and self-criticism. Moreover, in order to adapt themsleves to the special conditions of a modernized army, they must get fully acquainted with all the military activities, know the concrete conditions of the work and technical level of their respective units, learn with modesty the technical knowledge they need for their work, and guard against the subjectivist tendency of drifting away from reality. In this way political work in the army can be vigorously carried out under the new circumstances....

A modern revolutionary army must be equipped not only with modern scientific technique, but also with Marxism-Leninism and up-to-date military science....Besides intensifying our study of Marxism-Leninism and Comrade Mao Tse-tung's works, we must intensify our study of modern military science and technique, the art of commanding a modernized army in battle and new military systems. Unless we put greater effort into study of these things, we shall not be able to master and make use of the most up-to-date weapons, or command a modernized army in battle, and consequently we shall not be able to build up our army into an excellent modern revolutionary army.

APPENDIX 5

Speech by Tan Ch'eng, Head of the Political Department of the PLA, at the Eighth Party Congress, September 1956 (Extracts)

Negligence of our tradition of unity of officers and men and of higher and lower levels, and negligence of the function of democracy, have their ideological origins. Some people hold that in the past, because we had to defeat an enemy whose equipment was superior, we had to rely on the people and the soldiers, in other words, rely more on the human element. Hence the importance of the principle of unity of officers and soldiers, of higher and lower levels, of the army and the people and a democratic life under centralized leadership; hence it was proper for us to stress them. Now, after being re-equipped, our army has changed from a military force of a single arm to one of combined arms, and the demand for technique is greatly increased. Under such circumstances, they hold, we should only stress the function of technique and not that of political work and man. The function of technique, so they say, has leapt to a place of primary importance, while the function of political work and man has come down to a second place. In their opinion, in the past we fought with the help of political work, in future we shall fight with the help of technique.

Such ideas are evidently wrong. Those who hold such ideas forget our army's basic feature, namely, that our army is a people's army, and no amount of modernization will ever change this feature. On the contrary, we should make every effort to keep up and display this feature and bring out its superiority....

In modern warfare, the importance of technique is greatly enhanced. Without modern technical equipment and without joint operations of units of the combined arms which have attained a high level in military technique, the bravery of man by itself cannot win a war....It would be wrong to shut one's eyes to the development of military sciences and assume that we can win a war, just as we did in the past, with inferior weapons alone, with a single arm and simple techniques, and thereby underestimate the importance of technique and refuse to press ahead with the key task of raising our level of technique. But by emphasizing the importance of technique we do not mean to reduce the role played by man and the function of political factors. On the contrary, the human factor is always a determining factor in war, a factor that always counts. Under the circumstances where technical conditions are getting more complex from day to day, the diversity of arms in the army is increasing and the war is getting to be more cruel than ever, it is all the more necessary to bring into play the role of man. Technique is, after all, employed by man; no technique can be of any use if not combined with man. Further, mobility in warfare and co-operation in joint operations are possible only when there is political unity among men. Without this, there can be no mobility in warfare and no real joint operation in action.

We must give free scope to democracy if we want to consolidate unity inside our army....

Now as the unity within our Party is further strengthened and our society is advancing towards the elimination of the exploiting classes, the internal and external conditions contributing to the unity of our army are vastly different from those in any former period of our history. The elimination of the long-standing guerilla habits and mountain-toppism in our army is of great significance to the regularization of our army and to the attainment of a high degree of unification and centralism in our leadership. But under the new conditions, we cannot say there are no longer any problems about our internal unity. As I mentioned above, there are problems, only they have acquired new contents, that is, new contradictions. How to keep consolidating our inner-army unity and carry on our tradition of the unity of officers and men under the new conditions, so as to make our army always full of vitality and always invincible, is still a question that our army cannot afford to overlook. In this connection, it is extremely necessary for us, apart from strengthening the leadership of the Party and political work, to insist on democracy and on the practice of criticism and self-criticism, to combat the tendency towards renouncing democracy and criticism, and to struggle against the attempts to suppress democracy and retaliate upon those who criticize. By so doing, we will enable our officers and leading personnel to hear constantly opinions from below and keep soberminded, to be modest and prudent and not getting swell-headed and impetuous. Of course, the democracy we want to keep up and foster has nothing in common with the ultra-democracy we have all along opposed. Ultra-democracy and acts against discipline and detrimental to the organization such as refusal to carry out orders are impermissible at all times. Moreover, democratic life in our army must be placed under centralized leadership and kept within proper bounds; it bears no resemblance to ultra-democracy which defies all leadership and breaks all bounds.

In the past few years, another view has been prevalent in our army which is also harmful to the promotion of democracy, and should therefore, be criticized. This view is that officers should not be criticized openly, and that criticisms against them even inside the Party should be restricted. It is said that open criticism will impair the prestige of the officers. According to those who hold this view, officers should only be subject to supervision by leading organs and superiors, but not to supervision by the rank and file at the same time. In case officers commit mistakes, they should only be dealt with by the leading organs; the rank and file cannot look into the matter. This view is wrong. If it is followed, the officers would cut themselves off from the masses, and be liable to get swell-headed and self-conceited....

Since the modernization of our army, our military command has been highly centralized. But still all parts of our army should continue to receive, as before, the supervision of the local bodies of the Party, of the government and of the mass organizations. They should not reject such supervision on the pretext of centralized command. By supervision we mean: when any army personnel detach themselves from the people, violate the policies of the Party and the state and commit other offences against law and discipline, the local organizations may directly stop them from doing so or appeal to higher authorities. In addition, on certain questions and on certain kinds of work our army units should accept the leadership of competent local organizations, apart from accepting the leadership of higher levels in the army. For instance, in military engineering work, in questions like the purchase of farm land, removal of inhabitants and relocation of tombs from areas purchased, laying out restricted zones and collecting and managing labour power, the units concerned must accept the leadership of the local organizations and respect their opinions. The General Political Department put forth, in January 1954, a proposal that responsible comrades of army units should sit on local Party committees and information should be exchanged between local authorities and army units; the proposal, approved by the Central Committee of the Party, provides a proper mode of contact between Party committees of army units and local Party committees. Those army units which have not acted according to this proposal should do so. History and recent events have all proved the soundness of this system of dual leadership and the system that local organizations have supervisory power over army units. They have only done good to our army units and will not hinder the centralization of our command.

APPENDIX 6

Regulations Governing Political Work in the People's Liberation Army Adopted by the All-Army Political Work Conference in February 1963 and Promulgated by the Party Central Committee on 27 March 1963

Clause 1

The Chinese People's Liberation Army is an armed force of the People's Republic of China, is an army of workers and peasants created and led by the Chinese Communist Party and Comrade Mao Tse-tung and is a new type of People's army. The Marxist-Leninist political line and military line formulated by the Party and Comrade Mao Tse-tung is the fundamental guarantee for the winning of victory by our army. To closely stand together with the people and serve the people wholeheartedly is the sole aim of our army. Led by the Party and Comrade Mao Tse-tung, our army, together with people of the whole country, has waged protracted, hard struggles. The Chinese people had formed volunteers and with a high sense of patriotism, internationalism and brave and valiant actions, defeated the U.S. aggressors, fighting shoulder to shoulder with the Korean people. In the new historical China, our army is the defender and builder of the cause of socialism. It is necessary to continuously raise aloft the great red banner of the thinking of Mao-Tse-tung, raise high the three red banner of the general line for socialist construction the Big Leap Forward and the People's Communes, inherit and develop the glorious tradition of our army, build itself into a good, modern revolutionary army, strive for defending the country's sovereignty, territorial integrity and security, for liberating Taiwan, and for defending peace in the East and in the world, and strive for carrying out the Party's programme, lines and the cause of socialism and communism.

Clause 2

The thinking of Mao Tse-tung is the guideline for the Chinese people's revolution and socialist construction, and also the guideline for the building of the Chinese People's Liberation Army and for the political work of the army. Comrade Mao Tse-tung is a great contemporary Marxist-Leninist. The thinking of Mao Tse-tung represents the creatively developed Marxism-Leninism resulting from the application of the universal truth of Marxism-Leninism in the epoch when imperialism is heading towards collapse and socialism is advancing towards victory, in the course of the concrete practice of the Chinese revolution and in the collective struggle waged by the Party and the people. The thinking of Mao Tse-tung is a mighty ideological weapon against imperialism and a mighty ideological weapon against modern revisionism and doctrinairism. Comrade Mao Tse-tung not only laid down the correct political line of the Party, but also formulated the correct military line which is subordinated to the political line. The theories of Comrade Mao Tse-tung regarding the class struggle, proletarian revolution and proletarian dictatorship, regarding the general line, the theory of contradictions and the correct handling of contradictions among the people, regarding the inference that East wind prevails over the West wind and the general line on external politics, the theory that imperialism and all reactionaries are paper tigers, of strategically slighting the enemy and tactically attaching importance to him, regarding war and peace and that the decisive factor in a war is human beings, not materials, regarding the theory and policies on the general line for socialist construction, the Big Leap Forward and the People's Communes, the thesis on the relationship between economic construction and national defence construction, the thinking on people's war and the strategical and tactical principles of revolutionary wars, the theory regarding politics "red and expert", the theory regarding Party construction and democratic centralism, theory regarding Party's mass line and the working style of the Party, regarding the purpose and principles for the building of the people's army, regarding the Party's positive leadership over the army, the system of Party Committee, the system of political commissar and system of political work, regarding the basic principles on the political work for the unity of officers and men, unity of military and civilians and for thwarting the enemy troops, regarding the democratic system of the army and the militant style of work, regarding the militia system and the thinking that all people are soldiers, etc. etc., all these are not only the fundamental guarantee by which our army obtained victories in the past, but also the guidelines which must be observed in all future actions.

Clause 3

The Party Committees of various levels set up in the Chinese People's Liberation Army by the Chinese Communist Party serve as the core for the unified leadership and unity of army. The system of responsibility based on the division of labour by the leading officers under the unified collective leadership of the Party Committee is the fundamental system for carrying out the Party's leadership over the army. Except in a state of emergency which calls for opportune decisions by the leading officers concerned, all important questions in the army unit must first be fully discussed by the Party Committee and decision reached in accordance with the system of democratic centralism of the Party. Those pertaining to the field of military work will be put in the charge of military commanders for organising and carrying out; those pertaining to the field of political work will be taken charge of the political commissars for their organising and carrying out. Political commissars and military commanders are both commanders of the army units, and are jointly responsible for the work of the army units. In normal conditions, political commissar also takes charge of the routine work of the Party Committee. The Party established branches in the companies as the core for the unified leadership and unity of a company. It serves as the basic belt linking up the Party and the broad masses of officers and men.

The Chinese People's Liberation Army must also thoroughly carry out the system of dual leadership over the army by the military system under the unified leadership of the Party's

Central Committee and by the local Party Committees, so as to obtain the leadership and supervision over the army by the local Party Committees, to set up closer relations between the army and the local Party Committees, and to strengthen mutual co-ordination and mutual support in work.

Clause 4

The political work of the Chinese Communist Party in the Chinese People's Liberation Army is the lifeline of our army. The political work is the very work of the Party. The political organisation is the working organisation of the Party. The factor of political thinking represents the primary factor among the various factors on combat force. Our army must, in accordance with the directives given by the Party Centre and Comrade Mao Tse-tung in the past, place the human factor in the first place while handling the relations of weapon and human beings, give the political work the first place while handling the relations between various kinds of work and the political work, give the ideological work the first place in the political work. This is the orientation of our army's political work, also the orientation of the army's construction. The fundamental task of our army's political work is : To educate the troops in Marxism-Leninism and the thinking of Mao Tse-tung, elevate the proletarian consciousness of the entire personnel, thoroughly carry out the Party's programmes, lines and policies and the state laws and decrees, consolidate the Party's positive leadership over the army, cultivate the working style set out in the "Three Disciplinary Measures" and "Eight Points for Attention", maintain the high degree of concentration and unity and strict discipline of the army, enhance the unity inside and outside the army, strengthen internally the unity of officers and men, between upper and lower levels, between military and political work and other kinds of work and between various army units, strengthen externally the unity of the army and the people, between the army and local organisations and between our army and allied armies, and also carry out the work of thwarting enemy forces, so as to achieve the purpose of consolidating and raising the fighting efficiency of the army units, uniting ourselves and defeating the enemy.

Clause 5

The main content of the political work is as follows :

1. Give guidance to and ensure that army units thoroughly carry out the programmes and lines and policies of the Chinese Communist Party, observe the state laws and decrees, and fulfil all the tasks given by the Party and the State.

2. Organise the entire personnel to study Marxism-Leninism, and works of Comrade Mao Tse-tung, propagate the resolutions and directives of the Party, grasp the ideological trends of the army units, carry out vivid, ideological education, give citation to good persons and good events, overcome bad tendencies, and check the influence and erosion of modern revisionism and the bourgeois thinking. Educate the entire personnel to be loyal to the motherland, to the people and to the cause of the Party, show concern for State affairs, for the international communist movement, for the liberation movements of the oppressed nations and for the revolutionary struggles of the world people, hate, despise and slight imperialism and all reactionaries, develop patriotism, internationalism and revolutionary heroic spirit, enhance the fighting will and retain at all times the combat preparations.

3. Supervise the Party's ideological work and organisational work in the army, supervise the construction of the Party Committees at various levels and the Party organisations at the basic level, in accordance with the Constitution of the Chinese Communist Party. Give guidance to the work of the Communist Youth League organisations.

4. Carry on wartime political work, carry out incessant propaganda work, encourage the fighting morale, set a firm faith in victory, ensure that the troops resolutely carry out orders and fulfil fighting tasks.

5. Mobilise the entire armymen to actively study the military thinkings of Mao Tse-tung and the experience of fighting of our army, strive to study tactical skills, master in one's own trade, thoroughly carry out various decrees, rules and regulations and systems, constantly raise the military cultivation

of the army units, foster a strict organisational character, discipline and a fine militant working style, and ensure the completion of military training tasks.

6. Develop and cultivate the "Three Disciplinary Measures and Eight Points for Attention." The firm and correct political orientation, the working style of industry and thrift, the flexible and ingenious strategy and tactics, unity, tension, solemnity, the vivid working style—these are the criteria of fighting, training and all actions of our army. We must constantly carry on propaganda education, fully set in motion the masses and steel and cultivate them in the course of training and daily life.

7. Thoroughly carry out the Party's cadre policy of taking workers and peasants as the backbone and of uniting with and educating and transforming the intellectuals, persist in the principle of selecting and using cadres on the basis of taking into consideration both their qualities and ability; foster, fill out and check up on the cadres. Carry on the work of demobilisation of cadres, their transfer to other lines of work, their retirement and resettlement and the work regarding their dependents.

8. Carry on the work of defence, raise the political vigilance of troops, strictly keep the state secrets and military secrets, check the disruptive activities of the counter-revolutionaries, eliminate the hidden counter-revolutionaries. Wage struggle against all law-breaking criminal acts, and preserve the political and organisational purity of the troops.

9. Carry on the cultural work, master the Party's lines on art, and develop the cultural, recreational and sport activities on a mass scale. Organise cultural studies.

10. Develop the good tradition of respecting cadres and loving the soldiers, and enhance the unity of officers and men. Educate the cadres to show loving concern for the soldiers, to place strict demands on them through patient persuasion; educate soldiers to respect the cadres and to consciously observe the discipline and resolutely carry out orders. Develop political democracy, economic democracy and military democracy under the collective leadership, and fully bring into play the initiative and creativeness of the masses. Be concerned about the welfare of the entire personnel, and assist the departments concerned to

improve the material life of the army units. Carry out well the work of consolidating the troops, and check the reduction of non-combat personnel.

11. Develop the good tradition of supporting the administration and showing affection for the people, set up close ties with the local Party and administrative organisations, and cement the ties of the army and the masses of the people. Educate the army units to strictly observe the "Three Disciplinary Measures and the Eight Points for Attention", actively participate in the socialist construction and the political life of the state, and assist the local authority in the work of the masses.

12. Thoroughly carry out the policy of thwarting the enemy troops and of giving lenient treatment to the prisoners. Carry on the work of thwarting the enemy troops.

13. Carry on the political work in the research institutes for national defence science, and ensure that good results are obtained and talented persons are brought out.

14. Carry on the political work and political education in academies, and train cadres who are both "red and expert".

15. Carry on the political work in logistics, thoroughly carry out the line of building the army with industry and thrift, ensure the completion of materials supply, and the health and production tasks.

16. Assist the local Party and administrative organs to carry on the political work of the militia and in the recruiting of soldiers, and assist in the political work of demobilising soldiers and of their retiring from service in time of war.

17. Educate the entire personnel in developing the internationalist spirit, and seriously carry out well the work of uniting with the allied army and of consolidating and developing militant friendship between our army and allied armies.

18. Organise work inspection, sum up and popularise advanced experience, and strictly carry out the system of asking for instructions and reporting.

Clause 6

The political work of the Chinese People's Liberation Army

is necessarily to develop the working style of the Party, i.e. the style of combining theory with practice, the style of establishing close ties with the masses of the people and the style of self-criticism. The political work must carry out the principle of "coming from the masses and going back to the masses" and of "concentrating and persisting in it", and must apply the method of integrating the general calls with individual guidance, and the integration of leadership backbones and the broad masses, and develop democracy and thoroughly carry out the mass line under centralised leadership. In carrying on the political work, we must rely on the Party organisations at various levels, rely on the cadres and Party members and set in motion the broad sections of the masses, to see that everyone voices his opinion and everyone takes part in supervision and encourages and helps each other. In handling the internal relations and solving ideological questions, we must persist in the line of unity-criticism-unity, engage the method of persuasive education, raise the understanding, distinguish the right from wrong and enhance the unity. In the course of work, we must attach importance to investigation and research, turn our gaze at companies, penetrate into practice and solidly fix our work at the basic levels. All personnel dealing in political work should study hard Marxism-Leninism and the works of Comrade Mao Tse-tung, resolutely carry out the Party's lines and policies, stand firmly, adhere to principles, be brave in fighting, work enthusiastically, lead an industrious and thrifty life, establish ties with the masses and play an exemplary role in the course of fulfilling various tasks.

Clause 7

With a view to ensuring the positive leadership of the Chinese Communist Party over the Chinese People's Liberation Army, it is necessary to carry out Party work and political work in the army; political commissar and political organisations be installed in army units at and above the regimental level or in units equivalent to a regiment and above; political instructor be installed in a battalion or a unit equivalent to a battalion; political director be installed in a company or a basic-level unit equivalent to a company. If necessary, political assistants may be installed in the departments at the regimental level and above.

APPENDIX 7

Report to the Tenth Party Congress Delivered by Chou En-lai on behalf of the Central Committee, 24 August 1973 (Extract)

We should further strengthen the centralized leadership of the Party. Of the seven sectors—industry, agriculture, commerce, culture and education, the Army, the government and the Party—it is the Party that exercises overall leadership. Party committees at all levels should study "On Strengthening the Party Committee system," "Methods of Work of Party Committees" and other writings by Chairman Mao, sum up their experience and further strengthen the centralized leadership of the Party ideologically, organizationally, as well as through rules and regulations. At the same time the role of revolutionary committees and mass organizations should be brought into full play. We should strengthen the leadership given to primary organizations in order to ensure that leadership there is truly in the hands of Marxists and in the hands of workers, poor and lower-middle peasants and other working people, and that the task of consolidating the dictatorship of the proletariat is fulfilled in every primary organization. Party committees at all levels should apply democratic centralism better and improve their art of leadership. It should be emphatically pointed out that quite a few Party committees are engrossed in daily routines and minor matters, paying no attention to major issues. This is very dangerous. If they do not change, they will inevitably step on to the road of revisionism. It is hoped that comrades throughout the Party, leading comrades in particular, will guard against such a tendency and earnestly change such a style of work.

The experience with regard to combining the old, the middle-aged and the young in the leadership, which the masses created during the Great Proletarian Cultural Revolution, has provided us with favourable conditions for training millions of successors to the revolutionary cause of the proletariat in accordance with the five requirements put forward by Chairman Mao. Party organizations at all levels should keep on the agenda this fundamental task which is crucial for generations to come. Chairman Mao says : "Revolutionary successors of the proletariat are invariably brought up in great storms." They must be tempered in class struggle and two-line struggle and educated by both positive and negative experience. Therefore, a genuine Communist must be ready to accept a higher or lower post and be able to stand the test of going up or stepping down many times. All cadres, veteran and new alike, must maintain close ties with the masses, be modest and prudent, guard against arrogance and impetuosity, go to any post as required by the Party and the people and firmly carry out Chairman Mao's revolutionary line and policies under every circumstance.

APPENDIX 8

Report on the Revision of the Party Constitution Delivered by Wang Hung-wen at the Tenth Party Congress, 24 August 1973 (Extract)

We must strengthen the Party's centralized leadership and promote the Party's traditional style of work. The political party of the proletariat is the highest form of organization of the proletariat, and the Party must exercise leadership in everything; this is an important Marxist principle. The draft has incorporated suggestions from various units on strengthening the Party's centralized leadership. It is laid down in the articles that state organs, the People's Liberation Army and revolutionary mass organizations "must all accept the Party's centralized leadership." Organizationally, the Party's centralized leadership should be given expression in two respects: First, as regards the relationship between various organizations at the same level, of the seven sectors—industry, agriculture, commerce, culture and education, the Army, the government and the Party—it is the Party that exercises overall leadership; the Party is not parallel to the others and still less is it under the leadership of any other. Second, as regards the relationship between higher and lower levels, the lower level is subordinate to the higher level, and the entire Party is subordinate to the Central Committee. This has long been a rule in our Party and it must be adhered to. We must strengthen the Party's centralized leadership, and a Party committee's leadership must not be replaced by a "joint conference" of several sectors. But at the same time, it is necessary to give full play to the role of the revolutionary committees, the other sectors and organizations at all levels. The Party committee must practise democratic centralism and strengthen its collective leadership. It must unite people "from all corners of the country" and not practice mountain-stronghold sectionalism. It must "let all people have their say" and not "let one person alone have the say." The most essential thing about the Party's centralized leadership is leadership through a correct ideological and political line. Party committees at all levels must, on the basis of Chairman Mao's revolutionary line, achieve unity in thinking, policy, plan, command and action.

Constitution of the Communist Party of China (adopted by the Tenth National Congress of the Communist Party of China on 28 August 1973)

CHAPTER 1

General Programme

The Communist Party of China is the political party of the proletariat, the vanguard of the proletariat.

The Communist Party of China takes Marxism-Leninism-Mao Tse-tung Thought as the theoretical basis guiding its thinking.

The basic programme of the Communist Party of China is the complete overthrow of the bourgeoisie and all other exploiting classes, the establishment of the dictatorship of the proletariat in place of the dictatorship of the bourgeoisie, and the triumph of socialism over capitalism. The ultimate aim of the Party is the realization of communism.

Through more than fifty years of arduous struggle, the Communist Party of China has led the Chinese people in winning complete victory in the new-democratic revolution, great victories in socialist revolution and socialist construction and great victories in the Great Proletarian Cultural Revolution.

Socialist society covers a considerably long historical period. Throughout this historical period, there are classes, class contradictions and class struggle, there is the struggle between the socialist road and the capitalist road, there is the danger of capitalist restoration and there is the threat of subversion and aggression by imperialism and social-imperialism. These contradictions can be resolved only by depending on the theory of continued revolution under the dictatorship of the proletariat and on practice under its guidance.

Such is China's Great Proletarian Cultural Revolution, a great political revolution carried out under the conditions of socialism by the proletariat against the bourgeoisie and all other exploiting classes to consolidate the dictatorship of the proletariat and prevent capitalist restoration. Revolutions like this will have to be carried out many times in the future.

The Party must rely on the working class, strengthen the worker-peasant alliance and lead the people of all the nationalities of our country in carrying on the three great revolutionary movements of class struggle, the struggle for production and scientific experiment; lead the people in building socialism independently and with the initiative in our own hands, through self-reliance, hard struggle, diligence and thrift and by going all out, aiming high and achieving greater, faster, better and more economical results; and lead them in preparing against war and natural disasters and doing everything for the people.

The Communist Party of China upholds proletarian internationalism and opposes great-power chauvinism; it firmly unites with the genuine Marxist-Leninist Parties and organizations the world over, unites with the proletariat, the oppressed people and nations of the whole world and fights together with them to oppose the hegemonism of the two superpowers—the United States and the Soviet Union—to overthrow imperialism, modern revisionism and all reaction, and to abolish the system of exploitation of man by man over the globe, so that all mankind will be emancipated.

The Communist Party of China has strengthened itself and grown in the course of the struggle against both Right and "Left" opportunist lines. Comrades throughout the Party must have the revolutionary spirit of daring to go against the tide, must adhere to the principles of practising Marxism and not revisionism, working for unity and not for splits. and being open and above board and not engaging in intrigues and conspiracy, must be good at correctly distinguishing contradictions among the people from those between ourselves and the enemy and correctly handling them, must develop the style of integrating theory with practice, maintaining close ties with the masses and practicising criticism and self-criticism, and must train millions of successors for the cause of proletarian revolution, so as to ensure that the Party's cause will advance for ever along the Marxist line.

The future is bright, the road is tortuous. Members of the Communist Party of China, who dedicate their lives to the struggle for communism, must be resolute, fear no sacrifice and surmount every difficulty to win victory !

CHAPTER II

Membership

Article 1. Any Chinese worker, poor peasant, lower-middle peasant, revolutionary armyman or any other revolutionary element who has reached the age of eighteen and who accepts the Constitution of the Party, joins a Party organization and works actively in it, carries out the Party's decisions, observes Party discipline and pays membership dues may become a member of the Communist Party of China.

Article 2. Applicants for Party membership must go through the procedure for admission individually. An applicant must be recommended by two Party members, fill out an application form for Party membership and be examined by a Party branch, which must seek the opinions of the broad masses inside and outside the Party. Application is subject to acceptance by the general membership meeting of the Party branch and approval by the next higher-Party committee.

Article 3. Members of the Communist Party of China must :

(1) Conscientiously study Marxism-Leninism-Mao Tse-tung Thought and criticize revisionism;

(2) Work for the interests of the vast majority of people of China and the world;

(3) Be able at uniting with the great majority, including those who have wrongly opposed them but are sincerely correcting their mistakes; however, special vigilance must be maintained against careerists, conspirators and double-dealers so as to prevent such bad elements from usurping the leadership of the Party and the state at any level and guarantee that the leadership of the Party and the state always remains in the hands of Marxist revolutionaries;

(4) Consult with the masses when matters arise;

(5) Be bold in making criticism and self-criticism.

Article 4. When Party members violate Party discipline, the Party organizations at the levels concerned shall, within their functions and powers and on the merits of each case, take appropriate disciplinary measures—warning, serious warning, removal from posts in the Party, placing on probation within the Party, or expulsion from the Party.

The period for which a Party member is placed on probation shall not exceed two years. During this period, he has no right to vote or elect or be elected.

A Party member whose revolutionary will has degenerated and who does not change despite repeated education may be persuaded to withdraw from the Party.

When a Party member asks to withdraw from the Party, the Party branch concerned shall, with the approval of its general membership meeting, remove his name from the Party rolls and report the matter to the next higher Party committee for the record.

Proven renegades, enemy agents, absolutely unrepentant persons in power taking the capitalist road, degenerates and alien-class elements must be cleared out of the Party and not be re-admitted.

CHAPTER III

Organizational Principle of the Party

Article 5. The organizational principle of the Party is democratic centralism.

The leading bodies of the Party at all levels shall be elected through democratic consultation in accordance with the requirements for successors to the cause of the proletarian revolution and the principle of combining the old, the middle-aged and the young.

The whole Party must observe unified discipline : The individual is subordinate to the organization, the minority is subordinate to the majority, the lower level is subordinate to the higher level, and the entire Party is subordinate to the Central Committee.

Leading bodies of the Party at all levels shall regularly report on their work to congresses or general membership meetings, constantly listen to the opinions of the masses both inside and outside the Party and accept their supervision. Party members have the right to criticize organizations and leading members of the Party at all levels and make proposals to them. If a Party member holds different views with regard to the decisions or directives of the Party organizations, he is allowed to reserve his views and has the right to bypass the immediate leadership and report directly to higher levels, up to and including the Central Committee and the Chairman of the Central Committee. It is absolutely impermissible to suppress criticism and to retaliate. It is essential to create a political situation in which there are both centralism and democracy, both discipline and freedom, both unity of will and personal ease of mind and liveliness.

Article 6. The highest leading body of the Party is the National Party Congress and, when it is not in session, the Central Committee elected by it. The leading bodies of Party organizations in the localities, in army units and in various departments are the Party congresses or general membership meetings at their respective levels and the Party committees elected by them. Party congresses at all levels are convened by Party committees at their respective levels. The convening of Party congresses in the localities, in army units and in various departments and their elected Party committee members are subject to approval by the higher Party organizations.

Party committees at all levels shall set up their working bodies or dispatch their representative organs in accordance with the principles of close ties with the masses and simple and efficient structure.

Article 7. State organs, the People's Liberation Army and the militia, labour unions, poor and lower-middle peasant associations, women's federations, the Communist Youth League, the Red Guards, the Little Red Guards and other revolutionary mass organizations must all accept the centralized leadership of the Party.

Party committees or leading Party groups may be set up in state organs and popular organizations.

CHAPTER IV

Central Organizations of the Party

Article 8. The National Party Congress shall be convened every five years. Under special circumstances, it may be convened before its due date or postponed.

Article 9. The plenary session of the Central Committee of the Party elects the Political Bureau of the Central Committee, the Standing Committee of the Political Bureau of the Central Committee and the Chairman and Vice-Chairmen of the Central Committee.

The plenary session of the Central Committee of the Party is convened by the Political Bureau of the Central Committee.

When the Central Committee is not in plenary session, the Political Bureau of the Central Committee and its Standing Committee exercise the functions and powers of the Central Committee.

Under the leadership of the Chairman, Vice-Chairmen and the Standing Committee of the Political Bureau of the Central Committee, a number of necessary organs, which are compact and efficient, shall be set up to attend to the day-to-day work of the Party, the government and the Army in a centralized way.

CHAPTER V

Party Organizations in the Localities and the Army Units

Article 10. Local Party congresses at the county level and upwards and Party congresses in the People's Liberation Army at the regimental level and upwards shall be convened every three years. Under special circumstances, they may be convened before their due date or postponed.

Party committees at all levels in the localities and the army units elect their standing committees, secretaries and deputy secretaries.

CHAPTER VI

Primary Organizations of the Party

Article 11. Party branches, general Party branches or primary Party committees shall be set up in factories, mines and other enterprises, people's communes, offices, schools, shops, neighbourhoods, companies of the People's Liberation Army and other primary units in accordance with the requirements of the revolutionary struggle and the size of the Party membership.

Party branches and general Party branches shall hold elections once a year and primary Party committees shall hold elections every two years. Under special circumstances, the election may take place before its due date or be postponed.

Article 12. The main tasks of the primary organizations of the Party are :

(1) To lead the Party members and non-party members in studying Marxism-Leninism-Mao Tse-tung Thought conscientiously and criticizing revisionism;

(2) To give constant education to the Party members and non-Party members concerning the ideological and political line and lead them in fighting resolutely against the class enemy;

(3) To propagate and carry out the policies of the Party, implement its decisions and fulfil every task assigned by the Party and the state;

(4) To maintain close ties with the masess, constantly listen to their opinions and demands and wage an active ideological struggle so as to keep Party life vigorous;

(5) To take in new Party members, enforce Party discipline and constantly consolidate the Party organizations, getting rid of the stale and taking in the fresh, so as to maintain the purity of the Party ranks.

Constitution of the People's Republic of China (adopted by the Fourth National People's Congress of China at its First session on 17 January 1975)

PREAMBLE

The founding of the People's Republic of China marked the great victory of the new-democratic revolution and the beginning of the new historical period of socialist revolution and the dictatorship of the proletariat, a victory gained only after the Chinese people had waged a heroic struggle for over a century and, finally, under the leadership of the Communist Party of China, overthrown the reactionary rule of imperialism, feudalism and bureaucrat-capitalism by a people's revolutionary war.

For the last twenty years and more, the people of all nationalities in our country, continuing their triumphant advance under the leadership of the Communist Party of China, have achieved great victories both in socialist revolution and socialist construction and in the Great Proletarian Cultural Revolution, and have consolidated and strengthened the dictatorship of the proletariat.

Socialist society covers a considerably long historical period. Throughout this historical period, there are classes, class contradictions and class struggle, there is the struggle between the socialist road and the capitalist road, there is the danger of capitalist restoration and there is the threat of subversion and aggression by imperialism and social-imperialism. These contradictions can be resolved only by depending on the theory of continued revolution under the dictatorship of the proletariat and on practice under its guidance.

We must adhere to the basic line and policies of the Communist Party of China for the entire historical period of socialism and persist in continued revolution under the dictatorship of the proletariat, so that our great motherland will always advance along the road indicated by Marxism-Leninism-Mao Tse-tung Thought.

We should consolidate the great unity of the people of all nationalities led by the working class and based on the alliance of workers and peasants, and develop the revolutionary united front. We should correctly distinguish contradictions among the people from those between ourselves and the enemy and correctly handle them. We should carry on the three great revolutionary movements of class struggle, the struggle for production and scientific experiment; we should build socialism independently and with the initiative in our own hands, through self-reliance, hard struggle, diligence and thrift and by going all out, aiming high and achieving greater, faster, better and more economical results; and we should be prepared against war and natural disasters and do everything for the people.

In international affairs, we should uphold proletarian internationalism. China will never be a superpower. We should strengthen our unity with the socialist countries and all oppressed people and oppressed nations, with each supporting the other; strive for peaceful coexistence with countries having different social systems on the basis of the Five Principles of mutual respect for sovereignty and territorial integrity, mutual non-aggression, non-interference in each other's internal affairs, equality and mutual benefit, and peaceful coexistence, and oppose the imperialist and social-imperialist policies of aggression and war and oppose the hegemonism of the superpowers.

The Chinese people are fully confident that, led by the Communist Party of China, they will vanquish enemies at home and abroad and surmount all difficulties to build China into a powerful socialist state of the dictatorship of the proletariat so as to make a greater contribution to humanity.

People of all nationalities in our country, unite to win still greater victories !

CHAPTER ONE

General Principles

ARTICLE 1

The People's Republic of China is a socialist state of the dictatorship of the proletariat led by the working class and based on the alliance of workers and peasants.

ARTICLE 2

The Communist Party of China is the core of leadership of the whole Chinese people. The working class exercises leadership over the state through its vanguard, the Communist Party of China.

Marxism-Leninism-Mao Tse-tung Thought is the theoretical basis guiding the thinking of our nation.

ARTICLE 3

All power in the People's Republic of China belongs to the people. The organs through which the people exercise power are the people's congresses at all levels, with deputies of workers, peasants and soldiers as their main body.

The people's congresses at all levels and all other organs of state practise democratic centralism.

Deputies to the people's congresses at all levels are elected through democratic consultation. The electoral units and electors have the power to supervise the deputies they elect and to replace them at any time according to provisions of law.

ARTICLE 4

The People's Republic of China is a unitary multi-national state. The areas where regional national autonomy is exercised are all inalienable parts of the People's Republic of China.

All the nationalities are equal. Big-nationality chauvinism and local nationality chauvinism must be opposed.

All the nationalities have the freedom to use their own spoken and written languages.

ARTICLE 5

In the People's Republic of China, there are mainly two kinds of ownership of the means of production at the present stage : Socialist ownership by the whole people and socialist collective ownership by working people.

The state may allow non-agricultural individual labourers to engage in individual labour involving no exploitation of others, within the limits permitted by law and under unified arrangement by neighbourhood organizations in cities and towns or by production teams in rural people's communes. At the same time, these individual labourers should be guided on to the road of socialist collectivization step by step.

ARTICLE 6

The state sector of the economy is the leading force in the national economy.

All mineral resources and waters as well as the forests, undeveloped land and other resources owned by the state are the property of the whole people.

The state may requisition by purchase, take over for use, or nationalize urban and rural land as well as other means of production under conditions prescribed by law.

ARTICLE 7

The rural people's commune is an organization which integrates government administration and economic management.

The economic system of collective ownership in the rural people's communes at the present stage generally takes the form of three-level ownership with the production team at the basic level, that is, ownership by the commune, the production brigade and the production team, with the last as the basic accounting unit.

Provided that the development and absolute predominance of the collective economy of the people's commune are ensured, people's commune members may farm small plots for their personal needs, engage in limited household side-line production, and in pastoral areas keep a small number of livestock for their personal needs.

ARTICLE 8

Socialist public property shall be inviolable. The state shall ensure the consolidation and development of the socialist economy and prohibit any person from undermining the socialist economy and the public interest in any way whatsoever.

ARTICLE 9

The state applies the socialist principle : "He who does not work, neither shall he eat" and "from each according to his ability, to each according to his work."

The state protects the citizens right of ownership of their income from work, their savings, their houses, and other means of livelihood.

ARTICLE 10

The state applies the principle of grasping revolution, promoting production and other work and preparedness against war; promotes the planned and proportionate development of the socialist economy, taking agriculture as the foundation and industry as the leading factor and bringing the initiative of both the central and the local authorities into full play; and improves the people's material and cultural life step by step on the basis of the constant growth of social production and consolidates the independence and security of the country.

ARTICLE 11

State organizations and state personnel must earnestly study Marxism-Leninism-Mao Tse-tung Thought, firmly put proletarian politics in command, combat bureaucracy, maintain close ties with the masses and wholeheartedly serve the people. Cadres at all levels must participate in collective productive labour.

Every organ of state must apply the principle of efficient and simple administration. Its leading body must be a three-in-one combination of the old, the middle-aged and the young.

ACTICLE 12

The proletariat must exercise all-round dictatorship over the bourgeoisie in the superstructure, including all spheres of culture. Culture and education, literature and art, physical education, health work and scientific research work must all serve proletarian politics, serve the workers, peasants and soldiers, and be combined with productive labour.

ARTICLE 13

Speaking out freely, airing views fully, holding great debates and writing big-character posters are new forms of carrying on socialist revolution created by the masses of the people. The state shall ensure to the masses the right to use these forms to create a political situation in which there are both central-ism and democracy, both discipline and freedom, both unity of will and personal ease of mind and liveliness, and so help consolidate the leadership of the Communist Party of China over the state and consolidate the dictatorship of the prolet-ariat.

ARTICLE 14

The state safeguards the socialist system, suppresses all treasonable and counter-revolutionary activities and punishes all traitors and counter-revolutionaries.

The state deprives the landlords, rich peasants, reactionary capitalists and other bad elements of political rights for speci-fied periods of time according to law, and at the same time provides them with the opportunity to earn a living so that they may be reformed through labour and become law-abiding citizens supporting themselves by their own labour.

ARTICLE 15

The Chinese People's Liberation Army and the people's militia are the worker's and peasant's own armed forces led by the Communist Party of China; they are the armed forces of the people of all nationalities.

The Chairman of the Central Committee of the Communist Party of China commands the country's armed forces.

The Chinese People's Liberation Army is at all times a fighting force, and simultaneously a working force and a production force.

The task of the armed forces of the People's Republic of China is to safeguard the achievements of the socialist revolution and socialist construction, to defend the sovereignty, territorial integrity and security of the state, and to guard against subversion and aggression by imperialism, social-imperialism and their lackeys.

CHAPTER TWO

THE STRUCTURE OF THE STATE

Section 1. The National People's Congress

ARTICLE 16

The National People's Congress is the highest organ of state power under the leadership of the Communist Party of China.

The National People's Congress is composed of deputies elected by the provinces, autonomous regions, municipalities directly under the central government, and the People's Liberation Army. When necessary, a certain number of patriotic personages may be specially invited to take part as deputies.

The National People's Congress is elected for a term of five years. Its term of office may be extended under special circumstances.

The National People's Congress holds one session each year. When necessary, the session may be advanced or postponed.

ARTICLE 17

The functions and powers of the National People's Congress are : to amend the Constitution, make laws, appoint and remove the Premier of the State Council and the members of the State Council on the proposal of the Central Committee of the Communist Party of China, approve the national economic plan, the state budget and the final state accounts, and exercise such other functions and powers as the National People's Congress deems necessary.

ARTICLE 18

The Standing Committee of the National People's Congress is the permanent organ of the National People's Congress. Its functions and powers are : to convene the sessions of the National People's Congress, interpret laws, enact decrees, dispatch and recall plenipotentiary representatives abroad, receive foreign diplomatic envoys, ratify and denounce treaties concluded with foreign states, and exercise such other functions and powers as are vested in it by the National People's Congress.

The Standing Committee of the National People's Congress is composed of the Chairman, the Vice-Chairmen and other members, all of whom are elected and subject to recall by the National People's Congress.

Section II. The State Council

ARTICLE 19

The State Council is the Central People's Government. The State Council is responsible and accountable to the National People's Congress and its Standing Committee.

The State Council is composed of the Premier, the Vice-Premiers, the ministers, and the ministers heading commissions.

ARTICLE 20

The functions and powers of the State Council are : to formulate administrative measures and issue decisions and orders in accordance with the Constitution, laws and decrees; exercise unified leadership over the work of ministeries and commissions and local organs of state at various levels throughout the country; draft and implement the national economic plan and the state budget; direct state administrative affairs; and exercise such other functions and powers as are vested in it by the National People's Congress or its Standing Committee.

Section III. The Local People's Congreses And the Local Revolutionary Committees at Various Levels

ARTICLE 21

The local people's congresses at various levels are the local organs of state power.

The people's congresses of provinces and municipalities directly under the central government are elected for a term of five years. The people's congresses of prefectures, cities and counties are elected for a term of three years. The people's congresses of rural people's communes and towns are elected for a term of two years.

ARTICLE 22

The local revolutionary committees at various levels are the permanent organs of the local people's congresses and at the same time the local people's governments at various levels.

Local revolutionary committees are composed of a chairman, vice-chairmen and other members, who are elected and subject to recall by the people's congress at the corresponding level. Their election or recall shall be submitted for examination and approval to the organ of state at the next higher level.

Local revolutionary committees are responsible and accountable to the people's congress at the corresponding level and to the organ of state at the next higher level.

ARTICLE 23

The local people's congresses at various levels and the local revolutionary committees elected by them ensure the execution of laws and decrees in their respective areas; lead the socialist revolution and socialist construction in their respective areas; examine and approve local economic plans, budgets and final accounts : maintain revolutionary order; and safeguard the rights of citizens.

Section IV.   The Organs of Self-Government of National Autonomous Areas

ARTICLE 24

The autonomous regions, autonomous prefectures and autonomous counties are all national autonomous areas; their organs of self-government are people's congresses and revolutionary committees.

The organs of self-government of national autonomous areas, apart from exercising the functions and powers of local organs of state as specified in Chapter Two, Section III of the Constitution, may exercise autonomy within the limits of their authority as prescribed by law.

The higher organs of state fully safeguard the exercise of autonomy by the organs of self-government of national autonomous areas and actively support the minority nationalities in carrying out the socialist revolution and socialist construction.

Section V.   The Judicial Organs and the Procuratorial Organs

ARTICLE 25

The Supreme People's Court, local people's courts at various levels and special people's courts exercise judicial authority. The people's courts are responsible and accountable to the people's congresses and their permanent organs at the corresponding levels. The presidents of the people's courts are appointed and subject to removal by the permanent organs of the people's congresses at the corresponding levels.

The functions and powers of procuratorial organs are exercised by the organs of public security at various levels.

The mass line must be applied in procuratorial work and in trying cases. In major counter-revolutionary criminal cases the masses should be mobilized for discussion and criticism.

CHAPTER THREE

The Fundamental Rights and Duties of Citizens

ARTICLE 26

The fundamental rights and duties of citizens are to support the leadership of the Communist Party of China, support the socialist system and abide by the Constitution and the laws of the People's Republic of China.

It is the lofty duty of every citizen to defend the motherland and resist aggression. It is the honourable obligation of citizens to perform military service according to law.

ARTICLE 27

All citizens who have reached the age of eighteen have the right to vote and stand for election, with the exception of persons deprived of these rights by law.

Citizens have the right to work and the right to education. Working people have the right to rest and the right to material assistance in old age and in case of illness or disability.

Citizens have the right to lodge to organs of state at any level written or oral complaints of transgression of law or neglect of duty on the part of any person working in an organ of state. No one shall attempt to hinder or obstruct the making of such complaints or retaliate.

Women enjoy equal rights with men in all respects.

The state protects marriage, the family, and the mother and child.

The state protects the just rights and interests of overseas Chinese.

ARTICLE 28

Citizens enjoy freedom of speech, correspondence, the press assembly, association, procession, demonstration and the freedom to strike, and enjoy freedom to believe in religion and freedom not to believe in religion and to propagate atheism.

The citizens' freedom of person and their homes shall be inviolable. No citizen may be arrested except by decision of a people's court or with the sanction of a public security organ.

ARTICLE 29

The People's Republic of China grants the right of residence to any foreign national persecuted for supporting a just cause, for taking part in revolutionary movements or for engaging in scientific activities.

CHAPTER FOUR

The National Flag, The National Emblem and the Capital

ARTICLE 30

The national flag has five stars on a field of red.

The national emblem : Tien An Men in the centre, illuminated by five stars and encircled by ears of grain and a cogwheel.

The capital is Peking.

APPENDIX 11

A Comparative Study of the 1954 and 1975 Constitutions

In presenting his report on the revision of the Constitution to the First Session of the Fourth National People's Congress on 13 January 1975, Chang Chun-chiao claimed that the new Constitution of the People's Republic of China (PRC) was "the continuation and development of the 1954 constitution" and that "its basic principles are still applicable today." A Soviet commentary on the new Constitution of China, published in *Pravda* on 5 February 1975, on the other hand, asserts that the 1975 Constitution of the PRC "is not a modified variant of the old Constitution, as is claimed in (Chang Chun-chiao's) report" but "an entirely new Constitution, in which the principles of the 1954 Constitution have been radically changed." According to the Soviet commentator I. Alexandrov, the 1954 Constitution was replaced by a new one because the old one had become a hindrance to the "anti-people, anti-socialist policies of the dictatorship of the military-bureaucratic group of the Mao Tse-tung." Proceeding from the basic assumption that the Constitution of a country was "a mirror reflecting the social reality of that country" and judging the new Chinese Constitution in that light, the Soviet commentator comes to the conclusion that the Chinese society, "far from moving forward, has in many respects slided back through the fault of the Maoist leadership." The new PRC Constitution, he observes, "orients the development of China in a direction which has already inflicted heavy damage on the great Chinese people and which has led to a serious distortion of socialism in that country."

A dispassionate study of the two Chinese Constitutions, devoid of polemics, reveals certain very interesting features of the 1975 Constitution of the People's Republic of China, which undoubtedly deserve our attention. At places there appears a close similarity in the format and language of the two Constitutions—both of which are divided into a preamble and four chapters of the same description although one whole section in Chapter Two dealing with the office of the Chairman of State (which is now abolished) is omitted in the 1975 Constitution. At the same time, there are many changes, including some significant additions, in the new Constitution. The brevity of the new Constitution, is apparent from the fact that it consists of only 30 as against 106 articles in the old Constitution. The compactness of the new document appears to be the result of a deliberate policy and reflects a delicate compromise between the moderates and the radicals—the two contending groups within the top Chinese leadership.

Preamble

Like the old Constitution, the preamble of the new Constitution is an appraisal of the past and present domestic situation and a confirmation of existing domestic and foreign policies. Even Chang Chun-chiao conceded in his report on the revision of the Constitution, that the preamble in the 1975 Constitution had been written anew. It confirms the victory of the Cultural Revolution and calls for strict adherence to the basic policies and programmes of the Chinese Communist Party. The theory of continued revolution is sanctified and "Marxism-Leninism-Mao Tse-tung Thought" is given much prominence. Great stress is laid on the continuity of the class struggle throughout the entire historical period of socialism and opposition to hegemonism of the super Powers. China, the preamble declares, will uphold "proletarian internationalism" and will "never be a super Power." The phrases "dictatorship of the proletariat" and the "leadership of the Communist Party of China" are repeated five times and three times respectively in the preamble alone. In the 1954 Constitution, on the other hand, the concepts of people's democratic dictatorship, a broad people's democratic united front, the noble aims of peace, and indestructible friendship with the Soviet Union and People's Democracies were given much prominence. However, these concepts find no place in the new Constitution.

Chapter One : General Principles

Under Article I of the new Constitution, the "people's democratic state" of the 1954 Constitution has now become "a socialist state of the dictatorship of the proletariat." Article 2 is a significant addition. It speaks of the Chinese Communist Party as "the core of the leadership of the whole Chinese people" while the working class is stated to be exercising its leadership over the state through its vanguard—the CCP. Moreover, Marxism-Leninism-Mao Tse-tung Thought is declared to be "the theoretical basis guiding the thinking of our nation." In the old Constitution, there was no mention of either the CCP or of any guide to people's thinking.

While both the 1954 and 1975 Constitutions emphasize the equality of all nationalities, the sentence prohibiting "discrimination against, or oppression of, any nationality" is omitted in the present Constitution. Instead, it speaks of opposing both "big nationality chauvinism and local nationality chauvinism." Also missing in the new Constitution are provisions about the capitalist ownership of the means of production. However, by permitting cultivation of small plots for personal use and "limited side-line production," the 1975 Constitution takes care of the moderate (pragmatist) group's viewpoint as regards economic development. The principle "From Each According to his Ability to Each According to his Work," enshrined in the new Constitution, also reflected a pragmatic approach. However, it must not be forgotten that the use of the methods of the "Cultural Revolution" had not been completely given up. Thus, the right to hold extensive discussions and put up "big-character posters" (*Tatzupaos*) is protected in Article 13. Stress is also laid on "proletarian politics" and the need to study Marxism-Leninism-Mao Tse-tung Thought.

One of the most significant changes introduced in the new Constitution is the abolition of the post of Chairman of State, who was also Commander-in-Chief of the Chinese armed forces. The 1975 Constitution declares the Chairman of the Party Central Committee to be the Supreme Commander of the PLA, thereby openly affirming Party supremacy over the army. In accordance with Maoist military thinking, the PLA is stated to be a fighting force as well as a working force and a production force. Moreover, as compared with the 1954 Constitution, the new Constitution increased the sphere of the PLA's activities so as to "guard against subversion and aggression by imperialism, social-imperialism and their lackeys."

Chapter Two : The Structure of the State

As stated earlier, Chapter Two of the 1975 Constitution omits the entire section dealing with the election and duties of the Chairman of State. The second most significant feature of the new Constitution is that it places the National People's Congress—the highest organ of State Power—under the leadership of the Communist Party of China. The state apparatus is thus subordinated to the Party leadership. The powers and functions of the NPC, its Standing Committee, and the State Council (the Council of Ministers) have been reduced from 18, 19 and 17 specific duties, listed for each of these bodies in the 1954 Constitution, to six, five and four respectively in 1975 Constitution. Under the new Constitution, the NPC appoints and dismisses the members of the State Council, including the Prime Minister, "on the proposal of the Central Committee of the Communist Party of China." Thus, Party control over the State organs is formally asserted. The NPC no longer exercises control over the implementation or the enforcement of the provisions of the Constitution. It is also shorn of its power to decide questions of war and peace, general amnesties and changes in the state system, *i.e.* the status and boundaries of the provinces, autonomous regions and municipalities directly under the Central authority. An amendment of the Constitution, which under the 1954 Constitution required a 2/3 majority, can now be effected by a simple majority. Under the old Constitution, the NPC term of 4 years could be extended only in "exceptional circumstances," but the new Constitution allows the extension of its five-year term under "special circumstances" —a weak phraseology indeed.

The new Constitution contains no specific provision about a system of elections or electoral law as such although it speaks of deputies being "elected." Moreover, "when necessary", a certain number of patriotic personages could be "specially invited to take part as deputies" (Article 16). The local Revolutionary Committees at various levels are stated to be the permanent organs of the local People's Congresses. They have thus officially replaced the People's Councils which existed before the Cultural Revolution.

The new Constitution sanctifies the Cultural Revolution practice of public trials as it speaks of the "mass line" being applied in procuratorial work and in trying cases. It abolishes the peoples procuratorates and stipulates that "the functions and powers of procuratorial organs are exercised by the organs of public security at various levels." The latter are given considerable powers in matters of arrest and prosecution. Under the old Constitution, no citizen could be arrested without the permission of the local people's courts or of the people's procuratorates, which were responsible to local people's congresses at corresponding levels and exercised independent power in prosecuting officials or citizens free from the interference of local state organs.

Chapter Three : Fundamental Rights and Duties of Citizens

In this Chapter, there are some significant additions as well as omissions. The new Constitution makes it one of the fundamental rights and duties of citizens "to support the leadership of the Communist Party of China." (Article 26). The citizens are given two new freedoms—the freedom to propagate atheism and the freedom to strike, which, as Chang Chun-chiao stated in his report, had been included on the suggestion of Chairman Mao. Although the circumstances in which strikes could be permitted are not mentioned, but the very fact that permission has been given to workers to engage in "rebellious behaviour" is in itself significant and is bound to strengthen the hands of the radical left against the bureaucracy entrenched in power.

Among the significant omissions are the clauses relating to equality of citizens before the law; the provision about the state ensuring civic freedom "by providing the necessary material facilities" or conditions; the freedom of residence and change therein; and the legal protection in regard to the "privacy of correspondence." Moreover, unlike the 1954 Constitution, the clause on the right to work in the new Constitution contains no guarantee about ensuring that right "by planned development of the national economy" and gradually creating more employ-ment and better working conditions and wages. Similarly, the right to rest does not contain the previous commitment about the State prescribing "working hours and holidays for workers and office employees" and gradually expanding material faci-lities to enable working people to rest and build up their health. The right to material assistance in old age and in case of illness or disability is no longer accompanied by the guarantee that the State will provide "social insurance, social assistance and public health services" and gradually expand these facilities. Finally, the right to education in the 1975 Constitution is no longer supported by the statement that the State would estab-lish and gradually expand "the various types of schools and other cultural and educational institutions."

Both the 1954 and 1975 Constitutions contain a specific reference to the protection of the proper or just rights and inte-rests of the overseas Chinese. This provision affords ample opportunity to Peking to interfere in the internal affairs of countries, which have a large Chinese population. In place of "asylum", the word "residence" is now preferred in the new Constitution and this right is granted to those foreign nationals who are persecuted for supporting a just cause, for taking part in "revolutionary movements," (the 1954 Constitution used the phrase "peace movement") or for engaging in scientific acti-vities. This provision could also be misused by the Chinese authorities.

Chapter Four : National Flag, Emblem and Capital

The provisions of this chapter are the same as in the old Constitution, but they are summarized in one article.

Conclusions

The new Constitution consecrates the developments that have taken place both in the internal politics of China and its foreign policy. It represents a compromise between the two contending groups in the top leadership—the moderates and the radicals. It also reflects the present emphasis in Chinese politics on the Party leadership over all sectors of society.

Evidently, the framers of the 1975 Constitution were haunted by the ghosts of Liu Shao-chi and Lin Piao. They did not want any person occupying the post of Head of State or commander of the armed forces to ever be in a position to challenge the authority of the Party leadership at the Centre.

APPENDIX 12

Continuity and Change in the Party Central Committee, 1945-75

The 7th Central Committee had 44 regular and 33 alternate members. Of this total of 77 members, 64 (37 regular and 27 alternate members) were included among the 97 regular members of the 8th CC, and 3 among the 73 alternate members of the 8th CC. 23 regular members of the 7th CC, were regular members of the 8th CC, 9th CC, and 10th CC as well. (See Table 15)

Of the 97 regular members of the 8th CC, 35 were included in the 9th CC. Of these 35, 24 were included as regular members in both 9th and 10th CC (See Table 15), one (Teng Hua) was included as an alternate member in both the 9th and 10th CC. The remaining 10 (Chen Po-ta, Chen Yi, Cheng Wei-shan, Hsieh Fu-chih, Hsu-Hai-tung, Li Hsueh-feng, Lin Piao, Liu Ko-ping, Teng Tzu-hui and Wang En-mao) continued as members of 9th CC (the first 9 as regular members while the last one as an alternate) but they were not included in the 10th CC. Eight regular members of the 8th CC (Chien Cheng-ying (f), Li Ching-chuan, Li Pao-hua, Liao Cheng-chih, Tan Chen-lin, Teng Hsiao-ping, Ulanfu and Wang Chia-hsiang) were excluded from the 9th CC, but were included in in the 10th CC as regular members. The following 54 regular members of the 8th CC were included neither in the 9th CC nor in the 10th CC:

An Tzu-wen	Hsi Chung-hsun	Li K'o-nung
Chang Chi-ch'un	Hsiao Hua	Li Li-san
Chang Wen-t'ien	Hsiao K'o	Li Wei-han
Chao Erh-lu	Hsu Kuang-ta	Lin Feng
Ch'en Shao-min (f)	Hsu T'eh-li	Lin Po-ch'u
Ch'en Shao-yu	Hu Ch'iao-mu	Lin T'ieh
Ch'eng Tzu-hua	Hu Yao-pang	Liu Ch'ang-sheng
Chia T'o-fu	Huang K'o-ch'eng	Liu Hsiao
Ho Lung	K'o Ch'ing-shih	Liu Lan-t'ao

Liu Ning-yi	P'eng Chen	Wang Ts'ung-wu
Liu Shao-ch'i	P'eng Teh-huai	Wang Wei-chou
Liu Ya-lou	Po I-po	Wu Chih-p'u
Lo Jui-ch'ing	Shu T'ung	Wu Hsiu-chuan
Lo Jung-huan	Sung Jen-ch'iung	Wu Yu-chang
Lu Ting-yi	T'an Cheng	Yang Hsien-chen
Lu Cheng-tsao	T'ao Chu	Yang Hsiu-feng
Ma Ming-fang	T'eng Tai-yuan	Yang Shang-k'un
Ou yang Ch'in	Tseng Hsi-sheng	Yeh Chi-chuang

Of the 98 alternate members of the 8th CC (73 elected in September 1956 plus 25 elected in 1958), 20 were included in the 9th CC. Of these twenty, 13 (Chang Ta-chih, Chen Chi-han, Chen Hsi-lien, Han Hsien-chu, Hsu Shih-yu, Li Ta-chang, Liu Chien-hsun, Liu Tzu-hou, Saifudin, Sang-chi-yueh-hsi (Tien Pao), Wei Kuo-ching, Wu Teh, Yang Teh-chih) were included as regular members of both 9th CC and 10th CC; one (Tang Liang) was included as an alternate member of both 9th CC and 10th CC; while two (Fang Yi and Tan Chi-lung) were alternate members of the 9th CC but regular members of the 10th CC. The remaining 4 (Fan Wen-lan, Huang Yung-sheng, Pan Fu-sheng, and Wang En-mao) continued as members of the 9th CC (the first three as regular members while the last one as an alternate) but they were not included in the 10th CC. Thirteen alternate members of the 8th CC were excluded from the 9th CC but they were included in the 10th CC—7 of them (Chang Ping-hua, Chang Tsai-chien, Liao Chih-kao, Su Chen-hua, Li Chih-min, Tao Lu-chia and Yang Yung) as regular members and 6 (Chang Lin-chih, Chiang Hua, Chiang Wei-ching, Sung Shih-lun, Yao Yi-lin, and Yeh Fei) as alternate members. Sixty-five alternate members of the 8th CC were included neither in the 9th CC nor in the 10th CC.

Of the 170 regular members of the 9th CC, 122 were included as regular members in the 10th CC, (See Table 15) while 2 (Shen Mao-kung and Yang Fu-chen) became alternate members in the 10th CC. The remaining 46 were dropped in the 10th CC. Their names are:

Chang Kuo-hua	Chiu Kuo-kuang	Lai Chi-fa
Chang Tien-yun	Chou Chih-ping	Li Hsueh-feng
Chen Po-ta	Fan Wen-lan	Li Ssu-kuang
Chen Yi	Hsieh Fu chih	Li Tien-yu
Cheng Shih-ching	Hsu Hai-tung	Li Tso-peng
Cheng Wei-shan	Huang Yung-sheng	Liang Hsing-chu
Chiu Chuang-cheng	Kao Wei-sung	Lin Piao
Chiu Hui-tso	Kuang Jen-nung	Liu Chieh-ting

Liu Feng	Teng Tzu-hui	Wang Ping-chang
Liu Ko-ping	Tseng Kuo-hua	Wen Yu-cheng
Lung Shu-chin	Tseng Shan	Wu Fa-hsien
Ma Fu-chuan	Wang Chin-hsi	Wu Jui-lin
Nan Ping	Wang Hsiao-yu	Yeh Chun(f)
Pan Fu-sheng	Wang Hsin-ting	Yuan Sheng-ping
Tan Fu-jen	Wang Hui-chiu	
Teng Hai-ching	Wang Pai-tan	

Of the 109 alternate members of the 9th CC, 18 (Chang Yen-cheng, Chiao Lin-yi, Chin Tsu-min Fan Teh-ling, Fang Yi, Fu Chuan-tso, Han Ying, Hua Lin-sen, Keng Chi-chang, Kuo Hung-chieh, Kuo Yu-feng, Liang Chin-tang, Lo Hsi-kang, Ma Tien-shui, Tan Chi-lung Tsen Kuo-jung, Tsui Hai-lung, and Yu Tai-chung) were promoted as regular members of the 10th CC; while 62 continued as alternate members of the 10th CC (See Table 15). The remaining 29 alternate members of the 9th CC, who were not included in the 10th CC (either as regular or alternate members), were the following :

Chang Hsi-ting,	I Yao-tsai	Shu Chi-cheng
Chang Hsiu-chuan	Lan I-nung	Tseng Yung-ya
Chang Jih-ching	Lan Jung-yu	Wang En-mao
Chao Chi-min	Li Li	Wang Hsin
Chen Hua-tang	Li Shu-mao	Wang Wei-kuo
Chen Jen-chi	Li Tsai-han	Wei Tsu-chen
Chen Kan-feng	Li Yueh-sung	Wu Chun-jen
Chen Li-yun	Liu Hao-tien	Yang Huan-min
Fang Ming	Lo Yuan-fa	Yeh Chung-chuan
Huang Chih-yung	Nieh Yuan-tzu	

The ranking of the top ranking Party leaders (members of the Standing Committee of the Politburo or other members of the Politburo) had not been uniform in the various Central Committees. While Mao had throughout maintained his first position from 7th to 10th CC, Chu Teh's position has continuously declined from 2nd place in the 6th CC and the 7th CC to 5th place in the 8th CC, 6th in the 9th CC and 8th in the 10th CC. Chou En-lai, on the other hand, made a spectacular rise from the 24th place in the 6th CC to 4th place in the 7th CC, fell to 6th place in the 8th CC to rise again to 3rd place in the 9th CC and 2nd in the 10th CC. The ranking of other Politburo members had been quite irregular. For instance, Kang Sheng fell from 17th place in 6th CC to 18th in the 7th and 49th in 8th CC but rose to 5th place in the 9th CC and 4th in the 10th CC. Tung Pi-wu enjoyed 7th position in the 7th, 8th and 9th CC but 10th in the 10th CC. Yeh Chien-ying had 33rd place in 6th CC, 31st in 7th CC, 43rd in 8th CC, 9th in 9th CC and 5th in 10th CC. Liu Po-cheng was ranked 26th in 6th CC, 24th in the 7th, 20th in the 8th CC, 8th in the 9th CC, and 11th in the 10th CC. Teng Hsiao-ping rose from 30th place in 6th CC to 28th in 7th CC and 4th in the 8th CC but was excluded completely from the 9th CC. He was subsequently rehabilitated and included in the 10th CC. In January 1975, he was elevated to the position of Vice-Chairman of the Party Central Committee and Member of the Politburo Standing Committee. A correct estimate of the precise ranking of all the members of the 9th and 10th Central Committees is not possible because their names are listed in official Chinese news media in the order of the number of strokes in their surnames rather than in the order of their ranking in the Party. It seems that the recent practice of writing names in the order of the number of strokes has been adopted because there is no consensus about the ranking or seniority of members in the Party hierarchy among the various groupings.

Tables and Charts

TABLE 1

Party, Army and Governmental Structure of China, 1950-54

CHINESE COMMUNIST PARTY (CCP)

CENTRAL COMMITTEE OF CCP
44 members—meets twice a year

POLITBURO
13 Members
(Always in session)

| TENTACLES OF MILITARY CONTROL | | WEB OF CIVILIAN CONTROL |

People's Revolutionary Military Council (22 members)

State Administrative Council

General HQ of PLA

Judiciary, Finance, Communications, Trade, etc.

FIELD ARMIES   MILITARY REGIONS   SIX ADMINISTRATIVE REGIONS

First Field Army——	Northwest——	1. Northwest
Second Field Army—	South————	2. Southwest
Third Field Army—	East————	3. East China
Fourth Field Army—	Central-South—	4. Central-South
Fifth Field Army—	North———	5. North
Misc. PLA Units—	Northeast———	6. North East (Manchuria)
Mongol Military units—	Mongolian——	Inner Mongolian Auton. Region
PLA units in Tibet	Tibet	Tibet (Internal Autonomy)

Note: Each Field Army commander also commanded the Military Region.   Since he was also Chairman of the Military and Administrative (Political) Committee (for each region), he ruled all three.   Thus the military officers dominated in the control of the regions and provinces.

TABLE 2

Military Dominance over Regional Administrations, 1950-54

Field Armies	Military Regions	Regional Governments
1st FA Cdr : P'eng Teh-huai Pol. Csr : Hsi Chung-hsun	North-west MR Cdr : P'eng Teh-huai Pol. Csr : Hsi Chung-hsun	North-west MAC/AC Chm : P'eng Teh-huai Vc Chm : Hsi Chung-hsun & others
2nd FA Cdr : Liu Po-ch'eng Pol. Csr : Teng Hsiao-p'ing	South-west MR Cdr : Ho Lung Pol. Csr : Teng Hsiao-p'ing	South-west MAC/AC Chm : Liu Po-ch'eng Vc Chm : Teng Hsiao-p'ing, Ho Lung & others
3rd FA Cdr : Ch'en Yi Pol. Csr. Jao Shu-shih	East China MR Cdr : Ch'en Yi Pol. Csr. Jao Shu-shih	East China MAC/AC Chm : Jao Shu-shih Vc Chm : Su Yu & others
4th FA Cdr : Lin Piao Pol. Csr : Lo Jung-huan	Central-south MR Cdr : Yeh Chien-ying Pol. Csr : Lo Jung-huan	Central-south MAC/AC Chm : Lin Piao Vc Chm : Yeh Chien-ying & others
North China or 5th FA—direct army groups under control of the PLA GHQ, Peking Cdr : Nieh Jung-chen Pol. Csr : Po I-po	North China MR Cdr : Nieh Jung-chen Pol. Csr : Po I-po	North China AC Chm : Liu Lan-tao Vc Chm : Chang Su & others
North-east China garrisoned by units of 4th Field Army	North-east MR Cdr : Kao Kang Pol. Csr : Kao Kang	North-east People's Government/AC Chm : Kao Kang Vc Chm : Lin Feng, Kao Chung-min & others

Note : From 1949 to 1954 regional governments existed at an administrative level between the central government and the provinces. These were known as Military and Administrative Committees (MAC) to the turn of the year 1952-53 and as Administrative Committees (AC) thereafter. North China AC was under the Government Administration Council till Feb 1953 when it was recognized as a regional government.

TABLE 3

Five Field Armies During the People's Liberation Army Period, 1946-68

1946-54	1955-68 Military Regions
Ist Field Army (Northwest China M.R.)	Sinkiang Lanchow Chengtu
2nd Field Army (Central China M.R.)	Wuhan Tibet Kunming Chengtu
3rd Field Army (East China M.R.)	Nanking Foochow Tsinan
4th Field Army (Manchuria M.R.)	Shenyang Canton
North China or 5th Field Army (North China M.R.)	Tsinan Inner Mongolia Peking

TABLE 4

**Military Regions and the Dominant Field Army System,
1955-66**

Military Region	Dominant Field Army System
Mukden	4th Field Army
Canton	4th Field Army
Peking	5th Field Army
Tsinan	3rd & 5th Field Armies shared control
Nanking	3rd Field Army
Foochow	3rd Field Army
Wuhan	2nd Field Army
Chengtu	1st & 2nd Field Armies shared control
Kunming	2nd Field Army
Tibet	2nd Field Army
Lanchow	1st Field Army
Sinkiang	1st Field Army
Inner Mongolia	1st & 5th Field Armies shared control

TABLE 5

Military Regions and Provinces Ranked by Industrial Capacity

Military Regions	Percent of Total Industrial Capacity	Province	Percent of Total Industrial Capacity
Nanking	38	Kiangsu	34
		Anhwei	3
		Chekiang	1
Peking	18	Hopeh	11
		Inner Mongolia	4
		Shansi	3
Shenyang	12	Liaoning	9
		Kirin	2
		Heilungkiang	1
Wuhan	7	Hupeh	5
		Honan	2
Canton	7	Kwangtung	4
		Hunan	2
		Kwangsi	1
Chengtu	6	Szechwan	6
		Tibet	—
Foochow	4	Kiangsi	4
		Fukien	—
Lanchow	3.2	Kansu	2
		Shensi	1
		Ninghsia	0.1
		Chinghai	0.1
Tsinan	3	Shantung	3
Kunming	1	Yunnan	0.7
		Kweichow	0.2
Sinkiang	1	Sinkiang	1

Note : About 75% of all conventional weapons are produced in four
military regions, the traditional industrial regions of Nanking,
Peking, Shenyang and Wuhan.

TABLE 6

Military Regions and Military Districts

Military Regions	Military Districts
Canton	Hunan Kwangsi Kwangtung
Chengtu	Szechuan Tibet
Foochow	Fukien Kiangsi
Kunming	Kweichow Yunnan
Lanchow	Chinghai Kansu Ninghsia Shensi
Nanking	Anhwei Chekiang Kiangsu
Peking	Hopeh Inner Mongolia Shansi
Shenyang	Heilungkiang Kirin Liaoning
Sinkiang	—
Tsinan	Shantung
Wuhan	Honan Hupeh

TABLE 7

Political Control Structure of the PLA

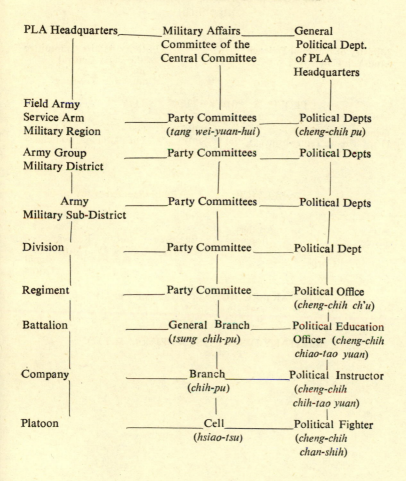

PLA Headquarters	Military Affairs Committee of the Central Committee	General Political Dept. of PLA Headquarters
Field Army Service Arm Military Region	Party Committees (*tang wei-yuan-hui*)	Political Depts (*cheng-chih pu*)
Army Group Military District	Party Committees	Political Depts
Army Military Sub-District	Party Committees	Political Depts
Division	Party Committee	Political Dept
Regiment	Party Committee	Political Office (*cheng-chih ch'u*)
Battalion	General Branch (*tsung chih-pu*)	Political Education Officer (*cheng-chih chiao-tao yuan*)
Company	Branch (*chih-pu*)	Political Instructor (*cheng-chih chih-tao yuan*)
Platoon	Cell (*hsiao-tsu*)	Political Fighter (*cheng-chih chan-shih*)

TABLE 8

Military Organization of China, January 1975
(Simplified)

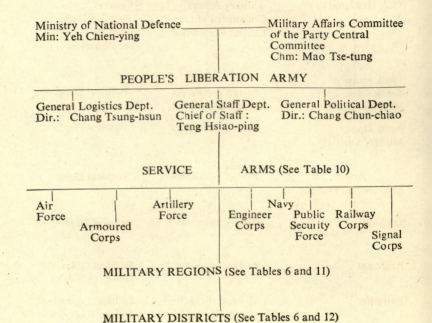

Ministry of National Defence———————Military Affairs Committee
Min: Yeh Chien-ying   of the Party Central
                                                            Committee
                                                            Chm: Mao Tse-tung

PEOPLE'S LIBERATION ARMY

General Logistics Dept.   General Staff Dept.   General Political Dept.
Dir.: Chang Tsung-hsun   Chief of Staff :   Dir.: Chang Chun-chiao
                                         Teng Hsiao-ping

SERVICE   ARMS (See Table 10)

Air   Artillery   Navy
Force   Force   Engineer Public Railway
              Armoured   Corps   Security Corps
              Corps   Force   Signal
                                                                            Corps

MILITARY REGIONS (See Tables 6 and 11)

MILITARY DISTRICTS (See Tables 6 and 12)

TABLE 9

Top Central Military Leadership, 1949-75

People's Revolutionary Military Council (1949-54)[1]

Chairman : Mao Tse-tung
Vice Chairmen (7) : Chu Teh (C-in-C)
                   Liu Shao-chi
                   Chou En-lai
                   Cheng Chien
                   Peng Teh-huai
                   Kao Kang
                   Lin Piao

Members (20) :

Chang Chih-chung	Liu Po-cheng
Chang Yun-yi	Lo Jui-ching
Chen Yi	Lung Yun
Fu Tso-yi	Nieh Jung-chen
Ho Lung	Sa Chen-ping
Hsi Chung-hsun	Su Yu
Hsu Hsiang-chien	Teng Hsiao-ping
Jao Shu-shih	Teng Tzu-hui
Li Hsien-nien	Tsai Ting-kai
Liu Fei	Yeh Chien-ying

National Defence Council, (1954-68)[2]

Chairman : Mao Tse-tung 1954-59
             Liu Shao-chi 1959-
Vice Chairmen :

Chang Chih-chung	1954-	Lo Jui-ching	1965-
Chen Yi	1954-	Lo Jung-huan	1954-63
Cheng Chien	1954-68	Lung Yun	1954-58
Chu Teh	1954-59	Nieh Jung-chen	1954-
Fu Tso-yi	1954-	Peng Teh-huai	1954-65
Ho Lung	1954-	Teng Hsiao-ping	1954-
Hsu Hsiang-chien	1954-	Tsai Ting-kai	1962-68
Lin Piao	1954-	Wei Li-huang	1959-60
Liu Po-cheng	1954-	Yeh Chien-ying	1954-

Military Affairs Committee of the Party Central Committee[3]
(at 1960-61) (sometimes referred to as Military Commission)

Chairman: ? Mao Tse-tung

Vice-Chairmen : Lin Piao
Ho Lung
Nieh Jung-chen
Members : Liu Po-ch'eng
Lo Jung-huan   d. Dec 63
Hsu Hsiang-chien
Yeh Chien-ying
Lo Jui-ch'ing
Hsiao Hua

Military Commission of the Party Central Committee (1971-72)

Chairman : Mao Tse-tung
Vice-Chairmen : Hsu Hsiang-chien
Nieh Jung-chen
Yeh Chien-ying
Members : Chang Ta-chih
Li Teh-sheng

Military Commission of the Party Central Committee, 1975

Chairman : Mao Tse-tung
Vice-Chairmen : Chou En-lai   probably
Wang Hung-wen   probably
Yeh Chien-ying
Teng Hsiao-ping   probably
Chang Chun-chiao   probably
Chen Hsi-lien   probably
Hsu Hsiang-chien
Nieh Jung-chen
Standing Member : Liu Po-cheng
Members : Su Yu
Li Teh-sheng
Chang Ta-chih

Ministers of Defence

Peng Teh-huai   Nov 54-Sep 59
Lin Piao   Sep 59-Sep 71
Yeh Chien-ying   Jan 75-

Chiefs of General Staff

Hsu Hsiang-chien   1949-1954
Su Yu   Nov 54-Oct 58

Huang K'o-ch'eng	Oct 58-Sep 59
Lo Jui-ch'ing	Sep 59-Nov 65
Yang-cheng-wu (Actg)	Aug 66-Mar 68
Huang Yung-sheng	Mar 68-Sep 71
Teng Hsiao-ping	Jan 75-

Directors of General Political Department

Lo Jung-huan	1950-Dec 56
T'an Cheng	Dec 56-1964
Lo Jung-huan (*de facto*)	1960-Dec 63
Hsiao Hua	Sep 64-1967
Li Teh-sheng	1969-Jan 75
Chang Chun-chiao	Jan 75-

Directors of Rear Services (Logistics) Department

Yang Li-san	1949-1954
Huang K'o-ch'eng	Nov 54-Dec 56
Hung Hsueh-chih	Dec 56-Oct 59
Ch'iu Hui-tso	Oct 59-Sep 71
Chang Tsung-hsun	Jan 75-

First Political Commissars of Logistics Department

Yu Ch'iu-li	1954-Feb 58
Li Chu-kuei	Feb 58-Mar 67
Chang Chih-ming	Jul 70-
Kuo Lin-hsiang	1974-

Notes :
1 It was the highest organ of military command of the State, exercising unified command and control over the PLA and other armed forces throughout the country.

2 It was a large body with 81 members in the first term (Sep 1954-Apr 1959), 99 members in second term (Apr 1959-Dec 1964), and 107 members in third term (Dec 1964-)—besides Chairman and 15 Vice-Chairmen. It had no direct control over the Ministry of Defence. Only its Chairman and Vice-Chairmen had power and influence.

3 As Secretary-General of the Party Central Committee, Teng Hsiao-ping was also probably a member of the MAC until he was disgraced. In 1967, Ho Lung, Hsu Hsiang-chien, Yeh Chien-ying and Lo Jui-ching were said to be replaced by Yang Cheng-wu, Hsiao Hua, Hsieh Fu-chih and Su Yu. In 1968, Hsiao Hua and Yang Cheng-wu were dropped and Huang Yung-sheng became a member of the MAC.

TABLE 10

Service Arms of Central Military Leadership, 1949-75

AIR FORCE

Cdr. :	Liu Ya-lou	1949-May 65
	Wu Fa-hsien	Sep 65-Sep 71
	Ma Ning	1974-
Pol. Csr. :	Wu Fa-hsien	1957-Sep 65
	Yu Li-chin	Sep 65-Mar 68
	Wang Hui-chiu	1968-1971

ARMOURED FORCE

Cdr. :	Hsu Kuang-ta	1951-Jan 67
Pol. Csr. :	Hsiang Chung-hua	Mar 58-1965
	Huang Chih-yung	1965-

ARTILLERY FORCE

Cdr. :	Ch'en Hsi-lien	1951-1959
	Chiu Chuang-cheng	? 1959-? 1963
	Wu K'o-hua	1965-Aug 67
	Chang Ta-chih	1969-
Pol. Csr. :	Ch'iu Chu'ang-ch'eng	1956-1961
	Chen Jen-chi	1961-?
	Yang Chih-sheng	1971-

ENGINEER CORPS

Cdr. :	Ch'en Shih-chu	Oct 52-
Pol. Csr. :	Huang Chih-yung	1958-1965
	Tan Fu-jen	? 1965-?
	Li Chen	Nov 69-

NAVY

Cdr. :	Hsiao Ching-kuang	Sep 50-
Pol. Csr. :	Su Chen-hua	Mar 57-Jan 67
	Li Tso-peng	Jun 67-Sep 71
	Su Chen-hua	1974-

PUBLIC SECURITY FORCE

Cdr. :	Lo Jui-ch'ing	1950-Sep 59
	Hsieh Fu-chih	1960-

Pol. Csr. :	Lo Jui-ching	Aug 53-Sep 59
	Hsieh Fu-chih	1960-

RAILWAY CORPS

Cdr. :	Teng Tai-yuan	1949-1954
	Wang Chen	Feb 54-1958
	Li Shou-hsuan	1958-Jun 68
	Chang Yi-hsiang	Jun 68-

Pol. Csr. :	Wang Chen	1954-1958
	Tsui Tien-min	? 1958-Aug 67

SIGNAL CORPS

Cdr. :	Wang Cheng	1957-
	Chiang Wen	?-?

Pol. Csr. :	Chu Ming	Mar 59-Dec 63
	Huang Wen-ming	Dec 63-

TABLE 11

Commanders and First Political Commissars of Military Regions, 1954-75

CANTON

Cdr. :	Huang Yung-sheng	1954-1958
	Li T'ien-yu	1958-1962
	Huang Yung-sheng	1962-Mar 68
	Ting Sheng (4th FA)	Mar 68-1973
	Hsu Shih-yu	1973-

Pol. Csr. :	T'ao Chu	1958-?
	Li T'ien-yu	?1962-?
	Liu Hsing-yuan	?-1971
	Jen Szu-chung	1971-?1973
	Wei Kuo-ching	Jan 74-

CHENGTU

Cdr. :	Ho Ping-yen	1954-d. Jul 60
	Huang Hsin-ting (2nd FA)	?-May 67
	Liang Hsing-chu (4th FA)	1967-1971
	Chin Chi-wei (2nd FA)	1971-

Pol. Csr. :	Kuo Lin-hsiang	1960-?
	Li Ching-ch'uan	Aug 65-May 67
	Chang Kuo-hua	May 67-d. Feb 72
	Yen Cheng	1971-?
	Liu Hsing-yuan	1974-

FOOCHOW

Cdr. :	Yeh Fei	1954-1960
	Han Hsien-chu	1960-1973
	Pi Ting-chun	1973-

Pol. Csr. :	Yeh Fei	1960-?
	Chou Chih-ping	?-1971
	Li Chih-min	1974-
	Liao Chih-kao	1974-

KUNMING

Cdr. :	Hsieh Fu-chih	1954-Oct 58
	Ch'in Ch'i-wei	Oct 58-?
	Wang Pi'cheng	1971-

Pol. Csr. :	Hsieh Fu-chih	1954-?
	Yen Hung-yen	?-1967

	Tan Fu-jen	1967-?
	Chou Hsing	1974-

LANCHOW

Cdr. :	Chang Ta-chih	1954-?
	Pi Ting-chun	1971-1973
	Han Hsien-chu	1973-
Pol. Csr. :	Hsien Heng-han	Dec 58-?
	Liu Lan-tao	?-Aug 67
	Hsien Heng-han	1967-

NANKING

Cdr. :	Hsu Shih-yu	1954-1973
	Ting Sheng	1973-
Pol. Csr. :	T'ang Liang	Jul 57-
	K'o Ching-shih	?-?
	Chiang Wei-ching	?-1968
	Chang Chun-chiao	1968-

PEKING

Cdr. :	Yang Ch'eng-wu	1954-Mar 59
	Yang Yung	Mar 59-1967
	Cheng Wei-shen	1967-1971
	Li Teh-sheng	1971-1973
	Chen Hsi-lien (2nd FA)	1973-
Pol. Csr. :	Chu Liang-ts'ai	Oct 55-
	Liao Han-sheng	?-1967
	Li Hsueh-feng	1967-1971
	Hsieh Fu-chih	1971-1972
	Chi Teng-kuei	1974-

SHENYANG

Cdr. :	Teng Hua	1954-1959
	Ch'en Hsi-lien	1959-1973
	Li Teh-sheng (2nd FA)	1973-
Pol, Csr. :	Chou Huan	1956-1959?
	Lai Ch'uan-chu	?1959-d. Dec 65
	Sung Jen-ch'iung	Dec 65-1968
	Tseng Shao-shan (2nd FA)	?-?

SINKIANG

Cdr. :	Wang En-mao (1st FA)	1954-1968
	Lung Shu-chin (4th FA)	1968-1971
	Yang Yung (2nd FA)	1971-
Pol. Csr. :	Wang En-mao	1954-1968

	Tsao Ssu-ming	? 1968-? 1974
	Sa'fudin	1974-

TSINAN

Cdr. :	Wang Hsin-t'ing	1954-Jul 58
	Yang Teh-chih	Jul 58-1973
	Tseng Ssu-yu	1973-

Pol. Csr. :	Shu T'ung	? 1958-?
	Wang Hsin-t'ing	1962-1964
	T'an Chi-lung	1964-1967
	Wang Hsiao-yu	1967-?
	Yuan Sheng-ping	?-1971
	Pai Ju-ping	1974-

WUHAN

Cdr. :	Ch'en Tsai-tao (2nd FA)	1954-Jul 67
	Tseng Ssu-yu (4th FA)	1967-1973
	Yang Teh-chih	1973-

Pol. Csr. :	Li Ch'eng-fang	1960-?
	Wang Jen-chung	?-1967
	Liu Feng	1967-1971
	Wang Liu-sheng	1971-

TABLE 12

Commanders and First Political Commissars of Military Districts, 1971-72 and 1974-75

Military District	Commander 1971-72	Commander 1974-75	First Political Commissar 1971-72	First Political Commissar 1974-75
Anhwei	Li Teh-sheng	Li Teh-sheng?	Liang Chi-ching Sung Pei-chang	—
Chekiang	Hsiung Ying-tang	?	Nan Ping	Tan Chi-lung
Chinghai	Chang Chiang-lin	Chang Chiang-lin	Sung Chang-keng	Sung Chang-keng
Fukien	Chu Yao-hua	Chu Yao-hua	Ni Nan-shan	Liao Chih-kao
Heilungkiang	Wang Chia-tao	Wang Chia-tao	Liu Kuang-tao*	
Honan	Chang Shu-chih	Chang Shu-chih	Liu Chien-hsun	Liu Chien-hsun
Hopeh	Ma Hui	Ma Hui	Tseng Mei	Tseng Mei
Hunan	Yang Ta-yi	Yang Ta-yi	Pu Chan-ya	Hua Kuo-feng
Hupeh	Hsin Chun-chieh	Hsin Chun-chieh	Chang Ti-hsueh	Chang Ti-hsueh ?
Inner Mongolia	—	Yu Tai-chung	Wu Tao	Wu Tao
Kansu	Chang Chung	Chang Chung	Lung Ping-chu	Lung Ping-chu ?
Kiangsi	Yang Tung-liang	Chen Chang-feng	Cheng Shih-ching	Cheng Shih-ching ?
Kiangsu	Huang Chao-tien	Huang Chao-tien	Wu Ta-sheng	Wu Ta-sheng
Kirin	Ho Yu-fa	Ho Yu-fa	Wang Huai-hsiang	Wang Huai-hsiang
Kwangsi	Chao Hsin-jan	Chao Hsin-jan	Wei Kuo-ching	Wei Kuo-ching

	Chang Ching-yao	Chang Ching-yao	Chen Te	Chen Te?
Kwantung			Su Ko-chih	—
Kweichow	Ho Kuang-yu	Ho Kuang-yu	Shi Hsin-an*	Li Tao-chih
Liaoning	Chang Hai-tang	Chang Hai-tang	Li Tao-chih	—
Ninghsia	Chiang Yu-an	Chiang Yu-an	Hsu Chung-po*	Yang Chun-sheng
Peking	—	Wu Chung	—	—
Shanghai	—	Chou Chun-lin	—	
Shansi	Hsieh Cher-hua	Hsieh Chen-hua	Liu Shih-hung	Liu Shih-lung?
Shantung	Tung Kuo-kuei	Tung Kuo-kuei	Tsao Chung-nan	Yuan Sheng-ping
Shensi	Huang Ching-yao	Huang Ching-yao	T'ang Chien-ju	Li Jui-shan
Szechuan	Chen Ming-yi	Hsieh Cheng-jung	Li Jui-shan	Liu Hsing-yuan
Tibet	—	Chen Ming-yi	—	Jen Jung
Tientsin	—	—	Jen Jung	Hsieh Hsueh-kung
Yunnan		Li Hsi-fu	Chou Hsing	Chou Hsing

* = 2nd Political Commissar

TABLE 13

National Congresses of the Chinese Communist Party, 1921-73

First : July 1921 (No records).

Second : July 1922. Hangchow, West Lake.
20 delegates representing about 100 Party members.

Third : June 1923. Canton.
20 delegates representing about 300 members, including Mao Tse-tung and Chu Chiu-pai.

Fourth : 22 January 1925. Shanghai.
Party had more than 1,000 members, while the Communist Youth Corps had a membership of over 9,000.

Fifth : 24 April 1927. Hankow.
Almost 100 delegates representing more than 500,000 Party members.

Sixth : 9 July 1928. Moscow.

Seventh : 2 April 1945-11 May 1945. Yenan.
755 delegates representing 1,210,000 Party members. Elected 44 regular or full members and 33 alternate members of the Party Central Committee. By 1950-51 the Party had a membership of more than 6 million.

Eighth : September 1956. Peking.
Delegates representing 10.7 million members elected 97 regular and 73 alternate members. In May 1958, the alternate membership was increased to 98 by adding 25 more persons.

Ninth ; 1-24 April 1969, Peking.
1,512 delegates elected 170 regular and 109 alternate members of the Party Central Committee.

Tenth : 24-28 August 1973, Peking.
1,249 delegates representing 28 million Party members elected 195 regular and 124 alternate members of the Party Central Committee.

TABLE 14

Continuity and Change in Top Party Leadership
The Politburo, 1945-75

7th Party Congress (1945)

Party Secretariat (5)

Mao Tse-tung	Chairman
Lin Shao-chi	Secretary
Chou En-lai	,,
Chu Teh (PLA)	,,
Chen Yun	,,

Other Members of the Politburo (5+8)

Chang Wen-tien	
Lin Po-chu	
Tung Pi-wu	
Jao Shu-shih	Purged in March 1955
Peng Chen	
Peng Teh-huai (PLA)	
Kao Kang	Possibly added in 1952 and purged in March 1955
Kang Sheng	Perhaps added in 1954
Lin Piao (PLA)	Since April 1955
Teng Hsiao-ping	Since April 1955

8th Party Congress 1956

(13 of the 7th Party + 13 New)

(in order of ranking)
Members of the Politburo Standing Committee (7)

Mao Tse-tung	Chairman
Liu Shao-chi	Vice-Chairman
Chou En-lai	,,

Chu Teh (PLA)	,,
Chen Yun	,,
Lin Piao (PLA)	,, (Since 1958)
Teng Hsiao-ping	General Secretary

Other Members of the Politburo (7+13+6 alternates)

Lin Po-chu	d. 1960
Tung Pi-wu	
Peng Chen	Purged in 1966
Lo Jung-huan (PLA)	d. 1963
Chen Yi (PLA)	d. 1972
Li Fu-chun	
Peng Teh-huai (PLA)	Purged in 1959
Liu Po-cheng (PLA)	
Ho Lung (PLA)	
Li Hsien-nien	
Ko Ching-shih	Since 1958 ; d. 1965
Li Ching-chuan	Since 1958
Tan Chen-lin	Since 1958

Alternate Members

Ulanfu	
Chang Wen-tien	Purged in 1959
Lu Ting-yi	Purged in 1966
Chen Po-ta	
Kang Sheng	
Po-I-po	

9th Party Congress (1969)

(9 of the 8th Party+16 New)

Members of the Politburo Standing Committee (5)

Mao Tse-tung	Chairman
Lin Piao (PLA)	Vice-Chairman ; Purged in 1971
Chou En-lai	Member
Chen Po-ta	Member ; Purged in 1970
Kang Sheng	Member

Other Members of the Politburo (5+16+4 alternates)

Chu Teh (PLA)

Tung Pi-wu

Liu Po-cheng (PLA)

Yeh Chien-ying (PLA)

Hsieh Fu-chih   Disappeared in 1970-71 ;
d. March 1972

Li Hsien-nien

Huang Yung-sheng (PLA)   Purged in 1971

Chiu Hui-tso (PLA)   Purged in 1971

Wu Fa-hsien (PLA)   Purged in 1971

Li Tso-peng (PLA)   Purged in 1971

Yeh Chun (f.) (Lin Piao's wife)   Purged in 1971

Chen Hsi-lien (PLA)

Hsu Shih-yu (PLA)

Chiang Ching (f.)

Chang Chun-chiao

Yao Wen-yuan

Alternate Members

Wang Tung-hsing

Li Hsueh-feng   Disappeared in 1970-71

Li Teh-sheng (PLA)

Chi Teng-kuei

10th Party Congress (1973)

(16 of the 9th Party+10 New)

Members of the Politburo Standing Committee (9+1)

Mao Tse-tung (82 years)   Chairman

Chou En-lai (76 years)   Vice-Chairman

Wang Hung-wen (35 to 40 years)   ,,

Kang Sheng (76 years)   ,,

Yeh Chien-ying (PLA) (76 years)   ,.

Li Teh-sheng (PLA) (61 years)   ,,

Teng Hsiao-ping (71 years)   ,,

                            Politburo member since January 1974 ; Vice-Chairman and Member of Standing Committee since January 1975

Chu Teh (PLA) (87 years)   Member
Chang Ch'un-chiao (65 years)   ,,
Tung Pi-wu (88 years)   Member ; d. 2 April 1975

Other Members of the Politburo (10+12+4 alternates)

Liu Po-cheng (PLA) (83 years)
Chen Hsi-lien (PLA) (62 years)
Hsu Shih-yu (PLA) (69 years)
Chiang Ching (f.) (61 years)
Yao Wen-yuan (44 years)
Li Hsien-nien (69 years)
Chi Teng-kuei
Wu Teh (61 years)
Hua Kuo-feng (60 years)
Wei Kuo-ching (61 years)
Wang Tung-hsing
Chen Yung-kuei   Peasant

Alternate Members

Ni Chih-fu   Model worker
Wu Kuei-hsien (f.)   Model worker
Su Chen-hua (PLA) (66 years)
Saifudin (60 years)

Notes :
1 In 1966 and 1967 Chou En-lai, Chen Po-ta, Kang Sheng and Li Fu-chun were called members of the Standing Committee.
2 The following were possibly added as members to the Politburo during the Cultural Revolution : Tao Chu, Hsu Hsiang-chien (PLA), Nieh Jung-chen (PLA), Yeh Chien-ying (PLA), Li Hsueh-feng, and Hsieh Fu-chih.
3 Age in parenthesis denotes age in 1975.

TABLE 15

Tenth Central Committee of the Communist Party of China, August 1973

Regular Members (195)

An Ping-sheng
Chang Chih-ming*
Chang Chun-chiao*
Chang Fu-heng*
Chang Fu-kuei*
Chang Heng-yun*
Chang Hung-chih
Chang Ping-hua
Chang Shu-chih
Chang Ta-chih*
Chang Ti-hsueh*
Chang Ting-cheng**
Chang Tsai-chien*
Chang Tsung-hsun
Chang Wei-min
Chang Yen-cheng
Chang Yi-hsiang*
Chang Yun-yi**
Chao Tzu-yang
Chen Chi-han*
Chen Hsi-lien*
Chen Hsien-jui*
Chen Kang**
Chen Mu-hua (f)
Chen Shih-chu*
Chen Yu**
Chen Yun**
Chen Yung-kuei*
Chi Peng-fei
Chi Teng-kuei*
Chiang Ching (f)*
Chiang Hsieh-yuan*
Chiang Li-yin*
Chiang Yung-hui*

Chiao Lin-yi
Chiao Kuan-hua
Chien Cheng-ying (f)
Chien Chih-kuang*
Chin Chi-wei
Chin Tsu-min
Chou Chien-jen*
Chou Chun-lin
Chou En-lai**
Chou Hsing*
Chou Hung-pao
Chou Li-chin (f)
Chu Chia-yao
Chu Mu-chih
Chu Teh**
Chuang Tse-tung
Fan Teh-ling
Fang Yi
Feng Hsuan
Fu Chuan-tso
Han Hsien-chu*
Han Ying
Hsia Pang-yin*
Hsiao Ching-kuang**
Hsieh Chia-hsiang*
Hsieh Ching-yi (f)
Hsieh Hsueh-kung*
Hsien Heng-han*
Hsing Yen-tzu (f)
Hsu Ching-hsien*
Hsu Hsiang-chien**
Hsu Shih-yu*
Hu Chi-tsung*
Hua Kuo-feng*

Hua Lin-sen
Huang Chen*
Huang Hua
Ismayil Aymat
Jao Hsing-li*
Jen Ssu-chung*
Kang Sheng**
Keng Chi-chang
Keng Piao*
Ku Mu
Kung Chao-nien
Kung Shih-chuan*
Kuo Hung-chieh
Kuo Mo-jo*
Kuo Yu-feng
Li Chen*
Li Chiang*
Li Chih-min
Lin Ching-chuan
Li Fu-chun**
Li Hsien-nien**
Li Jen-chih
Li Jui-shan*
Li Pao-hua
Li Shui-ching*
Li Shun-ta*
Li Su-wen (f)*
Li Ta
Li Ta-chang*
Li Teh-sheng*
Liang Chin-tang
Liao Cheng-chih
Lin Li-yun (f)
Liu Chien-hsun*

Liu Chun-yi*
Liu Hsi-chang*
Liu Hsiang-ping (f)
Liu Hsien-chuan*
Liu Hsing-yuan*
Liu Po-cheng**
Liu Sheng-tien*
Liu Tzu-hou*
Liu wei*
Lo Ching-chang
Lo Hsi-kang
Lu Jui-lin*
Lu Tien-chi*
Lu Yu-lan (f)*
Ma Ning
Ma Tien-shui
Mao Tse-tung**
Mo Hsien-yao*
Ni Chih-fu*
Nieh Jung-chen**
Nien Chi-jung*
Pa Sang (f)
Pai Ju-ping
Pan Shih-kao*
Paojihletai (f)*
Peng Shao-hui*
Pi Ting-chun*
Saifudin*
Su Chen-hua
Su Ching*
Su Yu**

Sung Pei-chang
Tan Chen-lin
Tan Chi-lung
Tang Chi-shan*
Tang Chung-fu*
Tao Lu-chia
Teng Hsiao-ping
Teng Tai-yuan*
Teng Ying-chao (f)**
Tien Hua-kuei*
Tien Pao*
Tien Wei-hsin
Ting Ke-tse
Ting Kuo-yu
Ting Sheng*
Tsai Chang (f)**
Tsai Hsiao
Tsai Hsieh-pin*
Tsai Shu-mei (f)*
Tsao Li-huai*
Tsao Yi-ou (f)*
Tsen Kuo-jung
Tseng Shao-shan**
Tseng Ssu-yu*
Tsui Hai-lung
Tsung Hsi-yun*
Tu Ping*
Tuan Chun-yi
Tung Ming-hui*
Tung Pi-wu**
Ulanfu

Wang Chao-chu*
Wang Chen**
Wang Cheng
Wang Chia-hsiang
Wang Hsiu-chen (f)*
Wang Huai-hsiang*
Wang Hung-kun*
Wang Hung-wen*
Wang Kuo-fan*
Wang Pi-cheng
Wang Shou-tao**
Wang Shu·chen (f)
Wang Shu-sheng**
Wang Tung-hsing*
Wei Feng-ying (f)*
Wei Kuo-ching*
Wei Ping-kuei*
Wu Kuei-hsien (f)*
Wu Ta-sheng*
Wu Tao*
Wu Teh*
Yang Chun-fu*
Yang Teh-chih*
Yang Yung
Yao Wen-yuan*
Yeh Chien-ying**
Yu Chiu-li*
Yu Hui-yung
Yu Hung-liang
Yu Sang*
Yu Tai-chung

---

* Also regular members of the 9th Central Committee
**Also regular members of the 7th (except Wang Shu-sheng who was not member of the 7th CC) 8th and 9th Central Committees

Alternate Members (124)

Chang Chi-hui*
Chang Chiang-lin*
Chang Huai-lien
Chang Kuo-chuan
Chang Lin-chih
Chang Ling-pin*
Chang Shih-chung*
Chang Ssu-chou*
Chang Ying-tsai*
Chao Feng*
Chao Hsih-chu
Chao Hsing-yuan*
Chen Pei-chen (f)
Chen Tai-fu
Chen Yu-pao
Cheng Chia-chung
Cheng Ho-fa*
Cheng San-sheng*
Chiang Hua
Chiang Pao-ti (f)*
Chiang Wei-ching
Chien Hsueh-sen*
Chilin Wandan*
Chu Hui-fen (f)
Chu Ke-chia
Chu Kuang-ya*
Fan Hsiao-chu (f)*
Feng Chan-wu*
Feng Pin-teh
Hsiang Chung-hua
Hsiao Ke
Hsieh Chen-hua
Hsieh Chia-tang*
Hsieh Wang-chun (f)*
Hsu Chih*
Hsueh Chin-lien (f)
Hu Chin-ti (f)
Hu Liang-tsai*
Hu Wei*
Huang Cheng-lien*
Huang Chih-chen
Huang Jung-hai*

Huang Ping-hsiu (f)
Huang Tso-chen*
Huang Wen-ming*
Janabil
Jen Jung
Juan Po-sheng*
Kang Chien-min*
Kang Lin*
Kao Shu-lan (f)
Kua Yao-ching
Li Hua-min*
Li Jih-rai
Li Shou-lin*
Li Ting-shan*
Li Tsu-ken
Li Yao-sung
Li Yuan*
Liao Chih-kao
Lin Li-ming
Liu Chen-hua*
Liu Chun-chiao*
Liu Hsi-yao*
Liu Kuang-tao
Lo Chun-ti (f)*
Lu Chin-lung
Lu Chung-yang
Lu Ho*
Lu Ta-tung*
Lu Tsun-chieh (f)*
Lung Kuang-chien*
Ma Chin-hua (f)
Ma Hsiao-liu
Ma Li-hsin
Ma Ming
Pai Tung-tsai
Pan Mei-ying (f)*
Pei Chou-yu*
Peng Chung*
Peng Kuei-ho*
Pu Ku-hsiang
Ruzi Turdi
(Joutzutuerhti)*

She Chi-teh
Shen Mao-kung
Shih Shao-hua*
Sun Chien
Sun Yu-kuo
Sung Ching-yu
Sung Shuang-lai*
Sung Shih-lun
Ta Leh (Ta Lo)*
Tang Ke-pi (f)
Tang Liang*
Tang Wen-sheng (f)
Teng Hua*
Tieh Ying
Tsui Hsiu-fan*
Wang Chiao-tao*
Wang Chien
Wang Chih-chiang*
Wang Ching-sheng
Wang Hsiang-chun (f)
Wang Kuang-lin*
Wang Liu-sheng*
Wang Mei-chi (f)
Wang Pai-teh
Wang Teh-shan
Wang Ti*
Wen Hsiang-lan (f)*
Wu Chin-chuan*
Wu Chung*
Wu Hsiang-pi
Wu Tsung-shu
Wu Yu-teh
Yang Chun-sheng*
Yang Fu-chen (f)
Yang Kuei
Yang Po-lan (f)
Yang Ta-yi
Yang Tsung (f)*
Yao Lien-wei*
Yao Yi-lin
Yeh Fei

*Also alternate members of the 9th CC

TABLE 16

Regional Party Bureaus, 1949-55 and 1961

Secretaries of Regional Party Bureaus

CENTRAL-SOUTH
(Honan, Hunan, Hupeh, Kiangsi, Kwangsi, Kwantung)

1949-54	1961-
1st: Lin Piao	1st: T'ao Chu
Yeh Chien-ying	2nd: Wang Jen-chung
Others: Lo Jung-huan	3rd: Ch'en Yu
Teng Tzu-hui	
T'an Cheng	
Li Hsueh-feng	
Li Hsien-nien	

EAST CHINA
(Anhwei, Chekiang, Fukien, Kiangsi, Kiangsu, Shantung)

1949-55	1961-
1st: Jao Shu-shih	1st: K'o Ch'ing-shih
T'an Chen-lin	2nd: Tseng Hsi-sheng
Others: Ch'en Yi	3rd: Li Pao-hua
Chang Ting-ch'eng	

NORTH CHINA
(Chahar, Hopeh, Pingyuan, Shansi, Suiyuan)

1949-54	1961-
1st: Po-I-po	1st: Li Hsueh-feng
Others: Nieh Jung-chen	2nd: Ulanfu
Chou Jung-hsin	3rd: Lin T'ieh
Liu Lan-t'ao	
Wang Ts'ung-wu	
Chang Su	
Liu Hsiu-feng	

NORTH EAST
(Heilungkiang, Jehol, Kirin, Liaohsi, Liaotung, Sungkiang)

1949-55	1961-
1st: Kao Kang	1st: Sung Jen-chiung
Others: Li Fu-ch'un	2nd: Ouyang Ch'in
Lin Feng	3rd: Ma Ming-fang

NORTH-WEST
(Kansu, Ninghsia, Shensi, Sinkiang, Chinghai)

1949-55	1961-
1st: Hsi Chung-hsun	1st: Liu Lan-t'ao
Others: Ma Ming-fang	2nd: Chang Teh-sheng
Ma Wen Jui	3rd: Hu Yao-pang

SOUTH-WEST
(Kweichow, Sikang, Szechwan, Yunnan)

1949-55	1961-
1st: Teng Hsiao-p'ing	1st: Li Ching-chuan
Ho Lung	
Others: Liu Po-ch'eng	
Sung Jen-ch'iung	
Chang Chi-ch'un	

Note: All the Regional Party Bureaus were abolished in mid-1955, but they were formally recreated in January 1961 by a decision of the 9th Plenum of the Party Central Committee. Kiangsi was under the jurisdiction of the Central-South Party Bureau during the 1949-55 period but it was shifted to the jurisdiction of the East-China Bureau in 1961.

TABLE 17

Provincial Party Leadership 1949-68

Provinces	First Secretaries	Tenure
Provinces (21)		
Anhwei	Tseng Hsi-sheng	1949-62
	Li Pao-hua	1962-
Chekiang	Tan Chen-lin	1949-52
	Tan Chi-lung	1952-55
	Chiang Hua	1955-
Chinghai	Chang Chung-liang	1949-54
	Kao Feng	1954-60
	Wang Chao (acting)	1961-62
	Yang Chih-lin	1962-
Fukien	Chang Ting-cheng	1949-54
	Yeh Fei	1954-
Heilungkiang	Chang Chi-lung	?-50
	Chao Teh-tsun	1950-54
	Ouyang Chin	1954-
Honan	Chang Hsi	1949-52
	Pan Fu-sheng	1953-58
	Wu Chih-pu	1958-61
	Liu Chien-hsun	1961-
Hopeh	Lin Tieh	1949-
Hunan	Huang Ko-Cheng	1949-52
	Chin Ming	1952-53
	Chou-Hsiao-chou	1953-59
	Chang Ping-hua	1959-
Hupeh	Li Hsien-nien	1949-54
	Wang Jen-chung	1954-
Kansu	Chang Teh-sheng	1949-54
	Chang Chung-liang	1954-61
	Wang Feng	1961-
Kiangsi	Chen Cheng-jen	1949-52
	Yang Shang-kuei	1953-
Kiangsu (North)	Hsiao Wang-tung	1949-52
(South)	Chen Pei-hsien	1949-52
	Ko Ching-shih	1952-55
	Chiang Wei-ching	1955-
Kirin	Liu Hsi-wu	1950-52
	Li Meng-ling	1952-?
	Wu Teh	1956-

Kwangtung	Yeh Chien-ying	1951-55
	Tao Chu	1955-65
	Chao Tzu-yang	1965-
Kweichow	Su Chen-hua	1949-54
	Chou Lin	1954-65
	Li Ta-chang	1965-65
	Chia Chi-yun	1965-
Liaoning (Liaohsi)	Kuo Feng	1950-54
(Liaotung)	Chang Wen-tien	1949-50
,,	Liu Lan-po	1950-50
,,	Chang Chi-lung	1950-53
,,	Kao Yang	1953-54
	Huang Ou-tung	1954-58
	Huang Huo-ching	1958-
Shansi	Cheng Tzu-hua	1949-51
	Lai Jo-yu	1951-51
	Kao Ko-lin	1952-53
	Tao Lu-chia	1953-65
	Wei Heng (Wei Han)	1965-
Shantung	Kang Sheng	1949-55
	Shu Tung	1955-60
	Tseng Hsi-sheng	1960-61
	Tan Chi-lung	1961-
Shensi	Ma Ming-fang	1949-52
	Pan Tzu-li	1952-54
	Chang Teh-sheng	1955-65
	Hu Yao-pang (acting)	1965-65
	Huo Shih-lien	1965-
Szechwan	Hsieh Fu-chih	1950-52
	Li Ching-chuan	1952-65
	Liao Chih-kao	1965-
Yunnan	Sung Jen-chiung	1951-53
	Hsieh Fu-chih	1953-59
	Yen Hung-yen	1959-

Autonomous Regions (5)

Inner Mongolia	Ulanfu	1949-
Kwangsi	Chang Yun-yi	1949-55
	Chen Man-yuan	1955-57
	Liu Chien-hsun	1957-61
	Wei Kuo-ching	1961-
Ninghsia	Pan Tzu-li	1949-51
	Chu Min	1953-?
	Wang Feng	1958-61
	Yang Ching-jen	1961-
Sinkiang	Wang Chen	1949-52
	Wang En-mao	1952-
Tibet	Chang Ching-wu	1956-65
	Chang Kuo-hua	1965-

Municipalities (2)

Peking	Peng Chen	1949-
Shanghai	Jao Shu-shih	1949-52
	Chen Yi	1952-54
	Ko Ching-shih	1955-65
	Chen Pei-hsien	1965-

Note :

During 1949-53, the senior Party secretaries were known simply as "secretaries" but in the 1953-55 period the ranking secretarial post was redesignated "first secretary."

During the Cultural Revolution (1965-68), almost all the First Secretaries of the Provincial Party Committees were disgraced or removed with the result that only Liu Chien-hsun of Honan and Wei Kuo-ching of Kwangsi survived criticism and continued in their posts in the post-Cultural Revolution period. (see Table 18)

TABLE 18

Provincial Party Leadership, 1968-75

Province	Chm. of Rev. Com.	First Secretaries of the PPC	
		1970-71	1974-75
Provinces (21)			
Anhwei	Li Teh-sheng (M)	Li Teh-sheng (M)	Sung Pei-chang¹
Chekiang	Nan Ping (M)	Nan Ping (M)* Tan Chi-lung†	Tan Chi-lung
Chinghai	Liu Hsien-chuan (M)	Liu Hsien-chuan (M)	Liu Hsien-chuan (M)
Fukien	Han Hsien-chu (M)	Han Hsien-chu (M)	Liao Chih-kao
Heilungkiang	Pan Fu-sheng	Wang Chia-tao (M)	Wang Chia-tao (M)
Honan	Liu Chien-hsun	Liu Chien-hsun	Liu Chien-hsun
Hopeh	Li Hsueh-feng	Liu Tzu-hou	Liu Tzu-hou
Hunan	Li Yuan (M)	Hua Kuo-feng	Hua Kuo-feng
Hupeh	Tseng Ssu-yu (M)	Tseng Ssu-yu (M)	Chao Hsin-chu
Kansu	Hsien Heng-han (M)	Hsien Heng-Han (M)	Hsien Heng-han (M)
Kiangsi	Cheng Shih-ching (M)	Cheng Shih-ching (M)* She Chi-teh (M)†	Chiang Wei-ching
Kiangsu	Hsu shih-yu (M)	Hsu Shih-yu (M)	Peng Chung
Kirin	Wang Huai-hsiang (M)	Wang Huai-hsing (M)	Wang Huai-hsiang (M)
Kwantung	Liu Hsing-yuan	T'ing Sheng (M)	Chao Tzu-yang

Kweichow	Li Tsai-han (M)	Lan Yi-nung (M)*	Lu Jui-lin (M)
Liaoning	Chen Hsi-lien (M)	Lu Jui-lin (M)†	Vacant
Shansi	Liu Ko-ping	Chen Hsi-lien (M)	Hsieh Chen-hua (M)
Shantung	Wang Hsiao-yu	Hsieh Chen-hua (M)	Pai Ju-ping
Shensi	Li Jui-shan	Yang Teh-chih (M)	Li Jui-shan
Szechwan	Chang Kuo-hua (M)	Li Jui-shan	Liu Hsing-yuan (M)
Yunnan	Tan Fu-jen	Chang Kuo-hua (M)	Chou Hsing
		Chou Hsing	
Autonomous Regions (5)			
Inner Mongolia	Teng Hai-ching (M)	Yu Tai-chung (M)	Yu Tai-chung (M)
Kwangsi	Wei Kuo-ching (M)	Wei Kuo-ching (M)	Wei Kuo-ching (M)
Ninghsia	K'ang Chien-min (M)	K'ang Chien-min (M)	K'ang Chien-min (M)
Sinkiang	Lung Shu-chin (M)	Lung Shu-chin (M)*	Saifudin
		Saifudin†	
Tibet	Tseng Yung-ya (M)	Jen Jung (M)	Jen Jung (M)
Municipalities (3)			
Peking	Hsieh Fu-chih	Hsieh Fu-chih	Wu Teh
Shanghai	Chang Chun-chiao	Chang Chun-chiao	Chang Chun-chiao
Tientsin	Hsieh Hsueh-kung	Hsieh Hsueh-kung	Hsieh Hsueh-kung

* = removed in Sep 1971
† = since Sep 1971
M = Military
PPC = Provincial Party Committees
Rev Com = Revolutionary Committees
1 = announcement made in July 1975

TABLE 19

Members of the Standing Committee of the Fourth National People's Congress, elected on 17 January 1975

Chairman: Chu Teh (PLA)**

Vice-Chairmen : (22)

Tung Pi-wu (d. April 1975)**	Tan Chen-lin*
Soong Ching-ling (f.)	Li Ching-chuan*
Kang Sheng**	Chang Ting-cheng*
Liu Po-cheng (PLA)**	Tsai Chang (f.)*
Wu Teh**	Ulanfu*
Wei Kuo-ching (PLA)**	Ngapo Ngawang-Jigme
Saifudin**	Chou Chien-jen*
Kuo Mo-jo*	Hsu Teh-heng
Hsu Hsiang-chien*	Hu Chueh-wen
Nieh Jung-chen (PLA)*	Li Su-wen (f.)*
Chen Yun*	Yao Lien-wei*

Members: (144)

---

 * Members of the Central Committee of the Chinese Communist Party.
 ** Member of the Politburo of the Party Central Committee

TABLE 20

State Council of China Appointed on the Proposal of the Central Committee of the Party by the Fourth National People's Congress at its First Session, 17 January 1975

Premier : Chou En-lai**

Vice-Premiers (12) (in order of ranking):

1.	Teng Hsiao-ping**	7.	Chen Yung-kuei**
2.	Chang Chun-chiao**	8.	Wu Kuei-hsien (f.)**
3.	Li Hsien-nien**	9.	Wang Chen (PLA)*
4.	Chen Hsi-lien (PLA)**	10.	Yu Chiu-li (PLA)*
5.	Chi Teng-kuei**	11.	Ku Mu*
6.	Hua Kuo-feng**	12.	Sun Chien*

Ministers (29):

Foreign Affairs	Chiao Kuan-hua*
National Defence	Yeh Chien-ying (PLA)**
State Planning Com	Yu Chiu-li (PLA)**
State Capital Construction Com	Ku Mu*
Public Security	Hua Kuo-feng**
Foreign Trade	Li Chiang*
Economic Relations with Foreign Countries	Fang Yi*
Agriculture & Forestry	Sha Feng (PLA)
Metallurgical Industry	Chen Shao-kun (PLA)
Machine-Building (1st Ministry)	Li Shui-ching (PLA)*
Machine-Building (2nd Ministry)	Liu Hsi-yao*
Machine-Building (3rd Ministry)	Li Chi-tai (PLA)
Machine-Building (4th Ministry)	Wang Cheng (PLA)*
Machine-Building (5th Ministry)	Li Cheng-fang (PLA)
Machine-Building (6th Ministry)	Pien Chiang
Machine-Building (7th Ministry)	Wang Yang (PLA)
Coal Industry	Hsu Chin-chiang
Petroleum & Chemical Industries	Kang Shih-en
Water Conservancy & Power	Chien Cheng-ying (f.)*
Light Industry	Chien Chih-kuang
Railways	Wan Li
Communications	Yeh Fei*
Posts & Telecommunications	Chung Fu-hsiang
Finance	Chang Ching-fu
Commerce	Fan Tzu-yu (PLA)
Culture	Yu Hui-yung*
Education	Chou Jung-hsin

Public Health	Liu Hsiang-ping (f.)*
Physical Culture & Sports Com	Chuang Tse-tung*

---

* Member of the Central Committee of the Chinese Communist Party (Sun Chien, Liu Hsi-yao and Yeh Fei are alternate members. All others are full members.)
** Member of the Politburo of the Party Central Committee
Com=Commission

Select Bibliography

BOOKS

Barnett, A. Doak. *Cadres, Bureaucracy, and Political Power in Communist China.* New York, 1967.

———. *Uncertain Passage : China's Transition to the Post-Mao Era.* Washington, 1974.

Bary Wm. Theodore De, ed. *Sources of Chinese Tradition.* New York, 1960.

Bobrow, Davis Bernard. *The Political and Economic Role of the Military in the Chinese Communist Movement, 1927-1959.* Ph.D. Thesis, Massachusetts Institute of Technology, 1962.

Brandt, Conrad, Benjamin Schwartz and John K. Fairbank, eds. *A Documentary History of Chinese Communism.* Cambridge, 1952.

Buchan, Alastair, ed. *China and the Peace of Asia.* London, 1965.

Carlson, Evans Fordyce. *The Chinese Army, Its Organization and Military Efficiency.* New York, 1940.

Chen, Jerome. *Mao and the Chinese Revolution.* London, 1965.

Ch'eng, J. Chester, ed. *The Politics of the Chinese Red Army.* Stanford, 1965.

Chi, Hsi-sheng. *The Chinese Warlord System.* Ph.D. Dissertation of the University of Chicago, 1967.

Chiang Kai-shek. *Soviet Russia in China.* New York, 1958.

Chiu Sin-ming. *A History of Chinese Communist Army.* Ph.D. Thesis of the University of Southern California, 1958.

Chu Teh. *On the Battlefronts of the Liberated Areas.* Peking, 1952.

Domes, Jurgen. *The Internal Politics of China 1949-1972.*

London, 1973.

Eighth National Congress of the Communist Party of China. 3 vols. Peking, 1956.

Elegant, Robert S. *China's Red Masters : Political Biographies of the Chinese Communist Leaders.* New York, 1951.

Erickson, John. *The Soviet High Command, 1918-1941.* London, 1962.

Far Eastern Economic Review. *Asia 1975 Yearbook.* Hong Kong, 1975.

Fraser, Angus M. *The People's Liberation Army.* New York, 1973.

Garthoff, Raymond L., ed. *Sino-Soviet Military Relations.* New York, 1966.

———. *Soviet Military Doctrine.* Glencoe, Ill., 1953.

Garvey, J. E. *Marxist-Leninist China Military and Social Doctrine.* New York, 1960.

George, Alexander L. *The Chinese Communist Army in Action.* New York, 1967.

Gelder, Stuart. *The Chinese Communists.* London, 1946.

Gillin, Donald G. *Warlord Yen Hsi-shan in Shansi Province, 1911-1949.* Princeton, 1967.

Gittings, John. *The Role of the Chinese Army.* London, 1967.

Griffith, Samuel B. II. *The Chinese People's Liberation Army.* New York, 1967.

Ho Kan-chih. *A History of the Modern Chinese Revolution.* Peking, 1959.

Ho Ping-ti and Tang Tsou. *China in Crisis.* 3 vols. Chicago, 1968.

Hinton, H. C. *An Introduction to Chinese Politics.* New York, 1973.

Hsiao Tso-liang. *Power Relations Within the Chinese Communist Movement, 1930-34.* Seattle, 1961.

Hsieh, Alice Langley. *Communist China's Military Politics and Nuclear Strategy.* Santa Monica, Calif., 1967.

Hsüeh Chün-tu. *The Chinese Communist Movement, 1921-1937.* Stanford, 1960.

———. *The Chinese Communist Movement, 1937-1949.* Stanford, 1962.

Hu Chiao-mu. *Thirty Years of the Communist Party of China.*

Peking, 1952.

Huang, T'ao. *Chung-kuo Jen-min Chieh-fang Chun ti San-shih Nien (Three Decades of the PLA)*. Peking, 1958.

Huntington, Samuel. *The Soldier and the State*. Cambridge, Mass., 1957.

Impey, Lawrence. *The Chinese Army as a Military Force*. Tientsin, 1926.

Janowitz, Morris. *The Professional Soldier : A Social and Political Portrait*. Glencoe, Ill., 1964.

Joffee, Ellis. *Party and Army : Professionalism and Political Control in the Chinese Officer Corps 1949-1964*. Cambridge, 1967.

Johnson, Chalmers A. *Peasant Nationalism and Communist Power*. Stanford, 1962.

Klein, Donald W. and Clark, Anne B. *Biographic Dictionary of Chinese Communism 1921-1965*. 2 Vols. Cambridge, Mass., 1971.

Lewis, John Wilson. *Leadership in Communist China*. Ithaca, 1963.

Lindbeck, John M., ed. *China : Management of a Revolutionary Society*. Seattle, 1971.

Liu, F. F. *A Military History of Modern China, 1924-1949*. Princeton, 1956.

Liu Shao-ch'i. *On Inner-Party Struggle*. Peking, 1952.

———. *On the Party*. Peking, 1952.

———. *How to be a Good Communist*. Peking, 1964.

MacFarquhar, Roderick. *The Origins of the Cultural Revolution, Vol. I, Contradictions Among the People, 1956-1957*. London, 1974.

MacNair, H. F., ed. *China*. California, 1951.

Mao Tse-tung. *Selected Military Writings of Mao Tse-tung*. Peking, 1963.

———. *Selected Works of Mao Tse-tung*. 4 vols. Peking, 1961-65.

Mitchell, General. *Outlines of the World's Military History*. Pennsylvania, 1949.

North, Robert C. *Kuomintang and Chinese Communist Elites*. Stanford, 1952.

O'Ballance, Edgar. *The Red Army of China*. London, 1962.

Powell, Ralph L. *The Rise of Chinese Military Power 1895-*

1912. Princeton, 1955.

———. *Politico-Military Relationships in Communist China.* Washington, 1963.

Pye, Lucian W. *Warlord Politics.* New York, 1971.

Rhoads, Edward J. M. *The Chinese Red Army, 1927-1963 : An Annotated Bibliography.* Cambridge, Mass., 1964.

Rigg, R. B. *Red China's Fighting Hordes.* Harrisburg, Penn., 1951.

Rue, John E. *Mao Tse-tung in Opposition, 1927-1935.* Stanford, 1966.

Schram, Stuart R. *The Political Thought of Mao Tse-tung.* New York, 1963.

———. *Mao Tse-tung.* New York, 1966.

Schurmann, Farnz. *Ideology and Organization in Communist China.* Berkeley, Calif., 1966.

Schwartz, Benjamin. *Chinese Communism and the Rise of Mao.* Cambridge, 1951.

Sha T'ing, *Chi Ho Lung (About Ho Lung).* Peking, 1958.

Sheridan, James E. *Chinese Warlord : The Career of Feng Yu-hsiang.* Stanford, 1964.

Smedley, Agnes. *China's Red Army Marches.* New York, 1934.

Snow, Edgar. *The Other Side of the River : Red China Today.* New York, 1962.

———. *Red Star Over China.* New York, 1956.

Strong, Anna Louise. *The Rise of the Chinese People's Communes—And Six Years After.* Peking, 1964.

Sun Tzu. *The Art of War,* Translated with an introduction by Samuel B. Griffith. London, 1963.

———. *The Art of War,* Translated by Lionel Gibs. Pennsylvania, 1949.

Swarup, Shanti. *A Study of the Chinese Communist Movement.* London, 1966.

Tang, Peter S. H. *Communist China Today.* New York, 1957.

T'ao Chu-yin. *Pie-yang Chun-fa Tung-chih Shih-ch'i (History of the Reign of the Warlords)* 6 volumes. Peking, 1957.

Thronton, Richard C. *The Comintern and the Chinese Communists, 1928-1931.* Seattle, 1969.

Tien Pu-i. *Pei-yang Chun-fa Shih hua (History of the Northern Warlords),* 6 volumes. Taipei, 1967.

Ti-szu-chun chi-shih (*A History of the Fourth Army*). Canton, 1949.

Ting Li. *Militia of Communist China.* Hong Kong, 1955.

Townsend, James R. *Political Participation in Communist China.* Berkeley, Calif., 1967.

Trager, Frank N., and Henderson, William, eds. *Communist China, 1949-1969, A Twenty Year Appraisal.* New York, 1971.

Treadgold, Donald W., ed. *Soviet and Chinese Communism: Similarities and Differences.* Seattle, 1967.

Whitson, William W. *Civil War in China, 1946-1950.* 2 volumes. Washington, 1967.

———, ed. *The Military and Political Power in China in the 1970s.* New York, 1972.

———, ed. *Military Campaign in China, 1924-50.* Washington, 1966.

———, ed. *PLA Unit History.* Washington, 1967.

———, with Chen-Hsia-Huang. *The Chinese High Command: A History of Communist Military Politics, 1927-71.* New York, 1973.

Wolfe, Thomas W. *Communist Outlook on War.* Santa Monica, Calif., 1967.

———. *Soviet Military Policy at the Fifty-year Mark.* Santa Monica, Calif., 1967.

Wright, Arthur F., ed. *Confucianism and Chinese Civilization.* New York, 1964.

ARTICLES

Ahn, Byung-joon, "The Cultural Revolution and China's Search for Political Order," *China Quarterly,* 58 (April/June 1974), pp. 249-85.

Baldwin, Hanson W., "China as a Military Power," *Foreign Affairs,* 30 (October 1951), pp. 51-62.

Bradsher, Henry S., "China: The Radical Offensive," *Asian Survey,* 13 (November 1973), pp. 989-1009.

Bridgham, Philip, "The Fall of Lin Piao," *China Quarterly* (July-September 1973) pp. 427-49.

Burton, Barry, "The Cultural Revolution's Ultra Left Conspiracy: The May 16 Group," *Asian Survey* (November

1971), pp. 1029-53.

Chai Winberg, "The Reorganization of the Chinese Communist Party 1966-1968," *Asian Survey*, 8 (November 1968), pp. 901-10.

Chang, Paris H., "Regional Military Power : The Aftermath of the Cultural Revolution," *Asian Survey*, 12 (December 1972) pp. 999-1013.

———, "Mao's Great Purge : A Balance Sheet," *Problems of Communism* (March-April 1969), footnote 37.

Charles, David A., "The Dismissal of Marshal P'eng Teh-huai," *China Quarterly* (October-December 1961), pp. 63-76.

Chen Yi, "Thirty Glorious Years," *People's China*, No. 15 (1 August 1957), pp. 14-9.

Cheng, Peter, "Liu Shao-chi and the Cultural Revolution," *Asian Survey*, 11 (October 1971), pp. 943-57.

Chieh-fang Chun-pao editorial, "Hold Aloft the Banner of Party Committee System," (1 July 1958), as translated in *Survey of China Mainland Press*, No. 1881 (24 October 1958), pp. 3-5.

———, "Raise Aloft the Great Red Banner of the Thought of Mao Tse-tung, Resolutely Implement Regulations Governing PLA Political Work," (8 May 1963), as translated in *Survey of China Mainland Press*, No. 2984 (22 May 1963), pp. 1-8.

———, "Resolute Carrying of Party's Military Line," (1 August 1958), as translated in *Survey of China Mainland Press*, No. 1881 (24 October 1958), pp. 1-3.

Chiu, Sing-ming, "The Chinese Communist Army in Transition," *Far Eastern Survey* (November 1958), pp. 168-75.

———, "Chinese Communist Military Leadership," *Military Review* (March 1966) pp. 59-66.

———, "Political Control in the Chinese Communist Army," *Military Review* (August 1961).

Chu Teh, "How the Chinese People Defeated the Chiang Kai-shek Reactionary Clique Armed by American Imperialism," *People's China*, No. 1 (1 July 1951), pp. 16-20.

———, "The Tasks of the PLA," *People's China*, No. 4 (16 August 1951), pp. 5-6.

———, "Twenty-five Years of the Chinese People's Liberation Army," *People's China*, No. 16 (16 August 1952), pp. 10-5.

Domes, Jurgen, "New Course in Chinese Domestic Politics :

The Anatomy of Readjustment," *Asian Survey*, 13 (July 1973) pp. 633-46.

————, "Some Aspects of the Cultural Revolution in China," *Asian Survey*, 11 (September 1971), pp. 932-40.

————, "The Cultural Revolution and the Army," *Asian Survey* (May 1968), pp. 349-63.

————, "The Ninth CCP Central Committee in Statistical Perspective," *Current Scene* (Hong Kong), 11 (7 February 1971), pp. 5-14.

————, "The Role of the Military in the Formation of Revolutionary Committees 1967-68," *China Quarterly* (October-December 1970), pp. 112-45.

Gayn, Mark, "Who After Mao ?" *Foreign Affairs*, 51 (January 1973), pp. 300-9.

Gelber, Harry G., "Nuclear Weapons in Chinese Strategy," *Problems of Communism*, 20 (November-December 1971), pp. 33-44.

Ghosh, S.K., "Crisis in Military Leadership in China," *News Review on China, Mongolia & The Koreas* (New Delhi) (February 1975), pp. 81-2.

Gittings, John, "China's Militia," *China Quarterly* (April-June 1964), pp. 100-17.

————, "Military Control and Leadership," *China Quarterly* (April-June 1966), pp. 82-101.

————, "The Political Control of the Chinese Army," *The World Today*, 19 (August 1963), pp. 327-36.

————, "The 'Learn from the Army' Campaign," *China Quarterly* (April-June 1964), pp. 153-9.

Hanrahan, Gene Z., "The People's Revolutionary Military Council in Communist China," *Far Eastern Survey* (May 1954), pp. 77-8.

Hsiao Hua, "Basic Experiences of the Past Two Years Concerning the Creation of 4-Good Companies in the Army," Report at the All-Army Political Work Conference, 2 February 1963, *Jen-min Jih-pao* (1 April 1963,) as translated in *Survey of China Mainland Press*, No. 2971 (3 May 1963), pp. 1-16.

————, "The Communist Party of China and the Chinese People's Liberation Army," *People's China*, No. 3 (1 August 1951), pp. 4-8.

Hsüeh Chun-wen, "Criticism of the 'Six Practical Principles',"

Kuang-ming Jih-pao (Peking) (2 January 1975) as translated in *Survey of People's Republic of China Press*, No. 5776 (20 January 1975), p. 2.

Hu Huang-tai, "The People's Liberation Army," *Peking Review*, No. 30 (28 July 1959), pp. 10-3.

Hung Chi (*Red Flag*) Editorial Department, "A Basic Summation of Experience Gained in the Victory of the Chinese People's Revolution," *Peking Review*, No. 45 (8 November 1960), pp. 15-21.

Hung Chou-wen, "The Absolute Leadership of the Party is the Basic Guarantee for the Victory of Our Army," *Kuang-ming Jih-pao* (26 December 1974), as translated in *Survey of People's Republic of China Press*, No. 5772 (14 January 1975), pp. 41-5.

Joffe, Ellis, "Contradictions in the Chinese Army," *Far Eastern Economic Review* (11 July 1963), pp. 123-6.

————, "The Chinese Army After the Cultural Revolution : The Effects of Intervention," *China Quarterly* (July-September 1973), pp. 450-77.

————, "The Chinese Army in the Cultural Revolution : The Politics of Intervention," *Current Scene* (December 1970), pp. 1-25.

————, "The Conflict Between Old and New in the Chinese Army," *China Quarterly* (April-June 1964), pp. 118-40.

Li Chih-min, "Military Expert of the Proleteriat Must Also Be A Practical Politician of the Proletariat," *Hung Chi* (*Red Flag*), No. 23 (1 December 1960) as translated in *Survey of China Mainland Magazines*, No. 242 (3 January 1961), pp. 1-10.

Lin Piao, "March Ahead Under the Red Flag of the Central Line and Mao Tse-tung's Military Thinking," *Peking Review*, No. 40 (6 October 1959), pp. 13-20.

————, "The Victory of the Chinese People's Revolutionary War is the Victory of the Thought of Mao Tse-tung," Special supplement to *China Reconstructs* (December 1960), pp. 1-15.

Lin Yun-cheng, "The Militia in the People's Revolutionary Wars of China," *Jen-min Jih-pao* (*People's Daily*) 28 June 1962) as translated in *Survey of China Mainland Press*, No. 2780 (18 July 1962), pp. 1-12.

Lo Jung-huan, "Early Days of the Chinese Red Army," *Peking Review*, No. 31 (3 August 1962), pp. 9-12,

Moody, Jr., Peter R., "The New Anti-Confucian Campaign in China : The First Round," *Asian Survey*, 14 (April 1974), pp. 307-24.

Nelson, Harvey, "Military Forces in the Cultural Revolution," *China Quarterly* (July-September 1972).

Nieh Jung-chen, "How the Chinese People Defeated the Japanese Fascist Aggressors," *People's China* (1 July 1951), pp. 20-31.

Peiris, Denzil, "Pragmatists vs. Ideologues," *Times of India*, 13 March 1975.

Peng Teh-huai, "Why the Chinese People's Volunteers Are Invincible," *People's China*, 4 (16 August 1951), pp. 7-8.

Powell, Ralph L., "Maoist Military Doctrines," *Asian Survey* (April 1968).

————, "The Increasing Power of Lin Piao and the Party Soldiers 1959-1966," *China Quarterly* (April-June 1968), pp. 38-65.

————, "The Military Affairs Committee and Party Control of the Military in China," *Asian Survey* (July 1963), pp. 347-56.

————, "The Party, the Government and the Gun," *Asian Survey*, 10 (June 1970), pp. 441-71.

Rigg, Robert B., "Red Army in Retreat," *Current History*, 32 (January 1957), pp. 1-6.

Robinson, Thomas W., "Chou En-lai's Political Style : Comparisons with Mao Tse-tung and Lin Piao," *Asian Survey*, 10 (December 1970), pp. 1101-6.

Shuang Yun, "The Marxist Military Line," *People's China* (1 September 1950), pp. 6-7.

Sims, Stephen A., "The New Role of the Military," *Problems of Communism*, 18 (November-December 1969), pp. 26-32.

Snow, Edgar, "Report from China—IV The Army and the Party," *The New Republic*, 164 (22 May 1971), pp. 9-12.

Solajic, Dragutin, "The Role of the Chinese Army," *Review of International Affairs* (Belgrade) 17 (20 December 1966), pp. 17-9.

Staar, John Bryan, "Conceptual Foundations of Mao Tse-tung's Theory of Continuous Revolution," *Asian Survey*, 11 (June 1971), pp. 610-28.

Vukadinovie, Radovan, "The Role and Strength of the Chinese Army," *Review of International Affairs* (Belgrade), 20 (5 December 1969), pp. 29-31.

Walker, Richard L., "The Chinese Red Army," *The New Republic*, 136 (13 May 1957), pp. 39-42.

Whitson, William, "The Field Army in Chinese Communist Military Politics," *China Quarterly*, (January-March 1969) pp. 1-30.

Wich, Richard, "The Tenth Party Congress : The Power Structure and the Succession Question," *China Quarterly*, 58 (April/June 1974), pp. 231-48.

Yeh Chien-ying, "Great and Decisive Strategic Battles," *Peking Review*, 32 (11 August 1961), pp. 12-7.

Index